THE INCREDIBLE DE FOE

DANIEL DE FOE

THE INCREDIBLE DE FOE

By

WILLIAM FREEMAN

KENNIKAT PRESS
Port Washington, N. Y./London

THE INCREDIBLE DE FOE

First published in 1950
Reissued in 1972 by Kennikat Press
Library of Congress Catalog Card No: 77-159085
ISBN 0-8046-1627-2

Manufactured by Taylor Publishing Company   Dallas, Texas

"His curiosity was insatiable. To write was as natural to him as to breathe. He made fiction seem like truth and truth like fiction. He was the perfect journalist. He could write on anything or nothing."

The Concise Cambridge History of English Literature.

CONTENTS

7

PART FOUR. ROBINSON CRUSOE

PART FIVE. THEREAFTER

LIST OF ILLUSTRATIONS

DANIEL FOE
Date of Birth Unknown
m. ROSE ......?
d. 1631

Children:

- DANIEL
- MARY
  - MARY b. 1645
- THOMAS d. an infant
- HENRY b. 1628
  - MARY b. 1657 m. FRANCIS BATHAM 1679
    - DANIEL m. 1. DOROTHY – 2. MARY WEBB
      - HANNAH d. 1759, unmarried
      - DANIEL d. young in 1708
      - TUFFLEY d. 1720
      - DANIEL d. young in 1724
  - ELIZABETH b. 1659 m. ROBERT DAVIS
- JAMES b. 1630 m. ALICE, 1656 d. bet. 1705–8
- DANIEL b. bet. July and Oct., 1660 m. Jan. 1, 1683 MARY TUFFLEY d. April 26, 1731
  - MARY d. 1688
  - BENJAMIN* m. 1718 HANNAH COATES d. 1737
    - SAMUEL b. abt. 1730 d. 1783
      - JAMES b. 1777 d. 1856
        - MARY
        - JANE AMELIA
          - JAMES WILLIAM
          - DANIEL b. abt. 1873
    - and 11 other children, 5 of whom are buried in St. Martin - in - the-fields
  - MARIA m. –LANGLEY
  - HENRIETTA m. JOHN BURTON d. 1760
  - MARTHA d. a child 1707
  - SOPHIA b. 1701 m. HENRY BAKER d. 1762
    - HENRY b. 1734 d. 1776
    - DAVID ERSKINE b. 1730 d. 1767
    - WILLIAM b. 1726 d. 1828 Rector of Lyndon, Rutlandshire
      - WILLIAM M.D. d. 1850
        - EMILY m. COL. DALLAS HUGH LATHAM R.A.
        - SOPHIA d. 1853
        - CHARLES BERNARD
        - WILLIAM Rector of Welton, Lincs.
        - HARRIET, ELIZABETH
      - HENRY DE FOE BAKER, d. 1845, clerk in Holy Orders
        - HENRY DE FOE BAKER Rector of Thruxton, Hants.
- A BROTHER (see p. 170)
- and probably other children.

* It should be especially noted that no reference has been made in this tree to Benjamin *Norton* De Foe, stated to be the illegitimate son of Daniel, and whose story is told in pages 122 and 271–3.

INTRODUCTION

THIS BOOK was planned as a tribute to a genius whom I regard as one of the greatest writers of English prose, and indisputably the greatest English journalist. And the very qualities that give him such supremacy involved me, in common with every other biographer of De Foe, in labyrinths of speculation and surmise which he himself would have been the first to appreciate and chuckle over.

Mr. George Sampson summarizes De Foe's life and work by stating that they defy summary, and then comparing him with Dickens, whom in some way he resembles. With the first statement I disagree, while agreeing with the second.

His effect upon the reader—and that, when all is said and done, is the measure by which every author must ultimately be tested—is the result of a combination of four qualities. Three of these are the hallmark of all first-class journalists—a capacity to select, an adequate vocabulary expertly used, and an ability (essential in every type of artist) to take an objective view of one's work. It was in a fourth quality that De Foe was superb, and indeed unique—his power to visualize not merely remembered facts, but events existing only in his own imagination.

This power he employs with such effect that the reader is totally unable to decide the point at which fact comes to a halt and leaves sheer invention to carry on. I fancy that De Foe himself became at times uncertain, and was like one who in his efforts to illuminate the dark forests of memory has lighted strange fires that leave him still more bewildered between truth and falsity.

De Foe, inevitably, has had a number of other biographers. I think I may claim to have read most of their works, and these I have chronicled in the bibliography at the end of this book. One of the earliest does, however, deserve special mention. He is so naïvely and delightfully diverting that it is a pity that the *Dictionary of National Biography* cannot find space for even a paragraph about him. His name was William

Chadwick, and his enthusiasm for De Foe suddenly bubbled forth nearly a century ago—to be exact, in the autumn of 1856.

He explains, with a gusto that defies syntax, the reasons that induced him to begin the book. "When anyone as inexperienced and untried as the writer presumes to take up pen on a subject so various and complex as that involved in one of the most stirring lives of the most stirring characters of the most stirring times in English history, he may well crave time for investigating the charge of presumption which fairly might be brought against him for attempting such a task." "How, it may be asked," he says, "came you to presume to write a life of Daniel De Foe? How indeed! I ask the question to myself—How?" He immediately answers it. He had arrived with a friend at Skipton, in Yorkshire, and left the company to visit a second-hand shop adjoining the hotel. He was rewarded by finding "sweepings from the library of the last of the Vavasours of Western Underwood", among which he discovered *A Tour Through England*. He began to read, and soon became so excited that he was "stimulated to enquiry as to the author. . . . This was followed by deeper investigation into the erratic waywardness of the ingenious writer and led me to take up pen myself in order, if possible, to throw some additional ray of light on one of Britain's greatest of geniuses, *Daniel De Foe*, the author of *Robinson Crusoe*. Also of *The Compleat Tradesman*,[1] a work which formed the background of the character of the great Benjamin Franklin, for the book is Franklin all over. Such is my apology for writing, such my preface."

After which he stuns the reader by stating that owing to the facts recounted in *The Tour* having been seen and encountered in 1732, whereas De Foe died in 1731, he is led to believe that the work is not by De Foe at all!

The inescapable fact confronting the ecstatic Chadwick and his better-trained, better-informed successors is that De Foe, in spite of his long, intensely active life, left comparatively little imprint of his personality upon those who knew him. We have no contemporary sidelights on his childhood, no intimate and human details of his emergence from lower-middle-class obscurity into a vivid and varied world in which for nearly half a century he was to play his own unique part.

---

[1] The title should, of course, be *The Compleat English Tradesman*.

De Foe, of course, shares this curious obliteration of
personality with another writer, the greatest of all. And
while it is true that biographers find it far easier to fill up the
years in De Foe's long life than those in Shakespeare's
comparatively short one, there is a similar absence of anything
in the way of contemporary description.

So far as his physical appearance is concerned, the
portraits of which any claim to authenticity can be made—
the caricatures are as fantastic as they are numerous—amount,
all told, to five. The earliest is that engraved by Van
der Gucht from a drawing by Taverner, published in 1703.
Another is one of De Foe looking over his shoulder, appearing in the second edition of *The True-born Englishman* in 1705.
The third—most often reproduced—is the "Laudatur et
Alget" portrait, commonly known as the *Jure Divino*, since
it formed the frontispiece to the folio edition of that book,
published in 1706. (There is a variation of this in Lee's
Biography.) The fourth, prefixed to the folio edition of his
History of the Union of Great Britain (1709) was engraved by
Skelton. The fifth—and least satisfactory—is an oval
portrait by Medland.

Unfortunately all of them present him in one of those full-
bottomed wigs which were nearly as effective in concealing
the wearer's personality as a mask. It surrounds a face which,
except for certain sardonic curves of the mouth, might have
passed for that of Addison or Steele or Richardson or a
hundred other plump, clean-shaven gentlemen of the late
seventeenth and early eighteenth centuries. (De Foe himself
might have devoted an entire essay to the Regulating Effect
of Full-bottomed Wigges upon the Countenances of Gentlemen of Breeding and Talent.)

For the biographer there remains the consolatory theory
that any artist, literary or otherwise, may be relied upon to depict, or at any rate reveal, himself sooner or later in
his works. Nevertheless there are a few who from natural
reticence or from deliberate self-obliteration contrive to
reveal almost nothing, and such a one was De Foe. In his
case the concealment is complicated, as already stated, by
his capacity to fuse fact and fiction beyond analysis. No
writer ever conveyed a passionate determination to tell the
truth, the whole truth, and nothing but the truth with such
ingenious and unscrupulous distortions. As we read, we are

left feeling that only the natural infirmities inflicted by time upon his memory are responsible for his lapses.

The first essential fact—the exact date of his birth—has so far eluded every biographer. Chadwick gives it as 1661; Chalmers the same; the *Dictionary of National Biography* gives the same date, but follows the statement with a hesitant (?). Professor Sutherland asserts that it is almost certain that he was born in the autumn of 1660; the late Mr. Wilfred Whitten says De Foe was born probably late in 1659,[1] quoting in support a letter from Mr. G. A. Aitken in *The Athenaeum*, while the latest edition of the *Encyclopaedia Britannica* dodges exactitude with a timid *"circa* 1659".

The precise date *might*, in many cases, be of little importance. But in this case it happens to be very important indeed, since whether he was born in 1659 or later affects the first-hand accuracy of one of his most famous works. Further uncertainties cloud our knowledge of his early boyhood.

Finally, we remain in the dark as to the exact date when he added the aristocratic "De" to the monosyllabic simplicity of "Foe", and why he did it.

Apart from the authorities mentioned in the Bibliography on pp. 297–8, other books, press cuttings and articles have gone to the composition of the picture I have tried to draw, particularly its background, since I decline to believe that any man can be properly appreciated if the circumstances and places and general atmosphere in which he lived are not clearly sketched in as part of his life. And De Foe's life was, to a more than ordinary extent, shaped and coloured by his period.

All, or at any rate most, of De Foe's writings of real importance are mentioned here. There remain, however, a very considerable number of lesser pamphlets and so forth to which no reference has been made, nor has a complete list of them been given. Either course would have involved an increase in the size and price of the book quite incompatible with any extra value that such an addition might have. Between three and four hundred "works" of De Foe have been traced and catalogued, some entirely ephemeral, many of no interest whatever except to the collector.

Finally, I should like to acknowledge my especial

[1] This is an obvious impossibility, since the register of St. Giles shows that a second daughter, Elizabeth, was born on July 19th, 1659.

indebtedness to Professor Sutherland for his recent investigations concerning De Foe, as mentioned in his biography; to the courtesy and helpfulness of the Librarian of the Royal Society of Arts and the officials at the Guildhall Library; to Mr. Alexander Leslie, and to Mrs. Margaret De Foe Latham, great-great-great-great-granddaughter of Daniel.

PART ONE

BACKGROUND

CHAPTER I

THE RESTORATION, AND AFTER

IN 1658, two years before the birth of Daniel De Foe—I am throughout, for the sake of simplification, using the "De" which he himself added, while referring to the rest of his family as Foe—the great Protector died. The date, September 3rd, was an anniversary of two decisive battles. In that some special significance was seen. There was further significance, said those attending him, in the tremendous storm which broke over England in the early hours of the following morning.

Cromwell's physician had diagnosed his prolonged illness as "a bastard tertiary ague"; in more modern, comprehensible English, a prolonged intermittent fever. It had been aggravated by the death of his daughter, Elizabeth Claypole, on August 3rd. His embalmed body, royally clothed, was publicly exhibited at Somerset House; its burial in Westminster Abbey did not take place until nearly three months after death.

The funeral ceremony was an affair, not merely of more than regal solemnity, as the poet Cowley records, but of more than regal expense. Sixty thousand pounds was allotted to meet the cost, and it is on record that in 1659 a further nineteen thousand pounds was still owing.

Within three hours of Oliver's death, Richard, his elder son, was nominated as the new Protector, and was accepted unopposed as Head of the State. "There is not a dog that wags his tongue, so great a calm are we in," wrote John Thurloe to Henry, Richard's brother, but added, significantly and less light-heartedly, "There are some secret murmurings in the army, as if his Highness were not a

general, as his father was." His new Highness certainly was
not. Tongues of men, to say nothing of dogs, began to wag.
The army leaders, after a meeting in October, decided to
petition Richard to appoint an efficient and professional
soldier as commander-in-chief. Richard refused, but
mitigated the refusal by increasing the military rates of pay.
There were other grievances, chiefly due to the country's
acute financial crisis, and there were negotiations, prolonged
but not unfriendly. Richard's own temperament, which
combined amiability, indifference and vacillation, was the
real problem. What can be done with a ruler who announces,
"I will not have a drop of blood spilt for the preservation
of my greatness", and of whom one contemporary—Thurloe
again—wrote, "I never saw or heard fraud or guile in him",
and another, "The sweetness of his voice and language has
won my heart"?

Unfortunately these qualities were no substitute for moral
strength and quick decisions. His prudent temper and his
gentle bearing would have been admirable in a constitutional
monarch, whose duties he would have accepted without
enthusiasm. But he was not a constitutional monarch.
Worse still, he had no real capacity or desire to govern.

The brief and colourless reign of "Queen Dick", if reign
it may be called, came to its inevitable end. The Puritan
army leaders quarrelled among themselves. Ninety of the
one hundred and sixty of the old anti-Puritan Parliament
returned to their seats and took over the business of govern-
ing; new armies under Monck in Edinburgh and Fairfax in
Yorkshire, the navy, and even the mobs in the street swung
over to the exiled Charles. Richard, so hard-pressed for
money that bailiffs were sent to Whitehall to seize his
property, finally escaped to Paris. For some years he lived
humbly as "John Clarke", "the whole diversion of him
there being drawings of landscapes and reading of books".
From Paris he moved to Geneva, but finally came back to
England about 1680, and lived at Cheshunt, still under the
name of Clarke. He died on July 12th, 1712, aged seventy-
six, and was buried at Hursley, in Hampshire.

Long before then he had faded into a legend, a mere
memory. And forty-two years before that date, on May
8th, 1660, Charles, the martyr's son, had landed, a swarthy,
loose-lipped young man who, commented shrewd old Isaac

d'Israeli, "wrote a fair little running hand, as if wrote in haste, or uneasy until it was done, as was to be expected from this illustrious vagabond, who could never get rid of his natural restlessness and vivacity".

Before he landed, the "vagabond" and his supporters had paved the way. On May 1st he had delivered his message to an enthusiastic Government, who in response had declared that the country ought to be ruled by Lords and Commons with the King over both, and rounded off this gratifying statement by voting fifty thousand pounds for "His Majesty's present occasions". Two days later the City and the fleet had declared for him.

On May 29th, his birthday, Charles made his triumphal entry into London, and in due course was rapturously received and crowned under the magnificent and inaccurate titles of King of England and Scotland, France and Ireland. And the country had swung violently from the excessive austerities of Puritanism to an equally violent, though more picturesque programme of wine, women and song.

Not to the exclusion of revenge, however, so far as the new King was concerned.

In November 1660 a Bill of Attainder against Cromwell and the regicides was passed. On January 26th, 1661, his body was disinterred, and four days later—the date being deliberately chosen to coincide with the anniversary of the martyred Charles's execution—was hung on the gallows in Tyburn. The body was subsequently buried under the gallows: the head set up on a pole at the top of Westminster Hall, an object lesson to all whose patriotism had suffered the double calamity of becoming obsolete and unpopular.

Existence under the glorious Restoration to middle-class Englishmen, if they were Londoners, might have suggested superficial parallels with the days of Elizabeth. The sovereign himself, after a frustrated, danger-haunted and exiled youth, had been welcomed, as Elizabeth had been welcomed, with hysterical delight to a throne darkened with clouds of intrigue and violence and grim and remorseless spiritual and political warfare. He had replaced, as she had replaced, a ruler whose convictions were as passionate as they were narrow, and—worst crime of all—whose regime had become antipathetic to the ingrained and natural instincts of the people. Elizabeth was shrewd beyond measure, cynical, disillusioned, occasionally moved to grim wit, and passionately English. Charles was shrewd, but not so shrewd, frequently witty, equally cynical, equally disillusioned, and English, but with reservations. Both gloried in pageantry, and in personal power, power derived from two sources, sovereignty and the prestige of their country. Both were completely unscrupulous. And under them both English ships sailed the seven seas with semi-piratical effrontery, attacked other ships—in Charles's case, chiefly the Dutch, their dogged, powerful, exasperated rivals.

Intrigue and counter-intrigue was the breath of their nostrils. Charles had been familiar with such an atmosphere throughout his exile; when he substituted "Rex" for "P" after his signature he also substituted English for Continental plotting. He scattered free pardons among his enemies, astutely conditioned by his new Parliament's willingness to forgive and forget, while concerning religious tolerance he wrote, "We declare a liberty to tender consciences, and that no man shall be disquieted or called in question for differences of opinion in matters of religion which do not disturb the peace of the Kingdom, and We shall be ready to consent to such an Act of Parliament as upon mature deliberation shall be offered to us for the full granting of that indulgence."

No monarch could have said more; no monarch could have meant it less. The Nonconformists were, at any rate, willing to believe him. They asked for a number of concessions, in return for which they were willing to accept a revised prayer-book. "So long as it is not made compulsory upon all and allows the Minister to offer free prayer some time." The King referred the matter to the Bishops: the Bishops replied evasively, and declined to take part in a joint conference. Charles metaphorically shrugged his shoulders. He was anxious to conciliate both the Puritan and Roman Catholic elements among his new subjects; if his suggestion were turned down, why, so much the better for his personal reputation for religious broadmindedness and generosity.

Parliament not only turned them down; it went a good deal further. It had already reinstated all the clergy, including those convicted of incompetency and scandalous living, dismissed during the Civil War. It now readmitted bishops to the House of Lords, and—far worse—passed the

Corporation Act, which excluded Nonconformists from all municipal bodies, and, in the case of boroughs elected by corporations even denied them a Parliamentary vote.

It was only the beginning. A year later Parliament passed the Act of Uniformity, under which Dissenters were described as "a great number of people following their own Sensuality and who, living without knowledge and due fear of God, do wilfully and schismatically abstain and refuse to come to their parish churches where . . . the work of God is used upon Sundays and other days ordained and appointed". By that Act, on or before the Feast of St. Bartholomew (August 24th) every minister was bound to give in public his unfeigned Assent and Consent to everything contained in the Book of Common Prayer. And all holders of ecclesiastical positions, all professors, and all university tutors had to conform to the Liturgy and to state that they regarded the Solemn League and Covenant as an unlawful oath. The alternative was immediate deprivation.

The result of all this malevolence was to drive some two thousand clergymen, including some of the best and wisest in the country, from the Established Church, and many more thousands of the sturdy and independent laity who had worshipped at their churches.

The King, still on the side of tolerance, though tolerance derived merely from a diplomatic sense of the value of give-and-take, suggested that he might be given powers of dispensation for the benefit of those with tender consciences. But Parliament and the Bishops were adamant. And in 1664 the Conventicle Act was passed. Its authors must have been the spiritual descendants of the Spanish inquisitors. Any person of over sixteen attending a Nonconformist service at which more than five people were present was liable to a fine of five pounds or to three months' imprisonment. For a second offence the penalties were doubled. For the third there was a fine of a hundred pounds, or transportation for seven years, at his own expense, "to one of His Majesty's foreign plantations", Virginia and New England being specifically excluded because a banished Nonconformist might find friends there.

A year later, in 1665, came the Five Mile Act. Anyone in Holy Orders who had not submitted to the Act of Uniformity, or who did not swear to refrain from taking up arms against the King or (the real crux) attempt any alteration in the Government of Church and State, was forbidden to come (except on a journey) within five miles of any place whatever in which he had previously held acres or even conducted services. The penalty for disobedience was forty pounds. To thousands of Nonconformist ministers this, apart from social ostracism, meant utter ruin, since they could not even act as tutors or schoolmasters.

That year was the year of the Plague. Small wonder that thousands of Nonconformists regarded the visitation and the Great Fire that followed it as the direct retort of an outraged Deity to the iniquities of the English Government.

A more reasonable sequel would have been a general relaxation of religious bigotry. And for a brief breathing-space there was. Efforts were actually made to modify the terms of conformity, and when in 1668 the first Conventicle Act automatically expired the Nonconformists plucked up heart. Their hopes were premature. Sheldon, Archbishop of Canterbury, persuaded the pliant Charles not only to enforce the previous acts, but to pass yet another, which contained this extraordinary clause:

"If any doubt should arise concerning the meaning of any part of this Act, it shall be determined in the sense that is contrary to the Conventicles, it being the intention of the House to suppress them in the most effective manner possible."

The next round in the struggle went with the King. His popularity as an individual he could always maintain, but the Dutch war and his entanglements with France had created a situation in which he dared not alienate any section of his people on a large scale. In 1671-2 he suspended the penal laws against the Nonconformists by a Declaration of Indulgence allowing certain persons to preach as Dissenters in certain specified places. He also abolished penalties against Roman Catholics (though their preaching was still forbidden).

Yet, in the end, the victory was to lie with the Commons, which formally asserted that "The Penal Statutes in matters ecclesiastical cannot be suspended but by Act of Parliament". Even among the Presbyterians there were many who realized the rightness of this, and Charles, realizing it too, called in his licences.

A sordid record of large-scale victimization. I have dealt

with it here in some detail only because it enables one to grasp the bitterness and despair which its infliction bred among families as sincerely and passionately adherent to their religious convictions as the Foes and their fellow-Dissenters were.

But there were, of course, other events to stir discussion and excitement. In 1662, for instance, the King went to Portsmouth to meet and marry the little Infanta of Portugal for the second time—the first time being merely by proxy. Her Highness's dowry was mixed but valuable—the island of Bombay in the East Indies, Tangier, and two million croisades, in consideration whereof thirty thousand pounds a year was settled upon her. And in July of the same year the Queen Mother came to England and took up her residence at Somerset House.

In 1663 "A Plot of Fanaticks" was discovered in the north; as a result "twenty-one conspirators were afterwards convicted in several places".

In 1664 exasperation with the Dutch came to a head. Rivalry between the two dominant seafaring nations had become increasingly intense and bitter. Compensation for innumerable wrongs inflicted in the course of innumerable conflicts, ranging from trivial clashes between Yarmouth and Dutch fishermen to slave raids and robberies of bullion in the Moluccas, had been demanded—and ignored—by both sides. In April a Committee of Trade issued its report, following which Parliament formally resolved that the Dutch, by invading the rights of the English in India, Africa and elsewhere, were the greatest obstruction to our foreign trade, and addressed his Majesty begging him to take some speedy and effectual course for redress thereof, assuring him that they "wou'd with their Lives and Fortunes assist him". And on June 11th the City lent His Majesty one hundred thousand pounds towards the Dutch wars. Both Houses thanked the City for the large sums they had lent the King. The City further responded by building, at its own charge, a man-of-war called *The Loyal London*, to replace a frigate of the same name which had been lost by fire.

War was formally declared in March 1665, and in the following month the King inspected a Grand Fleet including one hundred and seven battleships and fourteen fire-ships, prior to its sailing for Texel under the command of the Duke of York. Charles, assessing with his usual cynical detachment the useful distractions of a popular war, anticipated that when open hostilities began the fret and friction of religious difficulties would die down, and the nation be fused into patriotic unity. He was right. But he also thought that when it came to the final showdown Dutch prudence would avert a full-scale conflict. And in that he was hopelessly wrong.

CHAPTER II

THE PLAGUE

DE FOE, as a small, active, sharp-witted, sharp-eyed
boy, must have seen and heard much that lingered
all his life as isolated threads of memory. The streets
of London during those early, formative years were teeming
with incidents whose significance no child could completely comprehend, but which made them as thrilling a
playground as the assembly-place of a circus. There were,
of course, dangers; no doubt there were innumerable
exhortations and warnings from his mother, and punishments when they were disregarded.

In 1665 came excitements and terrors exceeding all others,
the Great Plague.

The adjective is not unnecessary. Many other visitations
of Plague had already swept not only the three known
continents but England itself. To-day we know at least its
main derivatives—gross overcrowding, almost complete
ignorance of the first laws of sanitation and hygiene;
prejudice, and a passive acceptance of such epidemics as part
of an incomprehensible system of divine punishment. That
such punishment fell almost entirely on the undernourished,
untaught, ill-clothed, ill-housed members of the community,
so earning it the name of the "Poor Man's Plague", merely
indicated that poverty was an additional form of sin.

There had been a number of outbreaks in London in the
sixteenth century. Collectively their stories make shocking
reading (a thousand died weekly in London alone in 1563).
By the time James I came to the throne the authorities seem
to have decided that some sort of large-scale and organized
preventive measures were necessary. For in that year, 1603,
matters came to a climax. The outbreak was so severe that
the Coronation was affected. The King was unable to enter
the City on his way to the Palace and had to travel deviously
through the fields about Stamford Hill to the Charterhouse,

and thence to Westminster. From Woodstock, where he and his Council had retreated for safety, a Royal Proclamation was issued. It ordained that in "the sinfully-polluted subburbes" no new tenants should be allowed to live in any infected houses until it be thought safe, none of the rooms "are to be pestered with a multitude of dwellers, and that such of them as were to be pulled down are to be rased accordingly, and not rebuilt".

It does not appear to have occurred to anyone that the result would be the still greater overcrowding of the remaining houses by what were vaguely and spitefully referred to as "dissolute and idle persons".[1]

Thirty-nine thousand people died during that particular visitation. There was another in 1609 (twelve thousand casualties, including many in the provinces); another in 1625 (thirty-five thousand casualties).

There was a peculiarly virulent outbreak in 1636, following which the Lord Mayor and all his aldermen were instructed to meet the justices of Middlesex, Surrey and Westminster every week "to advise them as to the courses taken on like occasions and as to the best means to be now taken". "The plagues," states a contemporary writer, "began the first time by a surfiet in *White Chapel*: the second time by seamen about the same place; the third by reason of Rotten Mutton at Stepney; the fourth with a Pack of Carpets from Turkey; the fifth with a Dogge that came over from Amsterdam."

The Plague presented many minor problems, one of these being the virtual impossibility of the parish clerks keeping, as in theory they were bound to keep, a record of the deaths arising from its visitation. At the beginning several did their best to conceal the outbreak; later on a number of the clerks themselves fell victims. The accuracy of the records they kept has been attacked. John Bell, the clerk to the Parish Clerk's Company, has left on record a spirited defence of himself and his colleagues, too long to quote here. It would probably be fair to say that they did their elderly best in a period of unique stress.

In discussing the Plague in its later and more ghastly phases, the seventeenth-century mechanism for grappling

[1] It is interesting to note that throughout Elizabeth's long reign of forty-five years no Act of Parliament was ever passed forbidding building development, though there were several outbreaks of plague in that period.

with illness of any type must be taken into account. To the Foes and their neighbours no doubt they appeared as scientific, intelligent and adequate as our own. But one wonders what a mid-twentieth-century medical officer of health or sanitary inspector would have to say to the following.

A College of Medicine which included nearly a hundred "doctors" who practised without its qualifications, as well as apothecaries—in itself a comprehensive and elastic term —who performed a doctor's duties. Many of both classes had never before seen a case of the Plague.

No compulsory certification of death. Notification was optional, the only officials directly concerned being aged female paupers, who were called "searchers", two being appointed by each parish. They were corrupt and ignorant; when a message came from a bereaved family that the local church bell should be tolled for a burial, they went to the house and "viewed" the body, or, if the family cared to bribe them with a shilling or so, did not even do that, but obligingly certified that death was due to any disease involving a minimum of trouble and inconvenience.

The fact that Jews, Quakers and other outside religious organizations refused to ask for a bell to be tolled complicated matters. They buried their dead without notification of any sort.

The contemporary Bills of Mortality have, inevitably, formed the chief sources of information concerning the numbers who died from the Great Plague. Nevertheless, they are farcically unreliable. From the "searchers" went reports from the clerk to each parish; from the clerks to the Company of Parish Clerks, from the Company to the Lord Mayor, and from him, if his lordship thought it worth while, to the Minister of State. After these prolonged official ramblings the statistics, classified alphabetically under "Parasites" and again under "Diseases and Casualties", were duly printed and published, together with a totally irrelevant "Assize of Bread, as set forth by the Lord Mayor and Court of Aldermen", from which it appears that a penny wheaten loaf must contain $9\frac{1}{2}$ ounces, a white loaf of the same weight being $1\frac{1}{2}$d.[1]

[1] In the Bill of Mortality, dated August 15th–22nd, 1565, appear the following causes of death: Chrisomes (9), Frighted (2), Head-mould-shot (1), Imposthume (8), Purples (2), Riting of the Lights (18), Tissick (9), Winde (4) and Suddenly (2).

The City itself was a standing invitation to every conceivable form of pestilence. Down the centres of the narrow,
concave, over-hung streets flowed sluggish streams, choked and
littered with refuse that made them literally open sewers,
except when rain-storms converted them into torrents.
Garbage, household filth and excrement, and every other
form of waste was piled high in the alleys, alongside windows
that opened straight from living-rooms. (So, indeed, they
were piled, incredible as it may seem, until a century ago.)
Even the dead played their part in poisoning the living; they
were buried thickly in City churchyards, and near those
same churchyards—St. Clement Danes, Cripplegate, St.
Brides—were wells from which the tainted water was pumped
for nearby citizens to drink and to wash with. In wet weather
the narrower streets were often ankle-deep in mud. And the
walls of the houses themselves, while their lathes and plaster
might keep out the rain, were ideal breeding-places for
rats and mice and lice.

Restoration officialdom did realize these handicaps to
sanitation, though only dimly. Under the title of "annoy-
ances" it classified neglect to cleanse sewers and town
ditches, standing pools of foetid water, the overcrowding of
churchyards, and the use by the poor of rotting foods. But
nothing was done, at any rate so far as the poor were
concerned; they remained in their hovels, resigned and
fatalistic, duly caught the Plague, duly died. The rich?
The rich went to live in the still more primitive but as
yet untainted country until the danger had passed.

Incidentally, the population of London at this time is
highly conjectural. But half a million, or a trifle under, is a
likely guess. (The second city in those days was, rather
surprisingly, Norwich, with about thirty thousand, Bristol
coming third with twenty-five thousand.)

Early isolated cases of Plague appeared at St. Martin's,
Westminster, and in St. Giles early in November 1664, the
beginning of a winter of extreme severity.

The origin of this particular climax in epidemics is
uncertain, and likely to remain so. One theory is that the
infection was carried in bales of merchandise arriving
from Holland; another, that it was introduced by Dutch
prisoners of war; a third, that it was not "imported" at
all, but merely a sudden terrific and culminating outburst

of what had always lain latent in seventeenth-century squalor.

On Christmas Eve occurred what Sherlock Holmes would have termed the Incident of the Comet, one which soared across the heavens leaving a blazing trail of light that people regarded from its coming as a portent, an omen, a warning of vague but terrific significance. During the following February and March the Thames was twice completely blocked by ice. In that refrigerator-like atmosphere the Plague bacillus was constrained to remain dormant. Few cases were reported; some of the few actually recovered.

But from early summer onwards there was no dormancy.

The great epidemic, *qua* epidemic, began at St. Giles-in-the-Fields. Boghurst[1] tells the story of that little section of London with vivid simplicity.

The heat brought vast numbers of flies. They invaded the houses in such multitudes that they lined the walls; "where any thread of string hung down, it was presently thick set with flies like a rope of onions. And covered the highways so thick that a handful at a time might have been taken up, and the croaking of frogs was loudly heard even before the ditches sheltering them could be seen".

Nor was the Plague the only epidemic. Between the church and the parish pound, he tells us, less than six score paces, forty families lay smitten with smallpox.

And in the meantime the guns of the Fleet thundered against the Dutch. Success swayed this way and that; with the country's trade half paralysed by the plague, and the plague itself filtering with horrible persistence further and yet further into the country districts and even among the ships, many of which were rotten and unseaworthy, England was in a desperate state, made more desperate still when the French joined the Dutch. On June 1st, 1666, the Duke of Albemarle met the enemy fleet. For the best part of a week the battle raged, and the roar of the guns off the Dutch coast echoed in the ears of waiting Londoners; then came the news that the ships which were their shield and pride

[1] William Boghurst was an apothecary living in St. Giles, and consequently a near neighbour of the Foes, a point of particular biographical interest. He left a manuscript dated 1666 (now in the British Museum) entitled *An Experimental Relation of the Last Plague of the City of London.* A man of high courage, he worked amid horrible sights and horrible perils; it is pleasant to record that he escaped infection.

had been almost battered out of existence by an enemy superior in numbers and equipment, though never in courage. The English vessels limped back to Sheerness to refit. With a French invasion imminent, they put to sea again half-way through July. On the 25th of that month Charles and his younger brother stood on the leads of Whitehall, once more listening to the mutter and rumble of the great brass cannon. And this time the silence that followed was the silence of victory. The English Admiral, landing at Schelling, had burnt two towns, a hundred and fifty ships in harbour, and a million pounds' worth of property.

The Queen Mother had left her London home on January 29th for France, where, under her physicians' instructions, she was to "drink the waters". The King accompanied her to Dover; from thence he went to the Nore, where the vessels that had lately soundly beaten the Dutch in another action off Lowestoft were anchored. . . . Heartening as it all was, the shadow of the Plague darkened the national rejoicings. At the official thanksgiving services held in every metropolitan church a collection on behalf of the sufferers from the Plague was made by the King's order. In the week that he had returned to London the recorded deaths had risen to four hundred and seventy. Some were in King Street, almost next door to the Palace gates. On July 6th a Royal Proclamation was issued, in which the full extent and distribution of the epidemic were stated. The High Court of Admiralty migrated to Winchester. On the 7th far more ominously significant news was published: His Majesty had departed from London for Syon House, Isle-worth. From there, two days later, the Court moved to Hampton Court, though further sittings of the Privy Council were still to be held at Syon House. Hampton Court was merely a stage in the royal retreat. Charles went on to Salisbury, adjourning Parliament until October, when he arranged to open it at Oxford, leaving the capital, the city with incomparably the largest population and infinitely the most vulnerable, to any form of pestilence, to swelter, and to be ravaged as it had never been ravaged since the Black Death. Guidance and direction, apart from the limited jurisdiction over which the Lord Mayor and his aldermen functioned, there was at first none.

From St. Giles, slowly and irregularly, but with devilish

persistence, the Plague percolated from west to east. In May forty-three cases had been reported; thereafter, month by month, the numbers rose to their ghastly zenith: 390 in June; 6,137 in July; 17,036 in August; 31,159 in September. By that time a third of the population had evacuated the City to find refuge in the country or elsewhere. A moderate estimate of the number who died in that year is 69,000. To them must be added another 2,000 in 1666, though the winter brought a sharp drop in the number of casualties.

The weather of 1665 remained a pitiless ally of the pestilence. The great frost was followed by an equally severe drought. No rain at all fell before the end of April, when there was a slight shower; from then until August there were only a few wet days. After them followed three weeks of sullen and suffocating heat, and finally, in September, rains so torrential that they extinguished the great fires that had been lit in the streets in the forlorn hope of destroying, or at least mitigating, the infection.

The physical effects of the Plague were horrible upon the living and hideous upon the dead. Many victims slept with their eyes half open, we are told, and, tormented by nightmares, twitched their heads continuously. A patient's suddenly screaming that he was on fire was recognised as indicative of a fatal symptom.

There were heroic doctors—far too few, of course—who stayed behind to fight for their patients' lives. Nathaniel Hodges, of Red Lion Court, was one of them. Dressed in his long black coat, knee-breeches, and formal cravat, and carrying his professional gold-headed cane, he entered each morning his consulting-room and did his limited but generous best for the crowds that thronged it. But in the houses of the victims there were only the "nurse-keepers", a race of thieving, brutal, uneducated women who would have made Dickens' Mrs. Gamp seem a Florence Nightingale by comparison; human vermin viler than the sleek black rats that battened on the neglected filth in the houses and streets and, with their fleas, were swift and deadly carriers of the infection.

Quacks of every kind with "infallible remedies" reaped magnificent harvests. Of these, a Frenchman named Angier was the most impudent and the most conspicuous. He claimed to have been successful in stopping the Plague in

Paris and other cities, and so much impressed the Secretary of State and the Privy Council that, after a trial of his remedy, which was by fumigation, the ingredients being brimstone and saltpetre with a dash of amber, the King was induced to give his support. Official advertisements were issued stating where Monsieur Angier's "fume" could be obtained, and the Mayor and Corporation were instructed to pay for it.

The Plague continued.

The College of Physicians had nostrums of their own. Unfortunately they proved no more effective than Monsieur Angier's. They also drew up a list of rules, of which the kindest thing that can be said about them is that they were well-meaning, and the unkindest that they were so vague as to be completely futile. Streets and houses were to be kept clean "as diligently as may be". The sale of corrupt food was to be "restrained". The poor were "to be relieved and put to work". Perhaps the most unfortunate of all were the inhabitants of Newgate and other gaols, since the prisons of those days had negligible water supplies and no sanitation whatever. The sick had inadequate supplies of medicine and in many cases might consider themselves indeed lucky if they had any at all. There was, of course, a general short-age of food and clothing.

Apart from quack medicines, and the street fires which the September torrents so ruthlessly extinguished, other more personal efforts were made to stem the disease. They were, by our present standards, pitifully ineffective.

Seventeenth-century methods of grappling with an epidemic were, basically, very much in line with those of the most backward African tribes in Victorian times. As with them, complete and ruthless isolation was the trump card. Not merely the sufferer, but everyone else who had the bad luck to be in the same house, was subjected to forty days' rigid quarantine. Entrances to such houses were officially marked with a large red cross, to which was added, as a pious official gesture, "God have mercy upon us". (The practice was no improvised emergency measure; it had the authority of established precedent, as a public proclamation of 1645 proves.) Customers at the few shops still functioning were required to place the exact amount of their purchases in pots filled with vinegar, the acid of which was supposed to be disinfectant. Written communications were sprayed with alcohol, and held, as a further precaution, at arm's length and read through magnifying-glasses.

It was advised that slaughter-houses should be removed outside the City. It was similarly advised that the corpses of Plague victims should be buried in quicklime.

Cats and dogs, regarded vaguely as plague carriers, were slaughtered wholesale; no one, however, seems to have bothered much about the real villains of the piece—the rats that swarmed everywhere. Tobacco-smoking was encouraged as part of a personal fumigatory process. Numbers of short clay pipes discovered in recent years in the vicinity of plague-pits testify to a belief demonstrably unsound.

The pits themselves deserve more than passing mention.

If there was one point at least on which every authority was in complete agreement it was that Plague victims should be buried with the utmost promptitude. And since single graves, even collective graves in the ordinary sense, were out of the question, pits, monstrously deep and wide, were the only solution. The chief, or at any rate the best known, of these was in Bunhill Fields, nicknamed by Southey "the Campo Santo of Nonconformity", and originally an open field. After the Plague it was surrounded by a wall and known as Tindall's Burying Ground. Among the one hundred and twenty-four thousand Dissenters who lie there are John Bunyan; George Fox, Founder of the Society of Friends; Isaac Watts; Susannah Wesley, mother of Charles and John Wesley; Henry, Richard and William Cromwell (descendants, though not sons, of Oliver Cromwell); Joseph Ritson, the antiquary; Joseph Hughes, founder of the Bible Society; Blake, the artist and poet; Thomas Stothard, the artist; and, of course, De Foe himself.

Other plague-pits were dug at the north end of Hand Alley (now New Street, Bishopsgate), in which De Foe himself lived for a time; Dead Man's Place, a Dissenters' burying ground in which Cruden, compiler of the *Concordance*, was buried; Early Street, Westminster; and Hounds-ditch, that follows the course of the old City wall. Since first paved in 1503 this last had been the resort of old-clothes dealers. The inhabitants, not very surprisingly, suffered severely from the Plague, and eleven hundred bodies were cast into a huge ditch which was dug to receive them. The churchyard of St. Olave's, Mark Lane, where a church has been in evidence since 1319, was another burying-ground for Plague victims, as the skulls over its entrance in Seething Lane bear witness. (It was these that inspired Dickens to nickname the place "St. Ghastly Grim" in *The Uncommercial Traveller*.) St. Olave's was Pepys's parish church. It contains a memorial to him as well as a monument to his wife. Both are buried in the vaults, she in 1669, he thirty-four years later.

St. Stephen's churchyard, in Coleman Street, was another of the chief burial places. De Foe makes special mention of John Hayward, the sexton, who remained on duty throughout that terrible summer, removing the dead from their houses and carting them to the pits. The church itself, a twelfth-century building, was destroyed by the Fire in the following year and rebuilt by Wren in 1676. Keats' father, as well as his brother Tom, are buried there.

The parish of St. Giles, focus of the Plague, had no pest-house to which the bodies could be taken direct, nor was there any available among London's one hundred and eighteen other parishes. St. Giles's overseers were commanded to find a site and build one. They did, in a field in rural Marylebone. The healthy inhabitants of that village protested violently. They were ironically given permission to share the building, if necessary, with the stricken parish.

In the City proper the Lord Mayor and his subordinate officials carried out their administrative duties efficiently, inasmuch as the dead were expeditiously collected and the needy survivors furnished with food. A curious aspect of the epidemic was that well-fed people, those on a higher physical level, could visit with impunity the plague-smitten districts, and even sleep in the beds of the dead before they (the beds, not the dead) were cold or cleansed of the stench.

What of the vast numbers who fled? The King might, with some justification, become an evacuee. But with him, with one or two exceptions, went the Privy Council in a body; as Mr. W. G. Bell points out, only three times during the seven months between July 1665 and February 1666, during which a hundred thousand people died, did the Privy Council ever concern itself with the Plague, and on two of those three occasions it was in connection with the King's and their own safety from infection.

Less highly placed but equally apprehensive citizens had begun to leave London as early as May. By midsummer the trickle of evacuees had become a flood. The rich could travel by road; for the poor there· was the river. The condition of the Port of London complicated their escape. Its intercourse with the outside world was partially cut off by a rigorous blockade on the part of the Dutch. Colliers who succeeded in evading the enemy vessels were not allowed to enter the Pool, which was completely deserted. Coal in vast quantities accumulated at Greenwich and Blackwall, to be removed by lighters after the vessels bringing it had departed. We have De Foe's statement that many of the watermen succeeded in taking themselves and their families up the river in boats "covered with tilts and furnished with straw", and lay alongside the shore, some setting up little tents made from their sails and lying under them during the day. The banks became lined with boats, and so remained as long as there was any food available. The local inhabitants were generous in helping these early evacuees, but, comments one authority dryly, "by no means willing to take them into their towns or houses".

In point of fact people living in barges or other vessels largely escaped infection; on the debit side it must be noted that the earliest places to be affected were on the river—Brentford, Greenwich, and Deptford. And Southampton, with Sunderland and Newcastle, was among the earliest to become Plague centres.

The Vicar of Stepney was among the noble minority who remained at their posts throughout. His parish, consisting of eight hamlets, had the greatest death-roll in London, although one of the latest to feel the full effects of the epidemic. Contrary to law, houses had been built over swamps and along the sea wall. And Ratcliffe Highway had become one of the most densely populated spots in London. The cemetery round the parish church soon filled, and a new one was constructed north of the Highway. Thousands of sailors spent their last leave in Stepney, and so many died that in the following year it was almost impossible to obtain the urgently needed recruits for the Navy from the neighbourhood. The deaths in July were only thirty, but of the total number for the year recorded in the ninety-seven parishes "within the Wall"—9,887—6,583 came from Stepney.

In St. Margaret's Westminster alone 3,000 people died.

A special part of the cemetery in Tothill Fields was set apart for Plague victims. Between two parts of the graveyard a deep ditch was dug, by order of the church-wardens, with a wall with doors in it, and a bridge crossing the ditch, "for the Reception of the poor visited of the Plague at the Pest House in Tuttle ffeildes".

Of the others who stayed to face the horrors of London's eight months' purgatory, the greatest was George Monck, Duke of Albemarle, who acted as a mysterious, benevolent and shrewd dictator, trusted and obeyed by the entire populace. His lieutenant, equally fearless, was the Earl of Craven. Less exalted heroes included the Lord Mayor, Sir John Lawrence, Sir Edward Berry Godfrey (years later to be violently and mysteriously murdered),[1] and a number of doctors.

Comparatively few deaths occurred within the City walls, the great majority being among the thousands living in a cesspool of poverty and dirt and crime in the areas beyond, chiefly in the east.

September came and passed, and October. The Court was still at Oxford, and it was November when there appeared the first number of a small bi-weekly, *The Oxford Gazette, Published by Royal Authority*, its editor being a journalist of established reputation named Muddiman. With the twenty-fourth number it changed its title to *The London Gazette*, and, as such, is still published twice a week as the official repository and disseminator of Court and legal information.

The daily list of casualties grew shorter and yet shorter. In the week November 14th–21st there were only six hundred and fifty-two cases. The faint-hearts who had taken refuge in the country "came crawling back as thick as they had fled".

Though the most horrible effects of the Plague had been eliminated or concealed—the death-carts, the unburied corpses—watchmen still guarded the infected buildings, and in other ways London must have seemed to their eyes more changed than it has been for us by a global war. No smoke rose from the shuttered and unoccupied houses to blur the winter sky. Along the echoing grass-grown cobbled streets shuffled multitudes of men and women beggars. And, most sinister of all, there were the vast, squat mounds that

[1] See pages 75 and 76.

marked the Pits—how many we do not know, nor are likely to know, since they were left in many cases unrecorded.

A severe frost, regarded, rightly, as an additional insurance against the risks of further outbreaks, brought the merchants and professional men back to their shops and offices. A process of stocktaking, social and financial, began. Accounts for services rendered during the Plague were rendered and settled ("*Paid the Common Hunt for Killing of Dogges in the Beginning of the Plague—£36.10.0*"). It was naturally a process that took some time. Five years later a special committee of the Common Council met to clear off the medical claims still outstanding.

The financial burden was not borne by London alone. From all over the country came contributions amounting to a generous total.

It is interesting to note that the losses in London's population through the Plague were more than made up for by new arrivals—six thousand a year—from the country. In forty years from the beginning of the century it actually rose by thirty-four thousand. Bell estimates the population after the Plague at about three hundred and fifty thousand.

Other cities, other towns and villages, had first-hand experience of the Plague. But none so tragic, so deserving of a saga of its own, as Eyam, the tiny village lying in a hollow of the Derbyshire hills.

Its inhabitants numbered three hundred and sixty people, and the Plague, hitherto unknown there, arrived in the latter half of September, its conveyance being a box containing tailor's samples and some old clothing, despatched from London to Edward Cooper, the village outfitter. The box was opened by George Vicars, his servant. The contents were damp, and he set them before a fire to dry. Within three days an unmistable plague-spot had appeared on his breast; three days later he was dead.

The village had no doctor. But there were two resident ministers, an old man about whom little is known, and a younger man, William Mompesson, whose quiet heroism has given him immortality.

Cooper followed his servant to the grave. Then there were four more victims, and in October, twenty-two. A lull came during the winter frosts, but in the next spring and summer the enemy sprang to life again, fifty-six dying in July alone.

The remaining inhabitants, panic-stricken, would have scattered. Mompesson, realizing what this would mean, succeeded in inspiring them with his own courage. A circle was drawn round the village, and its inhabitants, now heroes to a man, undertook never to cross it. Lord Devonshire, to whom Mompesson appealed, sent supplies of food.

Seventy-eight men and women of Eyam, including Mompesson's wife—their children had at the beginning been sent away to safety—died during August. Twenty-four more died in September, and fourteen in October, reducing the total population to thirty-three. Eight out of every nine who had remained in Eyam after the first outbreak had paid the price demanded of the highest type of heroism.

CHAPTER III

THE FIRE

THE FOE family, living as it did in the heart of the pestilence, survived unharmed, one might almost say triumphant, and certainly to become more prosperous. James Foe had met the situation with the calmness of a level-headed business man possessing complete faith in the justice of the God he had served so diligently all his life. Spiritually reinforced, he ordered his wife and children to retreat to the upper floors of the house, joining them there with a store of provisions after he had closed his shop, and leaving an employee on permanent duty in the street below to maintain connection with the outer world. For little Daniel it must have been a period with few compensating moments, and with dullness as the heaviest infliction. Continuous prayer and meditation are no substitute for the excitements of a busy street. Yet even harder to endure must have been the nights, hideous with the ghastly clanging of the bell that preceded the monotonous chant of "Bring out your dead", and the grinding creak of the plague-carts.

Autumn brought rain, cooler weather, fewer deaths, diminishing risks. The Foe family came downstairs, hygien-ically convalescent, spiritually exalted; the Lord had, indeed, protected his own. Daniel, though not allowed to wander, might at least sun himself on the doorstep and from there contemplate the familiar cobbles and unfamiliar weeds.

In less than a year he was contemplating a London ravaged—and purified—by fire.

The Plague had made itself known as a menace of excep-tional significance in the early summer of 1665. It was Nature's ultimatum after warnings repeatedly disregarded. The Fire came in the early autumn of the following year, also after repeated warnings, though this time uttered in good plain English. Many minds had been perturbed con-cerning what would happen if a serious blaze occurred among

41

those overhanging timber houses, and, defying the efforts of the authorities, passed completely beyond control. Three times in the past—in the eighth, tenth and twelfth centuries —the greater part of the City had been so destroyed. Those days were remote from living memory. But in 1633 there was a conflagration which should have produced a general overhauling of the city's fire-fighting organization, referred to in fuller detail elsewhere.[1] Charles himself had written to the Lord Mayor in the spring of 1665, emphasizing the dangers, insisting upon the necessity for following the regulations issued in 1651 and previous years, and authorizing severe punishment for those who ignored them. The need was stressed for building houses in brick and stone instead of timber. As to over-crowding, no building on new foundations was allowed within two miles of London or Westminster; "Jutties" and overhanging windows were not to be permitted, though balconies were. But building, legal and illegal, went on, and overcrowding became steadily worse.

One wonders if the Plague, with its overwhelming and paralysing grip on the minds of Londoners, drove even Royal commands from the official mind.

As the best-known chronicler of the epidemic we have a man of over sixty who infused what must have been a fantastic nightmare of his early childhood, though remaining a common topic of conversation for long afterwards, with the incomparable imagination which gave us *Robinson Crusoe*. He saw, of course, the Fire, too, and records many years later "how the despairing citizens looked on and saw the devastation of their buildings with a kind of stupidity". But concerning that he had comparatively little to say. Possibly its dramatic possibilities appealed less to him, or he may have felt that with all its horrific effects it formed a sequel inferior to his first story, as indeed most sequels are.

But the best-known chronicler of the Fire, which, in the words of E. V. Lucas, "ended an architectural era", was that volatile, ubiquitous diarist of genius, Samuel Pepys, aged thirty-three when the event occurred, Clerk to the Acts of the Navy, and resident above his office in Crooked Friars.

The date was Sunday, September 2nd, 1666. In the very early hours of the morning he was aroused by one of the

[1] See page 59.

maids[1] to say that there was a fire burning in the City. "So I arose, and slipped on my nightgown, and went to her window, and thought it to be at the back-side of Mark's Lane at the farthest."

However, "being unused to such fires as followed", as well he might be, Mr. Pepys decided that it was not worth worrying about, and rejoined Mrs. Pepys.

Almost at the same time the Lord Mayor, Sir Thomas Bludworth, was also roused. He exhibited not merely a lack of interest but active annoyance. "A woman might put it out!" he commented scornfully, and likewise went back to bed.

The fire, which had originated in the bakehouse of Farryner, the King's baker, in Pudding Lane, near Lower Thames Street, blazed on unchecked, encouraged by a brisk easterly wind. Pepys, getting up in earnest at about seven, was not even then particularly impressed by what he saw. But when presently Jane came along to tell him that she heard that three hundred houses had already been burnt down, he, with the little son of his friend Sir John Robinson for company, went out to see for himself. From "a high place" near the Tower he realized that the fire had reached London Bridge, destroyed all the houses that had survived the great conflagration of three years earlier, and was continuing its pitiless progress westward along the river bank.

At this juncture the Lord Mayor was given an opportunity of retrieving his character as the City's chief magistrate and of atoning for an error of judgment. Unfortunately for his fellow-citizens he let them down again. He was asked to isolate the fire by pulling down houses in its course. He refused, on the grounds that he had not the formal consent of the owners—red tape at its reddest! A suggestion made by a number of seamen that gunpowder should be used to break up the path of the flames was similarly ignored.

Pepys's reactions as the conflagration developed were unofficial and refreshingly different. His description of how he occupied himself during that catastrophic September morning has so much of the familiar Pepysian gusto that one is left with a sneaking conviction that on the whole, while

[1] The cook, Jane Birch, "a good-natured, quiet honest servant". Pepys appears to have had two other maids also named Jane.

he lamented the tragedy, he would have hated to miss seeing it happen.

"So down with my heart full of trouble to the Lieutenant of the Tower, who tells me that it hath burned down St. Magna [Magnus] Church and part of Fish Street already. So I go down to the waterside, and there got a boat and there saw a lamentable fire."

"Lamentable fire" was an understatement. London tradesmen of the seventeenth century lived over their shops, and the fire was destroying not merely their stocks, but their furniture, clothing and minor personal possessions. Since there was no concerted and organized attempt to fight the fire, the alternative was an endless series of pitiful individual tragedies. The scenes Pepys records were, indeed, comparable to those witnessed when a town was about to be invaded by a ruthless advancing enemy. Everything movable was piled upon carts, or, if near the river, into boats and barges; when there was time for neither method of transport, it was buried. Pepys reports, with that infinite capacity for appreciating the effective detail which he shares with De Foe, that the whole surface seemed to be covered with vessels piled high with furniture, so high that in many cases their cargo fell off into the water.

"Poor people," records the diarist, "were staying in their houses as long as till the very fire touched them, and then running into boats or clambering from one pair of stairs by the waterside to another. The pigeons," he adds, "were loth to leave their houses, but hovered about the windows and balconies, till they burned their wings and fell down."

After which he continues, with breathlessness of style entirely in keeping with the situation:

"Having seen the fire rage in every way, and nobody, to my sight, endeavouring to quench it, but to remove their goods; and having seen it get as far as the Steele Yard, the wind mighty high and driving it into the City; and everything, after so long a drought, proving combustible, even the very stones of churches; and, among other things, the poor steeple (of St. Laurance Pountney) by which pretty Mrs. —— lives, and whereof my old schoolfellow Elborough is parson, take fire at the very top, and there burned till it fell down; I to White Hall, with a gentleman with me who desired to go off from the Tower, to see the Fire in my boat;

and there up to the King's closet in the Chapel, where
people came about me, and I did give them an account
dismayed them all, and word was carried to the King. . . .
So I was called for, and did tell the King and Duke of York
what I saw, and that unless His Majesty did command houses
to be pulled down nothing could stop the fire."

His Majesty and the Duke "seemed much troubled". The
King sent Pepys to the Lord Mayor to tell him to spare no
houses, while "the Duke bid me tell him that if he would
have any more soldiers, he shall, and so did my Lord
Arlington afterwards, as a great secret".[1]

Pepys thereupon borrowed a coach, the property of
Captain Cocke, a friend whom he was lucky enough to meet,
and drove to St. Paul's, from which point he was compelled
to go on foot, "every creature coming away loaden with
goods to save, and here and there people carried away in
beds".

At last, in Canning (Cannon) Street, he met the unhappy
Lord Mayor, "like a man spent, a handkercher about his
neck". Pepys delivered the King's message. "'Lord,' he
cried, like a fainting woman, 'what can I do? The people
will not obey me. I *have* been pulling down houses, but the
fire overtakes us faster than we can do it!' " and crowned his
obstinacy and ineptitude by adding that he must go home to
rest and refresh himself.

Pepys, made of tougher fibre, was prepared to delay both
rest and refreshment. He walked slowly homewards,
"seeing people almost distracted, no manner of means used
to quench the fire; the houses, too, so very thick thereabouts
and full of matter for burning, such as pitch and tar in
Thames Street; and warehouses of oyle and wines and
brandy and other things". He dined, answered a Mrs.
Belcher's enquiries concerning two of her friends whose
house had been destroyed, and then with Moore, a companion, was once again "away, and walked through the
City, the streets full of nothing but people; and horses and
carts laden with goods, ready to run over one another, and
removing goods from one burned house to another". (The

---

[1] Arlington had just received a letter from Sir W. Coventry saying that
" the d. of York fears the want of workmen and tools, and wishes the Deputy
Lieutenants and Justices of Peace to summon the men to be there by break of
day. In some churches and chapels there are great hooks for pulling down
houses which should be brought ready against the morning ".

secretary's syntax at times seems nearly as much out of control as the fire.) "Among others I now saw my little Goldsmith, Stokes, receiving some friends' goods, whose house was burned the day after."

The indomitable Pepys continued his activities throughout what must have been a day of enormous mental and physical strain. He parted with Stokes at St. Paul's. From Paul's Wharf he hired a boat and took a Mr. Carcasse and Mr. Carcasse's brother to see the extent of the fire; met the King and his brother in their barge, and went with the royal couple to Queenhithe. There they called Sir Richard Browne to them, and gave him one order and one order only —to pull down houses apace. . . . But the fire was still advancing so fast that "little was or could be done". "Having seen as much as I could now," continues the diarist, "I away to Whitehall by appointment, and there walked to St. James's Park; and there met my wife and Credd and Wood and his wife, and thereupon the water again, and to the fire up and down, it still increasing and the wind great. . . . And all over the Thames, with one's faces (*sic*) in the wind, you were almost burned by a shower of fire-drops.

"When we could endure no more upon the water, we to a little ale-house on the Bankside, and there staid till it was dark almost, and saw the fire grow; and as it grew darker, appeared more and more, and in corners and upon steeples, and between churches and houses, as far as we could see up the hill of the City, in a most horrid, malicious and bloody flame, not like the fine flame of an ordinary fire . . . . We staid till, it being darkish, we saw the fire as one entire arch of fire from this to the other side of the bridge, and in a bow up the hill for an arch above a mile long, the churches, houses, and all on fire and flaming at once, and a horrid noise the flames made, and the cracking of houses."

The sight reduced Pepys to tears.

Tom Hater, yet another friend, arrived with a few of his goods from burnt-out Fish Street. Pepys gave both friend and goods shelter. But the news that the flames were coming nearer every moment compelled Pepys himself to prepare for removal, which he and household did by night ,"it being dry, and moonshine, and warm weather". He carried much of his goods into the garden, and brought his bags of gold and chief papers and his tallysticks into his office. Sir William

Batten had carts brought up from the country, and at four
o'clock in the morning Lady Batten obligingly sent Pepys one
to carry away his money and chief valuables. The cart finally
departed for Sir William Rider's house in Bednall Green,
with Pepys, clad in his nightgown, perched on the top.

Later, his heart eased "at having my treasure so well
secured", he returned to his own house. But neither he nor
his wife nor poor Mr. Hater, whom they still sheltered, got
much sleep.

On September 4th he reports, "Up by break of day to get
away the remainder of my things, which I did by lighter.
. . . Sir W. Pen and I to the Tower Street and there met the
fire burning three or four doors beyond Mr. Howell's whose
goods, poor man, his trayes and dishes, shovells etc. were
flung all along Tower Street in the kennels (gutters) and
people working therewith from one end to the other; the fire
coming in on that narrow street, on both sides, with infinite
fury. Sir W. Batten, not knowing how to remove his wine,
did dig a pit in the garden and lay it in there, and I took the
opportunity of laying in all the papers of my office that I
could not otherwise dispose of. And in the evening Sir W.
Pen and I did dig another and put our wine in it, and I my
parmizan cheese, as well as my wine and some other things.

"This night Mrs. Turner, who, poor woman, was removing her goods all day in the garden and her husband supped
with my wife and me in the office, upon a shoulder of mutton
from the cook's without any napkin or anything, but were
merry. Only now and then, walking into the garden, saw
how horribly the sky looks, all on a fire in the night, was
enough to put out of our wits; and, indeed, it is extremely
dreadful, for it looks as if the whole Heaven is on fire. I
after supper walked in the dark down to Tower Street, and
there saw it all on fire.

"Now begins the practice of blowing up of houses in
Tower Street, those next the Tower, which at first did
frighten people more than anything, but it stopped the fire
when it was done."

The "practice" was not the result of any change of heart
on the Lord Mayor's part, but of direct action on the part of
the King, who was always capable of taking a strong line
when occasion demanded. The workmen who blew up the
houses were sent from the Royal yards. Sir William Pen was

in charge, but the popular Charles and the less popular James were present in person to reward and encourage the workers.

Pepys's account of the last stages of the fire is so intimate and vivid that one is tempted to give it in full. On the 5th he writes, "I lay down in the office again upon W. Hewer's quilt, being mighty weary, and sore in my feet with going until I was hardly able to stand. About two in the morning my wife calls me up and tells me of new cryes of fire, it being come to Barkeing Church, which is at the bottom of our lane"[1] The tired man responded immediately. "I up, and finding it so, resolved presently to take her away, and took my gold which was about £2,350, W. Hewer and Jane down by boat to Woolwich, but Lord! what a sad sight it was by moonlight!"

At Woolwich there was fresh trouble. Pepys found the gates shut and left unguarded, and a rumour reached him that this was part of a French plot. He got the gate open, however, took his little party and his property to a friend's house, and after solemnly charging his wife never to leave his money unguarded, set out on the return journey, stopping en route to make sure that his goods were "well in the lighters at Deptford".

He was on the verge of exhaustion when he finished the journey, and so fearful that the fire had engulfed his house during his absence that he was afraid to make enquiries.

Begrimed, hungry, but incomparably observant to the last, he proceeded "to Mr. Wren's, and there eat a piece of cold meat, having eaten nothing since Sunday but the remains of Sunday's dinner". (He must have forgotten the shoulder of mutton the day before.) "Walked into Moorfields, our feete ready to burn, walking through the towne among the hot coles; drank there, and paid two pence for a plain penny loaf. And took up (which I keep by me) a piece of glasse of Mercers' Chappell, so melted and bucked with the heat of the fire like parchment. I also did see a poor cat taken out of a hole in the chimney joyning the wall of the Exchange, with the hair all burned off the bodie, and yet alive."

From the Tower, which would have been destroyed but for the blowing up of the adjoining houses, to the Temple,

[1] All Hallows, Barking, in Great Tower Street, almost opposite the end of Seething Lane. The church escaped, but narrowly.

whose church windows the flame nearly reached, the flames travelled. There they were halted.

"A strange sight to see how the River looks," laments Pepys on September 6th; "no houses nor church near it . . . . Strange it is to see Clothworkers' Hall on fire these 3 days and nights in one body of flame, it being the cellar full of oyle". On the following day: "Up by five o'clock"—one wonders whether he slept at all, and also what the reactions of the less enthusiastic Mrs. Pepys were—"and blessed be God! find all well: and by water to Pane's Wharf. Walked thence, and saw all the town burned, and a miserable sight of Paul's Church with all the roofs fallen, and the body of the quire fallen into St. Fayth's; Paul's School also, Ludgate, and Fleet Street. My father's house, and the Church, and a good part of the Temple the like."

The last flicker of the flames died down. Before that moment came, they had, in four days, destroyed thirteen thousand houses, obliterated four hundred streets, and razed ninety churches to the ground, including the great Cathedral itself. The London of the Elizabethans and Stuarts, of Shakespeare and Pepys, with its historic past and beauty and squalor, had gone. The actual value of what was destroyed in the process must for ever remain unknown. But—miraculously enough—only six people lost their lives.

Viewed in retrospect, the inactivity of the authorities, especially in their refusals to pull down buildings in the direct route of the fire, appears incredible. For this short-sighted timidity fear of subsequent action by house-owners was chiefly responsible. There was also the difficulty of obtaining effective assistance, owing to a widespread belief in a prophecy by a mythical "Mother Shipton" that London was doomed to hopeless and entire destruction. Who can be more wise than Destiny!

Five-sixths of the City proper was destroyed, only a small north-eastern segment escaping. The public buildings included the Royal Exchange, the Customs House, Newgate Gaol, most of the Guildhall, and fifty-two of the livery-companies' halls. Of ecclesiastical buildings, the Cathedral and eighty-four churches were destroyed.

The chief gains from the fire were both negative, but far from negligible. The city was cleansed, so far as further epidemics were concerned, with a ruthless thoroughness. It

had become a flaming altar great enough to satisfy all the
gods of Hygiene and Sanitation. And again, it had become
cleared, as it could have been cleared by no other means, for
the rebuilding and replanning of a new and better London.

Annesley,[1] in common with a number of other dispossessed
ministers, proved his mettle during the appalling months of the
Plague and the Fire by remaining and labouring in London
among the sick and dying, the demented, and the starving,
while the ministers of State of his Protestant Majesty were
finding safety, comfort and amusement in non-contaminated
Oxford and elsewhere.

His personal views of the King and the King's ministers
were expressed with a good deal more vigour than tact:

" London was in ashes, a byword and a proverb, a gazing
stock and an hissing, an astonishment to all that passed by;
it caused the ears of all to tingle that heard the rumour and
report of what the righteous hand of God had brought upon her.
A mighty city . . . made a fit place for Zini and Okim to take
up their abode in; the merciless element where it raged scarcely
leaving a lintel for a cormorant or bittern to lodge in, or the
remainder of a scorched window to sing in. A sad and terrible
face was there—in the place where God had been served, nettles
growing, owls screeching and thieves and cutthroats lurking.
The voice of the Lord hath been crying, yea roaring in the
City, in the dreadful judgment of Plague and Fire."

Mr. Annesley's fervour obviously exceeded his knowledge
of natural history.

The invasion of Zini and Okim and the equally remarkable
visit of singing cormorants and bitterns did not, at any rate,
prevent James Foe from reaping substantial advantages from
the fire. He had survived trade competitors who had been
less lucky, and he was not a man to let opportunities slide.
He abandoned the tallow-chandler's trade, and with his
savings set up as a butcher in Fore Street, then a narrow
thoroughfare among many other narrow streets running
along the City Wall, and near Moorfields, where after the
Fire was established a vast camp for homeless refugees.

[1] See pages 65–6.

CHAPTER IV

POST-FIRE

BEFORE the last flickers of the flames had died down life had begun to flow back into the empty, echoing streets, at first slowly, then in a steadily increasing torrent. Wherever men gather, whatever their purpose, authority must be evolved to plan and organize for the common good.

The Fire produced an inevitable crop of rumours concerning its origin. Two of the most popular were that it had been started by the Papists—one man swore on oath to seeing them busy at their infernal work—and that French troops, taking an unsporting advantage of the City's second and culminating disaster, had landed and were advancing to complete with the sword what plague and fire had begun. But many others attributed it to a second major punishment for the sins of the ungodly and unfaithful, while a minority of more scientifically minded citizens saw in the destruction of the most overcrowded slum areas a providential enforcement of the replanning and rebuilding so desperately overdue. Yet the unfortunate but inevitable corollary attached to the loss of so many dwellings, most of which had been grossly overcrowded, was the need for some sort of shelter, however flimsy, for the returning inhabitants. The near approach of winter accentuated the urgency.

The King's regulations concerning building have already been mentioned. The wholesale demolition of the wood-and-plaster houses that the Fire had spared, and which contrived to convert the narrow streets into half-lit tunnels, reeking from the streams of sewage that flowed down the centre, was an obvious measure. But there were many who thought that, while the need of accommodation was so acute, it would be madness to pull down any sort of human habitation, and that by far the most urgent task was the erection of more buildings of any type that could be run up on the nearest vacant fields beyond the City's borders.

The King and the wealthier sections of his subjects were in favour of the first course, taking the longer, but less sympathetic view, that what was needed was intelligent town-planning rather than indiscriminate mass-building. Four types of dwelling-houses were officially permitted, and these (as Mr. Brett-James points out) remained standardized well into the eighteenth century. The smallest, fronting on to side-streets, had two storeys, with garret and cellar; the next size had three storeys; the next, four storeys, while the most impressive and expensive was "a merchant's mansion house of great bigness, of four storeys only, and not to be built close to the street front".

Of the thirteen thousand houses destroyed, it is estimated that rather less than three-quarters were restored, the result inevitably being a general outward drift to the unbuilt-upon suburbs.

The story of post-Fire London is, in the main, one of individual replacement and of general improvements, but also of heartbreaking frustrations from the point of view of intelligent replanning. No architectural enthusiast, however gifted, however respected, was allowed to make more improvement in the general layout of the City than the timid and compromising minds of its official fathers could bring themselves to sanction. Apart from private opposition, there were almost insuperable problems arising from the privileges claimed and exercised by the City Guilds. None of the Londons that Wren and Petty and Evelyn and Barbon visualized remained more than vision. A new and nobler "Pauls" arose, a new Exchange, a new gaol. But the streets, though less narrow, were still crooked and uneven, ill-lighted, ill-paved, and with sanitation that mocked the word, so to remain for another century and a half.

As far as the Plague was concerned, the bitterest enemies of the Government must have hesitated to attribute it to human agency; an exasperated and vengeful Deity was obviously responsible. But the Fire was another matter.

One of the most widely prevalent rumours was that it had been deliberately started by the Government in order to destroy any plague-germs still dormant in the crevices of the old houses. Another, more serious, because supported by late but official confirmation, was that the Catholics were responsible. This was actually recorded upon the Monument erected fourteen years after the Fire, and two years after the discovery of "The Popish Plot", commonly known as Titus Oates' Conspiracy.[1] James II, being a Catholic, naturally deleted it; William III restored it. The poet Pope, a Catholic, commented bitterly,

> " Where London's column, pointing to the skies,
> Like some tall Bully, lifts its Head and lies."

It was not until the more tolerant era of William IV that the "lie" was finally removed.

Incidentally, the Monument recorded a second lie—at whose instigation remains unknown. It stated that the City was rebuilt in four years. London's bombed areas of to-day disprove the possibility of that, even with all our twentieth-century resources. Actually twenty-five years passed, an entire generation, before the post-Fire claim could be justified.

Concerning the Monument itself, about whose foundations Daniel as a small boy must often have watched the workmen busy, much has been written. Fish Street Hill, on which it is built, near the spot at which the Fire started, is directly in the line of approach to old London Bridge. It was planned in the year following the Fire and paid for by a levy of a shilling a chaldron on all coals brought into the Port of London.[2] Sir Christopher Wren was instructed to prepare several designs. His first suggestion was a pillar with flames of gilt bronze issuing from loopholes in the shaft, and a phoenix rising from the ashes on the summit. This was abandoned for a fluted column, crowned by a statue of the King fifteen feet high. The statue proved too costly, however, and His Majesty was then consulted. He suggested that though the statue would "carrie much dignitie and be more valuable in the eyes of foreigners and strangers . . . a ball of copper nine feet in diameter cast in severall pieces with the flames and gilt may well be done with the iron works and fixing for £350 . . . and this will be most acceptable of anything inferior to a statue . . . because one may go up into it and upon occasion use it for fireworks".

What ultimately materialized was a moulded cylinder, surrounded by a balcony and supporting a flaming vase of gilt bronze.

[1] See pages 75–8.
[2] Increased (1670–87) to 3s. and afterwards fixed at 1s. 6d.

The Monument as we know it is a Doric pillar of Portland stone, 120 feet high and 15 feet in diameter. Its total height with pedestal plinth is 202 feet, making it the tallest monument in London, Nelson's Column being 41 feet shorter. Begun in 1671, the work of construction took six years. De Foe described the total effect as like a candle with a handsome gilt frame. (It was an expensive candle, the cost being £13,450.) What he might have discussed, but did not, was the carving on the base, which indulged in an emblematical orgy that must have delighted the soul of Dickens,[1] with Latin inscriptions to match. The bas relief, designed by Caius Gabriel Cibber, a father of the dramatist Colley Cibber, included the City of London, excessively *décolleté*, her hair dishevelled, her hand resting on her sword; Time (complete with forelock); Peace; Plenty; a beehive (denoting Industry); a dragon; Charles II in Roman costume, with baton and a laurel-wreath, commanding Science (wearing a headdress of naked boys and carrying a statuette of Nature); Architecture and Liberty (going to the City's relief); the Duke of York; Justice and Fortitude; Labourers at work; and finally, "a Figure of Envy gnawing a Heart and emitting pestiferous Fumes from her Mouth".

"The general effect of this design," comments one authority, "has not been considered successful, but some of the details are excellent."

In other words, a perfect seventeenth-century example of the curate's egg!

Three hundred and eleven steps led—and for that matter, still do lead—the breathless and dogged visitor to the top, rewarding him with a view that is unique value for his sixpence and energy.

Seventeenth-century London was an aggregation of self-centred townlets, each cherishing its own outlook, traditions, prejudices and healthy contempt for the neighbouring townlets. And so, indeed, to a surprising and considerable extent, it remains to this day, the chief difference being that the townlets were fewer, smaller, and more sharply defined. The actual area ravaged by the Fire was, at its widest part, i.e., by the waterside, rather less than a mile and a half; its greatest depth, from Queenhythe Island, five furlongs, or

---

[1] He does, in fact, twice mention the Monument, once in *Barnaby Rudge*, and again in *Martin Chuzzlewit*.

a little over half a mile. Moorfields, with its new Bethlem Hospital, lay beyond the wall and the blackened and grass-grown area that the Fire had devastated. Due north the houses merely followed the irregular lines of the streets and were surrounded by open fields.

Architecturally, of course, London was left immeasurably and permanently poorer. But there was at least one supremely great successor to Inigo Jones. With characteristic energy and enthusiasm the diminutive Sir Christopher Wren prepared plans for the rebuilding of the City. Pepys's friend and fellow-diarist, John Evelyn, also prepared plans; so, too, did the great Sir William Petty (1623–85), who, after a career as mixed and melodramatic as De Foe's own, became Surveyor General of Ireland, a Fellow of the Royal Society, and (according to Evelyn) "the second counsellor in the Kingdom". Others were Nicholas Barbon (or Barebone), M.P., founder of the Phoenix Fire Insurance Company, and Mr. Richard Newcourt, whose plan for the new City consisted of hollow rectangular blocks of houses with a church in the centre of each, and in its mathematical regularity is interestingly prophetic of a modern American city.

CHAPTER V

LONDON

THE DIFFERENCE between the City of the Restoration and the London of to-day is so comprehensive and, quite literally, so vital that it is difficult to believe that young De Foe passed his boyhood as a normal young Englishman among normal fellow-countrymen. By any modern standards the seventeenth-century London scene was Oriental in its violently contrasting richness and squalor; in its abrupt transitions from narrow, dark and pestiferous streets to pleasant gardens; in its violent disregard of the most elementary rules of hygiene; in its drabness and gorgeousness of dress.

Approximately a tenth of England's population was concentrated there. Its outline, within the confines of the high City walls, was fantastically irregular; beyond those limitations a straggling, equally fortuitous fringe of houses was already forming suburban areas. Their spread during the seven decades that covered De Foe's lifetime was phenomenal; the population itself practically doubled. The Fire merely checked its development long enough for new regulations and modifications to become law.

In 1660 there were no buildings north of St. James's Park or west of St. Martin's—and St. Giles was still represented by the fields and meadows that fringed the northern side of Holborn. Southwark was bordered by marshy dikes; Kensington, Islington, and Hackney were country villages.[1]

Unfortunately, increases in population, and the conversion of fields into streets, bore no essential relationship to progress in civilized living. London, even after the Fire had branded its ruthless warning on the face of the City, was still regarded by country folk as the hot-bed and focus of every type of moral and physical danger. One could tell, even with one's eyes shut, when its boundaries were crossed.

[1] From Mr. Arthur Bryant's *The England of King Charles II.*

Firstly, by the sheer noise—the clatter and rattle of iron-shod wheels and hooves on its egg-shaped cobbles; or the cries of the shopkeepers and hawkers ("Buy a mouse-trap, or a tormentor for your fleas!") and the eternal quarrelling that arose from collisions.

Secondly, by the smells. The task of supplying a city of half a million people with pure and sufficient water for drinking, washing and flushing purposes had up till then never been treated as a major problem. In 1582 a Dutchman had obtained permission to pump water by a great water-wheel operating under one of the arches under London Bridge. The apparatus, an impressed observer records, could "throw water as high as the steeple of St. Magnus Church which was a thing never before known in England!" And in 1613 Sir Hugh Middleton had completed his New River Project of bringing water from Hertfordshire into London. Nevertheless, public water supplies remained gloriously haphazard. The middle classes drew what they needed from cisterns and fountains, called "cobs"; wealthy persons obtained what they needed from private pipes or "quills". As for drainage, Restoration London had to become late Georgian London—1815 to be exact—before the solid sewage was permitted to enter the pipes that carried away liquid filth. Only a century ago London was described as "one vast open cloaca, with the sewage of nearly three million people seething and fermenting in their midst".[1]

"Rivers of filth"—I again quote Mr. Bryant—"coursed down the centre of each street. . . . Even on a spring evening the citizen taking the air was sometimes driven indoors by the smells. . . ."

There were, too, many less personal offences to the nostrils. Brewers, soap-boilers, dyers and any others whose trades involved pungent by-products were the chief offenders. Furnaces that gave off pungent smoke added to the general darkness, grime and stench.

Yet London, beyond the immediate radii of all this foulness, could be, and was, challengingly gay. The oak-framed houses were carved and gilded, costumes were highly-coloured and gaudily rich and elaborate, while painted signs outside the narrow-fronted shops swung and

[1] Budd's *Principles of Sanitary Science and Public Health.*

creaked, and helped the less literate to identify butcher, baker and candlestick-maker. Despite the drifting but ever-present pall of smoke and fumes and the shadows cast by overhanging storeys, sunlight still contrived to find its way into those twisting streets. And to the southward there was always the Thames, so felicitously christened "liquid history" by a twentieth-century statesman.

It was indeed still a picturesque and gallant London, even after plague and fire had done their worst, and a fine place for well-bred, well-dressed, not-too-squeamish fine ladies and gentlemen . . . unless they were unwise enough to risk physical contagion and nausea by penetrating the slums in which the poor stifled and sickened and died and rotted.

Pavements were non-existent. But the broader thorough-fares had posts set up at intervals, not, as is so frequently assumed, for the tethering of horses, but as a general protection for pedestrians, and corresponding to our present-day railings at dangerous road-junctions. From the back of the main streets wandered inconsequent little lanes, sometimes leading to courtyards and mews and bright little gardens, sometimes leading to nowhere in particular, a planless maze that could be fascinating or sinister or merely exhausting, according to the explorer's mood.

Street lighting shared the same irresponsible individualism as sewage disposal and water supply. None but the main streets had any public lighting at all, and these streets were lit only in winter up to eleven o'clock at night. The street lanterns were reinforced by the lights in windows and houses —a semi-compulsory obligation between the Feast of All Saints and Candlemas. For the assistance of those abroad after dark there were the hordes of gamins known as link-boys, equipped with torches or lanterns; the private servants of the well-to-do accompanied their masters with lanterns and acted as a body-guard at the same time.

There were no police. Consequently the adjustment of individual quarrels became a matter of fisticuffs or duels, according to the status of the quarrellers, while the adjustment of large-scale differences—gang against gang, the butchers against the weavers, or the Wapping watermen against the Greenwich—had a habit of producing small-scale riots, frequently involving indiscreetly interested spectators.

There existed a fire-fighting service equipped with buckets, hatchets, and "crows"—long iron poles with hooks at the end to tear down burning thatch. There were even primitive, hand-operated pumps. But they belonged to, and were operated by, the newly-formed Fire Insurance Companies, and their use was limited to fires on the properties insured.

The Great Fire (which has necessarily been given a chapter to itself) was followed by extensive rebuilding. But the walls of the City were enormously thick and strong, practically indestructible, and as incapable of being changed by fire or any other calamity as the characters of Londoners themselves. Traders returned to their own traditional haunts, from the Lombard Street banker and goldsmith to the linen-drapers in St. Paul's Churchyard; the great markets of Hungerford, Billingsgate, Smithfield and Leadenhall were reopened on their old sites; the street vendors wheeled their barrows and cried their wares around Ludgate Hill and what is now New Bridge Street; the fine gentlemen sauntered, as in the past, through Covent Garden and Lincoln's Inn Fields—both of which, incidentally, the flames had spared. The same multitude of eating- and drinking-houses continued their trade, though the latter was already in process of being ousted, so far as the middle- and upper-class clients were concerned, by the coffee-houses.

Seven of London's gates remained. So, providentially, did the Tower, the high-spot of a visit to the capital for countryfolk, since it included, among other attractions, the Mint, the Royal Armoury, the Crown Jewels (which gained additional though purely metaphorical lustre by Colonel Blood's attempt to steal them in 1670). There was also a menagerie, eventually to become the nucleus of our familiar Zoo, that included lions and leopards and eagles. When the Tower but not the visitor was exhausted, there remained the Abbey, with its waxwork effigies, or, alternatively, as an edifying Sunday-afternoon expedition, Bedlam Hospital (made more entertaining still if one took buns to feed the lunatics) and innumerable side-shows. There were extra attractions in the dancing procession of millmaids down the Strand on the first of May, as well as St. Bartholomew's Fair in August, while November brought the Lord Mayor's Show.

Two licensed theatres existed—the King's, in Drury Lane, and the Duke of York's, in Lincoln's Inn Fields. There were also unlicensed theatres at Sadler's Wells and else-where, and, as alternatives to drama, cock-fighting and bear-baiting. For the less bloodthirsty, though not necessarily less sophisticated, there were the innocent delights of Kensing-ton, with its Grotto; or Moorfields or Knightsbridge, where there were mulberry-trees; or Hoxton, celebrated for farthing pies; or Rotherhithe, equally celebrated for cherries; or Vauxhall Gardens, where nightingales competed with the fiddlers to make music under the moon.

On summer evenings there were bowls and ninepins as well as cricket; football, played in the streets with dangerous vigour and a minimum of rules, was a popular winter sport.

The gentry travelled in their own magnificent carriages or on horseback; their ladies paid calls in sedan chairs. Middle-class folk, too, were horse-borne, or went by hackney carriages or coach. Both classes used the river, far dirtier, more crowded and noisier than it is to-day, and innocent of formalized embankments then and for many years to come.[1] Here watermen, occasionally jolly and young and proverbially profane, conveyed passengers up and down the river in broad open boats. For the élite, from Mr. Pepys to the King, there were rowing-barges, gilded and carved, and bearing no resemblance whatever to the squat, slow-moving, grimy vessels of to-day.

The seventeenth-century middle-class Londoner himself was an uncompromising individualist. His tastes were, by modern standards, crude; he expressed his thoughts in language as direct and unsubtle as the Bible; he ate and drank and sang and made love and worked and played and, in general, lived at his own pace and in his own way. He was primitive, unhurried, dogged, intolerant, childishly proud of being English because so childishly ignorant of every other nationality. He started his working day early; he finished it soon after noon. His spare time, like his spare money, he spent in pleasures as simple in their goodness or badness as a child's.

[1] Until recently a notice was still visible on the walls of a grimy little thoroughfare leading off Fleet Street. It ran: "Wait here for the Penny steamer". The optimistic passenger of to-day would have to wait a long time, since the whole width of a tarmac road, two paths and the granite wall of the Embankment intervenes.

Beer, of course, was the staple drink of the middle and lower classes. A sailor's allowance was a gallon a day. Imported wines, as well as a variety of fancy blends, were for the gentry and their ladies—hypocras (wine plus sugar and spice); syllabub (wine plus sugar and cream); purl (warm ale flavoured with herbs); buttered ale (ale drunk warm, and flavoured with sugar, cinnamon and butter); and "home-made claret", which was simply Devonshire cider plus turnip juice.

Dinner was a noontide affair and the focal meal of the day. Though Bacon had already discovered the preservative effects of refrigeration—and incidentally paid for the discovery with his life—the average Englishman's food remained edible just as long as unassisted Nature allowed it to be so. And transport being laborious and practically unorganized, it became necessary to eat food where it was slaughtered or caught or grown. A glut of oysters or greengages would have to be sold cheaply and consumed on the spot, since they would become uneatable before they could reach less glutted regions.

Food on the whole was plentiful, and, except among the poor, excitingly varied. Since there was only one main meal a day, there were no set dishes; no "breakfast menu" to contrast with the dishes appropriate to dinner. The visitor accepted without surprise whatever his hostess happened to have available. All the courses were put upon the table at the same time, and meals were frequently followed by singing, cards and wine-drinking. The seventeenth century was no time for the dyspeptic or melancholy.

Knives and forks were scarce, and used with regrettable irregularity and eccentricity. English diners continued to gnaw bones, and in general behave like healthy but famished animals; French visitors found our table manners shocking and had no hesitation in saying so. Contrariwise, as Tweedledee would say, there were extraordinarily elaborate codes of etiquette to regulate the attitude of the lower classes towards the upper, and of the upper towards Royalty. Charles might be a genial and democratically minded King, but no one was allowed to forget that he *was* a King.

Wages were low but not unbearably so. The artisan's fifteen shillings a week lost little from direct taxation and practically nothing from indirect. The best beef was only

threepence a pound, and bacon fourpence; beer was sixpence for a dozen bottles. Rush candles were dear—
fivepence a pound—but one could always economize by
going to bed early. Clothes were, admittedly, a problem.
The poor met it by wearing no undergarments at all. But
Daniel's middle-class parents would have considered that as
unthinkable as their descendants should think it to-day.
(Daniel's father, incidentally, would, either as a tallow-
chandler or a butcher, have worn traditional blue.)

The Channel contributed, as salt water has always
contributed, to the Englishman's spiritual as well as physical
isolation. It intensified his independence, his pride, his
reliance upon his own self-sufficiency. Of five million
inhabitants—roughly a quarter of those of France—a
million and a half lived in towns; of that million and a half
a third lived in London. Three and a half million—two and
a half million agricultural labourers—were left to populate
the rest of the country. The pastimes of the inhabitants of
isolated villages and hamlets were as primitive as their
work. The local landowner was their temporal chief, the
parson their spiritual. London, and the King, and the
King's merry and godless companions, were as remote and
inaccessible as the moon.

PART TWO

THE ADVENTURER

CHAPTER I

EARLY DAYS

THE COMPLICATIONS involved in tracing the ancestry of Daniel Foe, as he was known until 1703, begin two generations before he was born.

His paternal grandfather, after whom he was christened, lived in "moderately comfortable circumstances" in a microscopic, not to say mysterious, village called Etton[1] in Northamptonshire, five miles from Peterborough.

The name Foe is an old Northamptonshire one, and is assumed, with every justification, to be an Anglicized version of Faux, Vaux or "Devereux", derived from Flemish emigrants of Elizabethan days. The researches of the late Mr. Thomas Wright of Olney revealed the interesting fact that the records of Northamptonshire between 1608 and 1723 include the names of nine "Foes", one "Fooe" and one "Fow"—all in the neighbourhood of Etton.

It may be mentioned here that Daniel followed the then common custom of spelling his surname thus—"ffoe"— two small f's in place of the single capital. Chadwick writes: "With respect to De Foe's Northamptonshire origin, I am induced to believe from various enquiries at Elton, Elkington, Welton and their neighbourhoods, for Foes, Voes or De Voes or De Foes, or any name from which Foe could be expected to be derived, that James Foe . . . never had a

---

[1] Microscopic because it possessed under a hundred inhabitants, and, in spite of a parish church, is not mentioned in any of the recognized gazetteers, or at any rate any gazetteer I have been able to consult; mysterious because it has been confused by the contributor to the D.N.B., Monsieur Paul Dottin, and others with an "Elton" near the Northampton-Huntingdon border, or boldly placed under that name in Northamptonshire. No "Elton", microscopic or otherwise, exists in that county.

Northamptonshire origin, but that his ancestor probably came, in the reign of Queen Elizabeth, from the Spanish Netherlands, as a persecuted Protestant refugee and (a superb non-sequitur) that Daniel De Foe was of the genus or species of the London water-cress criers of our day."

Certain legends concerning the old man have come down to us. One is that the earlier Daniel lived at a house called Woodcroft, was a churchwarden, and kept a pack of hounds, the implication being that he was something of a country squire. Actually Woodcroft, notable as the focus of some very bitter fighting during the Civil War, was not his home, nor was he ever elected a churchwarden, that other hallmark of local eminence. His status was simply that of a yeoman farmer, but the existence of the hounds is beyond dispute, and so, too, is the huntsman in charge of the pack, who with a tactful impartiality worthy of the Vicar of Bray christened them Roundhead and Cavalier, Goring, Waller, and all the generals of both armies.

A further interesting point about Mr. ffoe is his will, proved only eight weeks after it was signed. He left ten shillings to the church; another ten to the poor; eighty pounds to his eldest son (Daniel the second, who died in 1647, leaving a daughter), when he came of age; fifty pounds to his daughter similarly, or when she married; and fifty pounds each to Henry and James, his other sons, when they came of age. His wife Rose, whom he appointed sole executrix, inherited the residue. Two hundred and thirty pounds divided among four children hardly suggests the opulence involved in fox-hunting, even in seventeenth-century fox-hunting on seventeenth-century pounds. But history does not disclose what the widow's residue amounted to.

James, the youngest son, was only a baby when old Daniel died. Of his earliest days very little is known. On leaving school he came to London, where he was bound apprentice to John Levit, a butcher. He seems to have been a shrewd and godly youth, a Puritan among Puritans. He was also fundamentally English in his hatred of tyranny, and an ingrained monarchist with a loathing of republicanism in any form.

Apart from omitting to marry his master's daughter, he carried out all the traditions of the good apprentice. When he had served his time, he set up for himself as a tallow chandler in St. Giles in Cripplegate, just outside the City boundaries. And in 1656 he married.

His wife was Alice; neither her other name nor anything else about her is known. Her distinguished son, who had so much to say concerning humanity in general and himself in particular, gives no more than an occasional oblique and tantalizing glimpse of her character. He was very young indeed when the first recorded clash between their two strong wills occurred. He threatened that unless he was allowed to go his own way he wouldn't eat his dinner, a threat uttered by small violent-tempered boys ever since there have been small boys to utter it. Mrs. Foe placidly accepted the challenge. And Daniel refrained from starvation.

The years young James Foe spent in London, from his apprenticeship onwards, were crowded with enough tumult, excitement and sheer horror to make the severest demands upon his common sense and adaptability, backed up though these admirable virtues were by an unshakable conviction that he had the support of an austere and narrow-minded but nevertheless just God, who stood very much in his relationship to his worshippers as a schoolmaster to a large and unruly class.

James, usually credited with a family of three, though a letter from his son Daniel to Lord Halifax makes it certain that there was another son,[1] would have had his hands sufficiently full with domestic and financial problems had he been living in times of normal tranquillity. He and his wife were godly folk: on Sunday they went to the dissenting chapel of St. Giles, then under the learned wing of the Reverend Doctor Samuel Annesley, Ll.D.

Annesley, born about 1620, was, says a biographer, "one of the most eminent of the later Puritan Nonconformists"— a description which is about as adequate as saying that De Foe was one of the most eminent of the later Puritan authors.

A considerable amount of mystery surrounds Annesley's earlier years. He was Warwickshire born, the son of John Aneley. This spelling of his father's name was "In order to support the baseless representation that he sought

[1] See page 170.

relationship with the Earl of Anglesey"[1]—although later he was acknowledged as the Earl's full nephew.

He went to Queen's College, Oxford, where, while naturally slow and sluggish, "he supplied this defect in nature by prodigious application. . . . Inclined to the Ministry", he was ordained, apparently twice, firstly by a bishop, secondly by a Presbyterian. He was appointed to *The Globe* man-o'-war, and was there chaplain to Lord Warwick, the admiral commanding the Parliamentary Fleet. Later, owing to "the great interest which he had with such as were then in power" he obtained the living of Cliffe, in Kent. He again went to sea with the Earl of Warwick. He left the sea finally in 1657, and held a succession of offices until 1662, when the strained threads which had been holding him to the Established Church snapped. Disregarding the pleas of his friends, he refused to conform, and was ejected from his living. For "keeping a conventicle", in other words, preaching in a meeting-house in Little St. Helens, his goods were distrained.

He died in 1696.[2] It probably needed very little persuasion on the part of Dunton, a bookseller who had married one of Annesley's daughters, to induce Daniel, already acquiring a reputation as a talented versifier, if not a poet, to write the elegy which has been frequently quoted.[3]

Though there is no record of young Daniel receiving any formal schooling prior to 1674 or thereabouts, it is extremely probable that the Foes, who themselves played a considerable part in his childish education, handed him over to receive some sort of training to the minister for whose courage and faith under persecution they had so much admiration.

Against an incredibly lurid background, a background that included civil warfare, political warfare, religious warfare, a life-and-death struggle at sea with Holland, the Plague, and the Great Fire, the early and formative years of young Daniel's life were passed. His mind, abnormally active, intelligent, and enquiring, must have been a continual source of pride to his father and mother. To both of them, although probably more to his mother, he owed that intimacy not only with the Scriptures and their meanings, but with

---

[1] *Vide* the Rev. A. B. Grosart's article in the *Dictionary of National Biography*.
[2] Wright gives the date as a year later.
[3] See page 116.

their vocabulary and style, which nourished and developed his genius throughout his life.

His general education continued, with Mr. Annesley as schoolmaster and Mrs. Foe as chief accessory. When he was able to read and write his mother set him the task of copying extensively from the Scriptures, so many portions he must have heard so often that he knew them by heart already. A little later, when rumours circulated that the Papists were using their influence with the King to have all the Bibles in London confiscated, Daniel was given the job, a stupendous one for a small boy, of copying out the whole of the Old and New Testaments.

He made a gallant beginning. Working, to quote his own words, "like a horse", he actually transcribed the entire Pentateuch. In addition to that, Annesley made the boy take notes of each weekly sermon, and from those notes build up the entire argument. How tired that small brain must have been; how aching those small fingers!

The God of the little family of Dissenters was a very real and personal God, intimate and ever present. And as real and ever-present were the Satanic hordes, from the Devil himself to his agents, demons, witches, sorcerers. Daniel, for all his faith, was terrified of the dark, and even more terrified of the moonlight and the apparitions that sprang to life from the checkered light and shade it created. He suffered from nightmares; superstition which the firmness of his belief in a wise and just Deity should have negatived haunted not only his boyhood but his entire life.

The Foes lived in what to-day would be regarded as the suburban fringe of the City. In Moorfields itself there were large and shady trees; in Silver Street, a little further south, was a colony of basket-weavers whose dexterity in twisting the rushes was guaranteed to provide endless interest to any small boy. Later on there was the thrill of watching the workman busy with the foundations of the Monument itself. Indeed, the four or five years following the Fire, crowded with little excitements spiced with an occasional dash of danger, must have provided Daniel with some of the happiest recollections of his life. Every normal boy is at heart an explorer; even the smallest house and the dingiest back garden become territories magically spacious, magically invested with romance. Daniel was supremely lucky in possessing a never-never-land whose borders began on the edge of his own doorstep and extended, beyond all comprehending, to the outermost rim of the City. His family background was thoroughly sound: his father was a God-fearing, well-to-do tradesman, a prominent and highly respected Dissenter and a member of the Corporation of Butchers, themselves almost exclusively Dissenters also. He was physically fit, and the possessor of a mind which was eternally inquisitive and acquisitive.

For a child in a middle-class London family of the seventeenth century he was considerable travelled. When he was only eight he had been taken to Harwich, and thence by boat up the Orwell on to Ipswich. He had even gone to Bath and, following the example of persons of quality, drunk the waters as a general preventive of scurvy and dysentery. He must have found the city an immense contrast after London's smoke and confusion. But all his life it was London that he really loved and understood.

The years slipped by. The boy reached an age when lessons under Mr. Annesley and at home, and self-education in the streets among other boys, had to be amended to a definite scheme of training as a prelude to earning his own living. James Foe was now well-to-do, or at least comfortably off, but he was the last man in the world to countenance an amiable inaction. Daniel's career was definitely envisaged, if not finally decided on. He was to enter the Church, the traditional career of the clever son of a middle-class family. Only in this case he would, of course, be limited to and handicapped by the dogmas of the Dissenters and the odium, so far as the Established Church was concerned, that such dogmas entailed.

To this end, he left Mr. Annesley when he was thirteen or fourteen, to be entered as a pupil at the Newington Green Academy, the alternative, a recognized grammar school followed by one of the universities, being out of the question.

The Academy was kept by the Reverend Charles Morton, a graduate of Oxford, where he had distinguished himself doubly as mathematician and antiquarian. In 1655, when he was twenty-eight, he was appointed Rector of Bilsan, in Cornwall, his own county. Seven years later he found himself one of the two thousand incumbents who were ejected from their livings by the Act of Uniformity. The

Great Fire destroyed much of the property he had in London, and he turned schoolmaster. He had, we are told, a reputation among his enemies of being "a rank independent". The epithet was probably deserved. But it would have been difficult to find a more ideal pedagogue for young De Foe.

A further note may be added here concerning Charles Morton. In 1686, weary of the eternal persecutions of his enemies, he departed, with his wife and nephew and a single pupil, for New England. (One is reminded of the migration of Samuel Johnson to London in 1737.) A suggestion had been made that he should become the first president of Harvard, but in the end the authorities appointed another man, and diplomatically offered Morton the post of vice-president, which he accepted. He was also inducted minister of the first church in Charlestown, and solemnized the first marriage there. He died in 1698. The only recorded blot upon his character was his support of the persecutions for witchcraft which disfigure the early history of Salem.

Morton's sermons, we are told, were "high but not soaring; practical but not low". His memory, adds a contemporary, a trifle ambiguously, was as vast as his knowledge. And to the last he was a believer in terseness and brevity, following the Greek maxim that "a great book is a great evil", and setting forth his view in small volumes (one of which, *Eutaxia*, describes a Utopian system of politics), and in language which was never "stale and studied, but always new and occasional".

Had De Foe gone to a typical grammar-school, and then to Oxford or Cambridge, he would probably have achieved something more than a superficial familiarity with the Classics. But his studies in French or any other language would have been negligible, and the same would have applied to mathematics. Above all, his knowledge of his own language would have remained limited to what he acquired incidentally from its everyday use, since English in those days was considered unworthy of serious study. It would be interesting, though entirely futile, to speculate upon the effect of a typical "superior" seventeenth-century education upon a youth of his mentality. My own view is that he was lucky to miss it.

Apart from his theological studies, he did receive what is

known as a "grounding" in Latin and Greek. Such was inevitable. But I have a conviction that dead languages made small appeal to him, possibly because they *were* dead; and because further studies of classical authors offered little attraction in a world so vivid with contemporary interests. French, Dutch, Spanish and Italian, these were worthwhile passports in an almost literal sense, and these he studied. And with them went history, natural science, geography, astronomy, physics and—an oddly incongruous but useful inclusion—a species of shorthand.

Thanks to his parents as well as to Annesley, he was already familiar with the Bible; incredibly familiar, considering his age. He had in the past copied out innumerable passages of its unique prose; he had been compelled to listen to innumerable discourses and sermons by Annesley, and to discussions among members of the Foe family and the friends of the family. Boy as he was, with all a normal boy's preoccupations and pleasures, he was already on the way to achieving a capacity for self-expression, unparalleled, with the single exception of the *Pilgrim's Progress*, in its inspired clarity and exactitude. (It is an interesting fact that on one occasion John Bunyan himself came to preach at Newington, and that most of the boys at Morton's Academy went to hear him.)

One realizes that James Foe must have been a great deal more than a successful butcher with powerful religious convictions which he had no hesitation whatever in expressing. From a psychologist's point of view, this forthright, honest citizen was the perfect father for his great son.

The boys at the Academy numbered fifty or sixty. Socially they were a mixture to gladden the heart of those who believe in the equality of opportunity where education is concerned. But collectively and individually they had one thing in common that separated them from others of their own social level, and made them outsiders, if not outcasts, in the new, gay, cruel days of the Restoration. Tailors' sons, butchers' sons, baronets' sons they might be. But they were all Dissenters. England was nominally Protestant, and a Protestant was, in the beginning, a Dissenter. Nevertheless the England of Charles II would have forgiven them more readily if they had belonged to the Church of Rome.

The Academy included among its scholars Samuel

Wesley, father of John and Charles. Another was one who was "so great a textuary that he could pray for two hours together in the Scripture language". But it is not by this slender and priggish claim that he became famous, but because De Foe borrowed his surname for "the most popular hero in all fiction".[1] The youthful prodigy was called Timothy Cruso.

Three years was the normal time spent at the Academy by theological students. De Foe, however, was an exception; he remained for about five years.[2] In that time he must have seen many leave to become ministers. Yet he himself did not become one; the father who had had proud dreams was never to see these dreams come true. Not all the influence of the master he so profoundly admired and respected, nor a familiarity with the Scriptures strong and deep enough to colour not only his writing but his whole attitude to life, nor—perhaps most powerful of all—the tremendous leverage of his parents' wishes, were strong enough to hold him to that career.

Personally I regard this breakaway not as a retreat but rather as a tribute to the sturdy and clear-headed common sense of De Foe's own character. In the course of those academic years the dark-skinned, thin-faced boy had not merely grown into what was, by seventeenth-century standards, a man, but one, moreover, who had absorbed a knowledge of men and things far beyond that formalized learning which could have little value outside the dusty limitations of the pulpit. Those deep-set eyes had seen too many strange sights, that saturnine mouth spoken to too many strange people. . . . And, even more, in rebellion against the endless repetition of rigidly framed beliefs was, I suggest, a fount of natural and inextinguishable honesty, and at least some inkling of the fact that life, or at any rate his life, was an exciting quest, an inescapable pilgrimage, far beyond the conventional duties of the ministry. "My Destiny and France demand it," asseverated Napoleon, defending his divorce from Josephine. De Foe's destiny and England's demanded that he should become her greatest journalist, instead of a dissenting minister handicapped

---

[1] *Vide* the late Wilfred Whitten.
[2] The exact period is uncertain, but the date of his leaving the Academy is specifically stated to be the autumn of 1676.

rather than equipped by a scathing tongue and a brilliantly inventive pen. He declined to dedicate his life to the service of the Church—and it is reasonably certain that there was the devil to pay when he announced the fact to his family.

As a youth of eighteen he was still legally under the control of his father; as Daniel De Foe, genius and incorrigible individualist, he remained under the control of no one but himself to the end of his life.

Yet he did not abandon the ministry entirely without regret. Terming it "none of my office", he continues: "It was my disaster first to be set apart from the honour of that sacred employ." Had he lived two centuries later he might have compromised; the born wanderer and critical observer might have been shaken by the kaleidoscope of life into becoming a missionary, a revivalist, or even the founder of a new sect. It is not unlikely that James Foe offered to take his son into partnership. If so, the offer was declined; the lifelong prospect of slaughtering, dismembering and selling animals, and the sight and smell of their blood, did not appeal to him, apart from the fact that a butcher's business was not one to provide opportunities for conversing with amusing and intelligent people, or of seeing anything of the world beyond the horizon of the City.

Yet he had no objections whatever to trade as such. Furthermore, in the years immediately following the Fire London became a City in which trading not only achieved a new dignity and status but opened a new and exciting avenue to wealth. Shopkeepers were becoming merchants, and merchants were becoming rich. Money talked, if not always with refined accents, loudly enough to command the material comforts and luxuries coveted by the parvenu, and grocers, linen-drapers and such were beginning to realize that there were other ways of making it than by humbly serving the gentry from the further side of the counter. London itself was in process of rebuilding in brick and stone in place of the Elizabethan timber and plaster. And the streets they built were wider, and the outlook and ambitions of Londoners metaphorically widened, too.

To James Foe and his contemporaries the changes must have seemed as revolutionary and exciting as television and the rocket-plane seem to the older generation to-day.

Since 1620 there had been newspapers. The earliest single sheets, printed on both sides and called "corantos", were followed by bulkier "newsbooks". Their titles were remarkable. *Mercurius Pragmaticus, Mercurius Fumigosus, The Faithfull Scout, The Man in the Moon, Mercurius Democritus in Querpo;* their information erratic and skimpy. The Plague year, as stated elsewhere, saw the birth of *The Oxford Gazette,* later *The London Gazette,* and to-day the oldest European newspaper in existence.[1] By 1680 the Government had taken charge of the youthful Press, which, after the manner of youth, showed indications of getting altogether too independent and out-of-hand. "Newsbooks or Pamphlets of News" could only be published under licence. But the titles grew, if anything, more fantastic: publications for 1681 and 1682 include *News from Parnassus, The Weekly Discoverer Strip'd Naked, The Mock Press, The Encounter of Harry Lungs and Jasper Hem,* and *Weekly Memorials for the Ingenious.* And the expression of their views became if anything more violent.

By 1688 there was also a penny post, though it did not extend beyond the City. Fire (though not life) insurance was coming into its own and represented yet another phase of the new realization of the value of civic and commercial operations. A third was the sudden, indeed dangerously sudden, development of the joint stock company, and the attendant experts, the stock jobber and the share speculator.

Trading companies needed capital; the flourishing tradesman with get-rich-quick ambitions hurried to supply it. Life was an extremely exhilarating business to any brisk and self-confident young man of the period.

Brisk and self-confident and quick-witted and imaginative, and with an instinctive ability to unite all these qualities to secure his own advancement—such was Daniel De Foe of the 1680s; the ideal merchant-adventurer in embryo, but for an eternal inquisitiveness and an overriding restlessless that all his life made the further side of the hill more important than the side already explored.

He became apprenticed to a Mr. Charles Lodwick, of Cornhill, an importer of wines and an exporter of hosiery and cloth. A humdrum beginning, no doubt, for a beginner possessed of the turbulent temperament of De Foe, living in

[1] See page 38.

times calculated to encourage and inflame that turbulence. The Plague and the Fire and the war ·with the Dutch belonged to his vanished boyhood, but religious warfare, more fierce, more relentless than any secular enmity, still raged.

The London apprentice of Restoration days belonged to a small but important and well-defined section of society. He had traditional rights, privileges, perquisites and punishments. His life might be said to represent boyhood and adolescence in a perpetual state of uncertain equilibrium, more or less comparable with that of a naval cadet or first-year undergraduate. Not that De Foe's temperament, whatever his calling, would ever have permitted him to become typical. Added to which, he entered the business older than the average apprentice, as well as being very much better educated. Thomas Lodwick, his employer's son, seems to have realized the fact from the beginning, and treated him as an equal. His progress was rapid; the early stages of apprenticeship, involving the performance of those small menial duties which are the junior's in every business organization, were soon left behind. Within a couple of years Daniel had become sufficiently trusted to be allowed to deal directly with other business men as a representative of his firm.

Of the details—the intimate Pepysian details of his daily life—we have no record, beyond such as may be submerged in the fiction-disguised-as-fact and fact-disguised-as-fiction writings of his later years. We do not know, for example, whether he slept in the Cornhill premises, as was the custom with apprentices, or whether, when the day's work was done, he walked home to the butcher's shop in Moorgate where James Foe still had his business.

James had at least one consolation to offset his son's defection from the ministry. Lodwick was a Dissenter, though one who kept his religious views subservient to his business, and his apprentices, Dissenters also, were allowed very considerable liberty in their spare time to demonstrate against the Papist infiltration.

It is interesting to note that when in later years his enemies taunted him with being apprenticed to a hosier—in those days one who dealt in a considerable number of other items, including gloves and night-caps—De Foe denied the charge vehemently. But the denial seems to have had its stress on the word "hosier" rather than on "apprentice". It is obviously unlikely that he would have become a trader in goods of any description without some preliminary period of training.

Moreover, the life of an apprentice, with its organized and frequently rowdy fellowships, offered endless opportunities for youthful daring, initiative, and, as a result, leadership, which must have had very considerable attractions to young De Foe.

One outstanding event of 1678 may have had considerable influence upon his future career. In the autumn of that year Titus Oates, son of a Norwich ribbon-waver but born at Oakham, and destined to plot and vilify in London for nearly thirty years, laid before Sir Edmund Berry Godfrey, a well-known London magistrate, secret and lurid details of what became popularly known as the Papist, or Papistic, Plot. Of this despicable and ill-favoured villain it need merely be said that the *Dictionary of National Biography* heads his biography simply *Titus Oates, Perjurer*—a unique distinction —and concludes a summary of his character by quoting from a contemporary writer:[1]

"His mouth was the centre of his face, and a compass there would sweep his nose, forehead and chin within the perimeter. . . . He was a most consummate cheat, blasphemer, vicious, perjured, impudent and saucy, foul-mouthed wretch, and were it not for the truth of History, and the great emotions in the Public he was the cause of, not fit to be remembered."

The "great emotions he was the cause of" were great enough to convulse the Government, and indeed all England, as nothing else had done since the discovery of the Gunpowder Plot. Oates's story, supported by the evidence of a fanatical parson named Tonge and a bundle of documents, concerned a Papist plot, organized abroad, in which the Pope himself was involved, together with the King of France, the General of the Jesuits, two Irish archbishops and numerous other important though lesser fry. Its alleged object was to murder Charles while in residence at Windsor, place James on the throne, and thereafter to reimpose Catholicism. A band of ruffians was to set fire to the newly built City, while three thousand other ruffians were to massacre its citizens.

[1] Roger North.

All this, of course, focused the limelight upon James, Duke of York, the King's younger brother and heir-presumptive to the Throne.

About James most historians have found it difficult to write with enthusiasm.[1] He was unmistakably a Stuart, but he lacked the essential kingliness and dignity that went with his father's wrong-headedness, and the infectious wit and vitality that made so much of his brother's selfishness and open immorality forgivable. The first Charles possessed fanatical adherents throughout his ill-starred life, and indeed long after it had ended; the second Charles died one of the most popular kings in England's long line of rulers.

To revert to Oates. He was an unmitigated scoundrel, but he was also extraordinarily plausible—history records few unmitigated scoundrels who were not. The public at large believed in him and Tonge and the documents, veri-similitude being added to the story by the disappearance of Sir Edmund Berry Godfrey, and the discovery five days later of his body in a ditch. An extra macabre touch was given by evidence which showed that he had had nothing to eat for two days before his death, and that he had first been strangled and then transfixed by his own sword, which had been left in the wound. That he had been "kidnapped and murdered" by Papists to prevent any revelations seemed obvious. An enraged mob bore his body through the City. Catholics wisely barricaded themselves in their houses and were silent.

All London, all England, was aflame with rumours and sus-picions. Charles, shrewd and immensely experienced in the ways of panic-spreaders, alone remained unmoved and incred-ulous. When Oates appeared to give evidence against some unfortunate Jesuit priests, he examined the witness in person and more than once caught him out. Charles's position was, in point of fact, a delicate one. He urgently needed money for the navy and army. He could only obtain it through Parliament, which was reassembling on October 21st, and, as always, his personal popularity and powers of persuasion were his chief assets in so obtaining it. This preposterous plot, in whose bloody ramifications he had no belief what-

[1] Dislike and mistrust of James had reached such a pitch that in June, 1680, the Earl of Shaftesbury " presented " the Duke to a grand jury at Westminster as a Popish Recusant. (But he was not definitely excluded from the Throne.)

ever (though he did believe in a movement to introduce
Popery and stated as much privately to a friend), had
wrought the country into an almost hysterical pitch of
loyalty; he could literally not afford to dissipate it. Extreme
tact was required. Charles announced that he had heard of
the plot, but would forbear to express an opinion, preferring
to leave the matter to the law. . . .

The unspeakable Oates became a hero, a patriot of the
first water, whose safety demanded an armed bodyguard; a
denouncer of Popery whose mere word was enough to send
any suspect to prison, and the recipient of a State pension of
twelve hundred pounds a year.

He continued to earn his country's gratitude. The
culmination came when, in November, he accused the
unfortunate Queen, a Catholic, of having secretly plotted
with Wakeman, her physician, to poison the King, to
whom she had never been anything but devoted, utterly
faithless though he had been from the earliest months of their
marriage. Charles for once rose completely to the occasion
and supported her openly and courageously.

For the rest of the unedifying, but, to the student of the
period (and of panic-stricken human nature at any period),
immensely interesting story, there is no space here. Oates's
fortunes rose and fell; his villainies were unmasked, he
earned the hatred he deserved. But his effrontery, adaptability and, one might add, his good luck never deserted him.
He lived to be fifty-six, a plotting, foul-mouthed liar to the
last. He was, says one historian, "distinguished for the
effrontery of his demeanour no less than by the superior
villainy of his private life". And on that note we may leave
him. He impinged upon the world of London; that world
was De Foe's, and De Foe records the fact as part of the
bizarre background against which his own bizarre life was
enacted.

The whole atmosphere of the City was tense with excitement under Oates's revelations, excitement to which the
London apprentices contributed with the utmost gusto and
enthusiasm. For once animal spirits were gloriously supported by public opinion. Organizing themselves into
bands, they patrolled the streets, including in their crusade
against Popery not only the beating-up of any persons
suspected of Jesuitical plotting but the raiding of taverns

suspected of harbouring them, to say nothing of the brothels which for years had been the scandal of Moorfields. Un-offending pedestrians ran additional risks from hordes of lurking robbers, cut-throats and other riff-raff, who, taking advantage of the general hysteria, were apt to rush out from dark courts and alleys to attack any passer-by who looked fair game. These, too, the apprentices dealt with.

The "truncheon" carried by these impromptu special constables was known as a "Protestant flail", and consisted of two clubs joined together by a leather lash. De Foe makes an interesting reference to this. He writes:

"I remember in the time of the Popish plot, when murthering men in the dark was pretty much in fashion, and every honest man walked the streets in danger of his life, a very pretty weapon which soon put an end to the doctrine of assassination; this was a Protestant flail . . . a pistol is a fool to it; it laughs at the sword or the cone;[1] for you know, there's no fence against a flail. . . . Though I never set up for a hero, yet when armed with this scourge for a Papist, I remember, I feared nothing."

De Foe also tells the story of how one evening a band of other apprentices, drinking in a tavern, overheard a customer ask the landlord for news of the conspiracy. Whereupon one of them, probably De Foe himself—the joke is entirely typical—told the newcomer that six Frenchmen had attempted to carry off the Monument, unfinished though it was, and but for the watch, who stopped them as they were going over the bridge and compelled then to take it back again, they might, "for all we know, have carried it over to France". If he needed proof, added the inventor of a practical joke worthy of Charles Lamb, he could go and see the crowd that was watching the masons busy resetting the stones.

The victim, one of the innumerable anonymous characters who flit across De Foe's ironic pages, never to appear again, departed properly impressed.

There is here an exasperating gap in our knowledge of exactly what De Foe did and where he went during the next three or four years. Nearly all biographical statements commonly accepted as truth are nothing more than assumptions based upon references scattered so profusely and irregularly through his own books. How many of them are

[1] A helmet with a conical top.

to be taken seriously or with a grain of salt only the mocking genius who recorded them could have said. But it is fairly certain that, released from his apprenticeship, he spent a couple of years on the Continent. It is equally certain that Mr. Charles Lodwick did not drop out of the picture.[1]

What appears most likely is that De Foe travelled in Spain and Portugal as a negotiator or agent for certain goods, linking English traders and exporters, Lodwick, and probably others, with the foreign buyer, the Continental trip following English journeys, including one to Liverpool. It is further probable that he went to Portugal in a coaster, visiting Oporto and other important ports; that he joined a caravan of merchants whose journey took them through Madrid and Pampeluna; that after spending some months in the South of France he crossed the Alps on a tour in Italy, and finally returned to London via Paris and Calais.

A Grand Tour, minus the grandeur, but plus experiences and intimacies that no bear-led sprig of the aristocracy could hope to achieve; what finer possible training could there be for a writer whose understanding not only of his fellow-countrymen but of his fellow-creatures was to be among his greatest assets? He had little passion for exploration for its own sake, or for voyages that merely revealed unfamiliar seas or mountains; it is noteworthy that his fictitious travellers are invariably seasick. All his life his abiding interest lay in humanity itself; a man's environment and period might make him a rarer or more familiar specimen, but to De Foe they were no more than a background.

His likes and dislikes are typically exhibited in his comparisons between the Spaniards and the Portuguese. The former he liked, though one Spaniard did his furious but ineffective best to swindle him. They were noble in sentiment and haughtily polite, a characteristic also inherited from their Moroccan ancestor. He noted, however, their tendency to boast; their jealousy, frequently justified; their ferocity where their women were concerned. They were lazy, too, and incapable of sustained effort. And their religious fanaticism and terror of the Inquisition shocked his Puritanical upbringing. But they were a surprisingly sober race, like the Southern French, and for that and other qualities he endured them.

[1] See page 83.

He also endured the French, chiefly for their politeness, and their gaiety even in the midst of misfortune. But he condemned, somewhat surprisingly, the carefulness of the lower classes in their money affairs. And he regarded the Frenchman's sprightliness and instability and impulsiveness with the amused superiority common to the British tourist abroad to this day. (One would have given a great deal for a Frenchman's first-hand impression of young De Foe.)

The morals of the Italians frankly scandalized him; his most generous explanation of their licentiousness was to attribute it to their excessive use of spices. And their hypocrisy and pride, particularly the pride of the Venetians, seemed to him revolting. The Portuguese were also on his black list. He refers to them as "a proud and effeminate nation whose commerce has declined", which may have been true. He also regards their sailors with contempt, and accuses the Portuguese in general as being "worse than the Turks" in their cringing submission to their superiors and their brutal tyranny towards inferiors. He sums up by deciding that the features of the inhabitants exhibit certain negro characteristics, and that they are a mongrel race, combining the vices of both blacks and whites.

It is an odd but understandable fact that this saturnine wanderer from London, with his deep-set, ever-inquisitive grey eyes and his rigidly Puritanical upbringing, should have found the lives of the inhabitants of Italy and France and Spain and Portugal far more interesting and worth recording than those of the Netherlands or Germany. It was not an active dislike, though the comparatively little he saw of the Germans was enough for him to label them drunkards; while so far as the Dutch were concerned he admired them greatly. Perhaps this neglect was simply because they were so much less exciting from the journalistic point of view.

He specialized as every good journalist does or tends to do. The current punishment meted out to heretics and others would have had a limited field of investigation to-day, but it was a wide one three centuries ago. In Portugal he witnessed, and subsequently described in detail, the infliction by the Inquisition of torture by fire. In Spain he saw a ceremonial hanging, and made special mention of the executioner's noble badge and of his equally noble humanitarianism. In Germany he met an official whose boast it was that he never needed more than two strokes to sever a client's head from his body. In Amsterdam he found a house of correction where an ingenious arrangement compelled prisoners to pump incessantly as the alternative to being drowned in their cells. He witnessed yet other executions in Paris.

Not all his visits were morbid, of course. But wherever he went and whatever he saw, from irrigating cisterns to bull-fights, from the parading of the gorgeously-uniformed Swiss guards of Louis XIV to the exquisite ladies who took the air in the gardens of the Tuileries; from Spanish bull-fights to the priestly processions in the City of the Popes—all was material for comment and comparison. No child having its first glimpse of London could have been more naïvely thrilled and excited than this grown-up Londoner amid the wonders of the cities of other countries.

Enough can be legitimately deduced from his writings to make one reasonably certain that he actually saw and experienced the European adventures he describes. But it was part of what may be called the infernal credibility of De Foe—the quality appears in every subject his pen touches—that his description of events in the West Indies, in Madagascar, Tobago and other regions about which he can only have read or heard wears the guise of truth seen at close quarters.

One rather curious aversion emerges from De Foe's account of his travels. Either because they interfered with his smooth progress from country to country, or because their sheer immensity was something to which England could show no parallel, or possibly from a combination of both reasons, he loathed mountains. They infuriated him. He abused them as being frightful, horrible, appalling, and worse than crossing the sea.

His Continental journey came to an end. He returned to England via Harwich (his delight at returning being temporarily, but only temporarily, dimmed by the dishonesty of the traders there). The feverish colours and gay life of Paris and Versailles and of Spain and Italy became things of the past. London was his home, where he was understood, where an industrious and shrewd and intelligent and broadly educated young man of twenty-four might make a fortune and a reputation.

Given the industry and the genius of De Foe, the second was inevitable. But, given his eternal restlessness, not the first.

In *The Compleat English Tradesman*,[1] the first part of which was published when the author was forty-five and the second two years later, De Foe devotes an entire section to warning young tradesmen against the troubles which are likely to follow if they marry too young. He begins:

"It˜was a prudent provision which our grandfathers made in the indentures of tradesmen's apprentices, that they should not contract matrimony during their apprenticeship; and they bound it with a penalty that was then thought sufficient, however custom has not taken the edge off it since, viz. that they who did thus contract matrimony should forfeit their indentures; that is to say, should lose the benefit of their whole service, and not be made free."

While from a purely grammatical point of view De Foe has shown less than his usual certainty of touch, the general effect of his advice is clear enough.
He continues:

"Doubtless our fathers were better acquainted with the advantages than we are; and saw further into the desperate consequences of expensive living in the beginning of a tradesman's setting out into the world than we do; at least it is evident that they studied more and practised more of the prudential part, in those cases, than we do.
"Hence we find them very careful to bind their youth under the strongest obligations they could to temperance, modesty, and good husbandry, as the grand foundations of their prosperity in trade, and to prescribe to them such rules and methods . . . as they thought would best conduce to their prosperity. Among these rules, this was one of the chief, viz. that they should not wed before they had sped; it is an old homely rule coarsely expressed, but the meaning is evident, that a young beginner should never marry too soon. While he was a servant, he was bound to it, as above, and when he had his liberty, he was persuaded against it, by all the arguments which ought, indeed, to prevail with a considering man, namely, the expenses that a family necessarily would bring with it, and the care he ought to take to be able to support the expense."

[1]See pages 281-2.

After which admirable sentiments, there is an amplification of the marriage-theme. Not only may a bad wife ruin a tradesman who has been imprudent enough to wed too early in his career, but the same may happen when she is a good wife. De Foe does indeed cover the whole ground with depressing thoroughness, quoting personally-known examples of young men who married prudently and young men who, disregarding all warnings, did not. Perhaps the outstanding quality of the whole essay is the extraordinarily up-to-date quality. It might, as they say, have been written yesterday.

No counsel could have been more indisputably right. But De Foe himself did not follow it. Possibly James Foe, two of whose daughters were already married, was anxious for his son to settle down in London, doubly stabilized with a business and a wife of his own. Possibly, though somehow one does not feel that this was the primary reason, he himself was in love. There must have been family councils of which we have no record. With these Charles Lodwick must have concerned himself, for on December 28th, 1683, the following notice appeared in the office of the Vicar General.

"Charles Lodwick, of St. Michael's, Cornhill, applies for Daniel Foe of the same parish 24 and a bachelor merchant, and Mary Tuffley, of St. Botolph's, Aldgate, spinster with consent of her father. At St. Botolph's, Aldgate, St. Giles, Cripplegate, or St. Lawrence, Jewry."

One wonders what precisely the grounds were which involved Lodwick applying for the licence when the bridegroom was a man of twenty-four or in his twenty-fourth year. Perhaps he was still bound under the terms of his apprenticeship. And why, since the ceremony took place only four days later, three churches are mentioned as being in the running for the ceremony.

St. Botolph's was the one selected, the Reverend Mr. Hollingsworth officiating. With the delightfully casual spelling of the period, "Foe" has now become "Ffoe", on the register, "batchelor", "batcheller", and his wife's maiden name "Tufflie".

James Foe could hardly have wished for a more satisfactory alliance. Mr. Tuffley, an ardent Dissenter, who settled later at Newington, where he conducted a "conventicle", gave his daughter the extremely satisfactory sum of three thousand seven hundred pounds as a marriage dowry. He had two sons: Charles, who went to sea, and Samuel, who stayed at home to run a successful business at Hackney. It was indeed a thoroughly worthy if unexciting *ménage*. But one may hazard the guess that Daniel, to whom the commonplace and unexciting were anathema, suffered considerably from boredom in the Tuffley circle.

In Mary herself he was luckier than he deserved to be. One feels that the celebrated epitaph on Lady Jones—"she was bland, passionate, and deeply religious"—was almost perfectly applicable. But where business affairs were concerned, she put all her energies and all her intelligence at her husband's disposal; her household was managed, says a chronicler, "with enthusiasm and good taste". And if James Foe had wanted his son to continue the family line he had every reason to be satisfied. In course of time—and not a particularly long time—eight children appeared: Daniel and Benjamin, followed by six daughters, Mary, Hannah, Henrietta, Maria, Martha and Sophia. Mary and Martha died young, but the others throve.

It is curious that nowhere in De Foe's pages is his sister Mary mentioned.

He does not even refer to her marriage to Mr. Francis Bartham, shipwright and bachelor, aged thirty, at St. Mary Magdalen, Bermondsey, "Co, Surrey". The date was May 20th, 1679, and the bride is officially designated as "Mrs. Mary Foe, of St. Swithin, London, Spinster, about 20. . . . With her father's consent", adds the parish record.

It is difficult to believe that De Foe was not present at the ceremony. If he was, it is even more difficult to believe that he saw and heard nothing worth recording.

Reference to his brother occurs once; other relations— a schoolmaster in Somerset; another relation in Dorsetshire; a London cousin whose reputation outside his business was nothing to boast about—do appear, but only incidentally. One would probably be right in putting De Foe among those who find more to interest and amuse them among their friends and acquaintances than among their relations. To such, though blood may be thicker than water, it is considerably less attractive.

At some time during 1683, obviously after his marriage, De Foe was established on his own account in business.

The shop was in Freeman's Court, facing the entrance to Change Alley. A great fire in 1759 which virtually wiped out Cornhill included De Foe's premises in its path. In the eyes of a Londoner of to-day it would have been difficult to realize that they constituted a retail place of business.

Nothing would have been exhibited in the windows, with their tiny panes; the shop-owner or one of his apprentices would have stood at the entrance to proclaim to the passersby the merits of what might be purchased in the cramped and dimly-lit interior, with an accent on the variety rather than on the quantity of the stock.

In later years De Foe was always stung to exasperation when his enemies alluded to him as a seller of stockings. It would be more accurate to say that, following the business in which he had served his apprenticeship, he included stockings among the items in which he dealt as a general exporter on his own account. At a later stage he added drugs and perfumes to the lists. These included civet, largely used for blending with scents, a fact which gave his enemies a further opportunity of sneering at him as the Civet Cat Merchant.

But as a business man De Foe was not to succeed. He was, indeed, doomed by temperament to be a failure. He was far too volatile, and—worse—far too impatient. Ironically enough, that passion for exactitude in everyday details, for analysing and dwelling upon the familiar trivialities of life, the very qualities which infuse his literary work with peculiar and perennial charm, seem to have been conspicuously absent when he was a shopkeeper. His nimble mind found no worthy outlets in the daily management of a small business. His irritation developed into intensified dislikes— of the Jews, for example, with their eyes unwaveringly fixed upon any deal in which there were possibilities of profit, however small. His heart was set upon the acquirement of a reputation for the wit and bearing of the young aristocrats who swaggered past in the streets outside. His restless, arrogant, snobbish—yes, snobbish—spirit soared above the slow building up of a fortune, or, hitching his wagon to a lesser star, the maintenance of his family and himself, by the sound and unspectacular methods of his father.

Yet his new duties and responsibilities were morally and legally inescapable. "My brother," says a character in one of Chesterton's *Father Brown* stories, "is, I regret to say, not a domesticated person". Neither was De Foe. His enthusiam for married life, never much more than tepid, ebbed. The arrival of babies in a house already inconveniently cramped probably helped the ebbing process. His eternally active brain, always dominating his heart, found the close-linked claims of home and business intolerable. He had not the safety-valve of a convinced and active revivalist; to the rigid creeds and dogmas of his father and Morton he gave little more than detached and diplomatic recognition. And in the meantime, heard amid a never-ceasing chorus of pettifogging domesticity, sounded the syren voices of travellers from foreign lands, of traders, agents and customers who came to talk of spices and wines and fabrics, and stayed to discuss and balance their own experiences against those of the eager, fluent, wide-travelled Mr. De Foe.

One's sympathies go out to his wife, as indeed they may well do to the wives of all geniuses. But in her case there was no dreaming, unworldly poet or painter or musician to mother, to adore and to weep over, but an intensely practical and clear-headed (though frequently wrong-headed) young man whom mothering would only reduce to exasperation, and tears to a cold comparison with the emotional reactions of the ladies of France or Spain.

If, allowed such frailties and diversions, he could only have minded his own business, and made the little shop in the City the focus of his world, as it was the focus of hers! But even in 1683, the first year of their marriage, he had shown alarming symptoms of dabbling, with more vigour than discretion, in politics. His pen—she must have dreaded watching it in action—he used from the first with the same lethal simplicity with which he used his tongue. The problem of Austria inspired him. Her territory had been invaded by the Turks, who gave every indication of advancing still further into Europe. The Whigs in England, detesting the Austrians and their Popish rulers, regarded the invaders as instruments of God, and wished them well. But De Foe, although a Whig, regarded them as a curse and a menace; infidels to whom Catholicism, however bigoted, was infinitely preferable, and said as much. Unfortunately we have no copy of this, his first political excursion.

Within three years of his marriage his first three children were born. Mary must have had her hands heartbreakingly full. The nature of Daniel's business gave him innumerable excuses for travelling; the reproaches of an overworked wife and the less articulate pleading of three infants did not detain him, and between 1684 and 1688 he contrived to travel, chiefly on horseback, frequently with a companion, over most of the main roads of Britain. An incorrigible wanderer makes an unsatisfactory husband and father. (And yet, when his children were old enough to understand and appreciate him, and for him to understand and appreciate them, what a gloriously exciting story-teller he must have been!)

Riding was always De Foe's favourite method of travelling; it left him at liberty to think undisturbed and uninterrupted; his speed was his own; he could stop as often as he pleased. A horse, too, emphasized his social status.

His powers, his talents, opened like flowers in the sunshine of popularity; his wit, no less than his effective oratory, made him welcome among other wits and orators. And popularity is heady stuff; it can hardly be wondered at if Mary noted changes in Daniel that made the tie between them still more tenuous. She had her religion, her family, her friends to sustain her, but there must have been many recriminations in public, and much bitterness when she was alone.

What of the stocking, wines, and perfumes business? Its fortunes fluctuated; there were times of opulence; when they were the reverse, there was Mary's *dot* to fall back on, and even when that had gone, her father, and the sailor brother Charles, and the comfortably-off brother of Hackney, to say nothing of Daniel's father, were at hand, and could, and doubtless did, come to the rescue.

CHAPTER II

INTERLUDE FOR REBELLION

IN 1685 King Charles regretfully and apologetically died, after a reign of twenty-five years. He had begun to reign when he was thirty, returning from exile a cynical, astute stranger; he ended it one of the most popular sovereigns in our history. His physical and mental tenacity should have given him a longer reign, but his physicians defeated Nature and by sheer persistence in drugging, bleeding, and generally harassing a sick man killed him in his fifty-fifth year. Had he been a heretic fallen into the hands of the Inquisition, his end could have been scarcely more painful, and would certainly have been quicker. Judged by modern standards, seventeenth-century doctors were ruthless though well-meaning ignoramuses and bunglers.

It was entirely typical of Charles that, while a sworn upholder of the Protestant faith, and while the bishops about his bed and the crowd surrounding the Palace were praying for his recovery, he had a Catholic priest in waiting to admit him into the Church of Rome and to administer the Last Sacrament.

His successor was, of course, his younger brother, to whom Charles once acidly retorted, when James expostulated about the absence of a bodyguard: "Do not be afraid—they will never kill me to make you King!"

"They", Charles's subjects, never did. Now they were James's subjects, and they did not love him. Yet, Catholic as he was known to be, and despotic at heart, he swore solemnly to protect the Church of England and to keep the laws inviolate. And London, at any rate, accepted these promises with general enthusiasm, tempered, so far as the Dissenters were concerned, with justifiable doubt.

For James, stubborn, narrow-minded and tactless, possessed the mentality of a politician, admiral or general of the traditional hide-bound type which has stumped across the comic stage since the first curtain rose on the first comedy. As King, no longer subject to the shrewd control of his brother, he simply hardened into a despot who regarded any concession to those opposing him as a rank betrayal of his office. One example may be quoted. When the Whigs opened a subscription in March 1686 for the relief of the Huguenots, its success was immediate, not merely because the average Englishman sympathized with suffering Frenchmen, but because it gave the average Englishman a chance of recording his detestation of the French King who had inflicted those sufferings, and of his Catholic Court.

James, of course, was infuriated. He did his best to prevent the money being distributed. Meetings of Dissenters, at coffee-houses and elsewhere, became more frequent, more urgently charged with plans for action, more secret.

At one such meeting De Foe met an old school friend, John Dunton, who had married a daughter of Samuel Annesley, and had, furthermore, visited Charles Morton in his new sphere at Harvard. Dunton and De Foe became firm allies.

It is hardly to be wondered at that as the days passed the new King's popularity, such as it was, steadily ebbed. The fact that James was a bigoted Tory made him anathema to the Whigs; that he was an active Papist roused clouds of suspicion and hatred among his Protestant subjects. And the complete absence of that easy-going charm and sagacious affability that were such enormous assets to his brother handicapped James very badly indeed. . . .

Small-scale rioting broke out in London. It was rigorously suppressed. De Foe's family were there, but De Foe himself was by this time in the West Country. Monmouth, ill-starred illegitimate nephew of James,[1] had returned from exile and landed at Lyme. There, amid the frantic cheering of the inhabitants—though the gentry discreetly held aloof —he proclaimed himself the Protestant champion of the people. His supporters, fired with the reckless enthusiasm which is so much less dangerous than calculated plotting by a small band of cold-blooded fanatics, because so transitory,

[1] He was the spoilt favourite of Charles, and officially recognized and ennobled by him, though in point of fact doubts have been expressed as to whether he really was Charles's son. There is ground for supposing that the easy-going King may have been hoaxed for once.

issued a proclamation in which they charged the new King
with being the instigator of the Great Fire and—an odd
descent in crime—of the murder of Sir Edmund Berry
Godfrey.

The time was high summer; young De Foe was cantering
in the neighbourhood of Wimborne, from which Lyme is
not far distant. The syren voice of Adventure had called.
He had no particular domestic or business entanglements;
on the other hand, he had a deep-seated and traditional
detestation of the Popery which menaced his country, and
a conviction that immediate action was needed to combat it.
All about him impatient patriots were joining the rebels;
had their leader not been the most impatient of them all,
and had he not made the cardinal mistake of proclaiming
himself King instead of waiting for Parliament to offer him
the throne when the unpopular James had vacated it, a
different page, indeed a different volume, of English history
might have been written.

De Foe, with the journalistic instinct to be where things
were happening, had allowed himself to run the immense
risk of joining the marching rebels.

Thirty-five years later, shortly after *Robinson Crusoe* had
been published, appeared *The Memoirs of a Cavalier*.[1] No
author's name appeared upon the title-page, but the work
was undoubtedly by De Foe, and bears on every page
unmistakable evidence of his style. The Edinburgh edition
of 1809 says: "It must undoubtedly . . . be allowed to
reflect additional lustre, even on the author of *Robinson
Crusoe.*"

It may have done. But to-day it would be a reasonably
safe bet to wager that eighty out of every hundred average
Englishmen have never heard of the *Memoirs*, or, alternatively, could not name their author, and ninety-five per
cent have never read the book. Its preface contains the
familiar truth-for-truth's-sake-at-all-costs nonsense concerning the Cavalier's family and antecedents. "The name,"
said the publisher, "bestowed upon the Cavalier is purely
suppositious. . . . The laboured attempts of our Author
to investigate the matter, and to authenticate the manuscript, are so many proofs of his amazing skill in bestowing
real life upon the phantoms of his own genius. . . . It is

[1] See page 254.

impossible to read his book without a full persuasion of its being written by the identical person to whom it relates."

De Foe was not even born when the battles it describes in such detail (together with the inevitable statistics, coincidences, and moralizings) took place; the King for whom his fictitious cavalier fought and endured had ended his life on that bleak January morning in 1649.

But De Foe *had* taken part in the defeat which ended the career of the wretched grandson of Charles the Martyr and of his followers in the summer of 1685. And that he did not make use of his experiences there to lend verisimilitude to his account of his Cavalier hero's life I refuse to believe.

Whether he actually fought in the doomed ranks of the little army, numbering, as it did, no more than six or seven thousand all told, and indifferently armed at that, is unknown. History tells us that in a preliminary skirmish near Bath Monmouth achieved a definite advantage, and that if he had followed it up, he would have stood every chance of complete victory. Instead, he fell back to Sedgmoor, where his forces were bloodily annihilated. De Foe was lucky enough to escape. Unknown locally, and inconspicuous in the confusion of the rout, he found refuge with a relation, a schoolmaster at Martock. Monmouth himself, detected in hiding, was taken to London. His grovelling appeals for clemency were disregarded, and he was beheaded on Tower Hill ten days later. Less eminent rebels, hunted down ruthlessly, had no better fate. The notorious Judge Jeffreys, his natural sadism inflamed by acute ill-health, was sent down to the West Country to remind His Majesty's subjects of the penalties attached to rebellion. Among others, three of De Foe's fellow-students at Newington, Battersby, Hewling, and Jenkyns, were caught and executed; Tutchin,[1] an acquaintance, an active Whig politician who was to play a prominent part in De Foe's life, later on received the fantastically degrading sentence of being "whipp'd in public through all the towns in Dorset every year for seven yeares". He was further ordered to pay a fine of a hundred marks, and find security for good behaviour for the rest of his life.

John Tutchin, born a year after De Foe, was in some respects extraordinarily like the older man. He came of a

[1] See also pages 130 and 165.

family of Nonconformist ministers; his father had settled in London and was a freeman of the City. In addition to De Foe's courage, youth and wit, he had the same capacity for deadly sarcasm and the same recklessness in employing it. He had also the same belief in the inalienable freedom of the subject. A few months before Sedgmoor he had published a volume of poems; to these the egregious Jeffreys referred when sentencing him. (Incidentally, though Tutchin admitted to being a friend of Monmouth, there was no evidence whatever that he had been actively involved in the rebellion. Probably the truest charge against him was that he had been instrumental in recruiting for the Duke's army.)

"You," thundered Jeffreys, "are a rebel, and all your family have been rebels since Adam. They tell me you are a poet. *I'll* cap verses with you!"

The sentence followed. The indomitable Tutchin promptly petitioned the King to grant him the favour of being hanged with the other condemned fellow-prisoners. His Majesty declined. The sequel was a sordid anti-climax. Jeffreys was bribed to recommend a pardon; when, not long afterwards, the judge himself had been committed to the Tower and Tutchin visited him there, Jeffreys, according to Macaulay, excused himself by saying that he had acted only according to instructions.

De Foe remained precariously in hiding until the first fury of denunciation and arrests had died down, and then unobtrusively made his way by easy stages back to London.

The story of his escape, told as he might have told it, would have made magnificent reading. Unfortunately discretion prevailed; he remained silent. For once resembling Gilbert's Duke of Plaza Toro, "he found it less exciting".

In April 1687 James issued a second Declaration of Indulgence, cancelling the first.

It appeared, on the face of it, to be a broad-minded effort to solve the problem of religious freedom by treating it as no problem at all. He proposed a coalition of Catholics and Nonconformists. He said that the Nonconformists could freely return to their conventicles; that in future they could be under his Royal protection. The Bill of Test was abolished. No one was to be persecuted; each was to be at complete liberty to worship after his own fashion.

From the Stuart point of view, this must have indicated a magnificent broadmindedness and generosity. It did not occur to him that his offence lay in something entirely divorced from religious tolerance, in conceiving that he had the personal right to issue anything of the sort. So far from placating both Papists and Dissenters, the Declaration was precisely calculated to arouse a fury of protest from every religious body in the kingdom, including the Parliament, who alone was entitled to give it final authority, and whose right James had so gratuitously flouted.

"Was anything ever more absurd?" demanded De Foe, "than this conduct of King James and his party in wheedling the Dissenters, giving them liberty of conscience by his own arbitrary dispensing authority, and expecting they should be content with their religious liberty at the price of the Constitution!"

Apart from any constitutional rights, the Declaration concealed a trap, and a clumsy trap at that. If the Bill of Test was removed from the Statute Book, Catholics could be, and indubitably would be, appointed to all the highest offices of the Church, from the archbishoprics downwards. The Established Church would be thrust into the background, the Dissenters reduced to complete impotence. It would be a reversion to the days of Bloody Queen Mary. The mere prospect was unendurable.

The Archbishop of Canterbury and seven bishops, my Lords of Asaph, Ely, Chichester, Bath and Wells, Peterborough, and Bristol, petitioned the King to dispense with their reading or distributing the hated Declaration. They were ordered to enter into their recognizance to appear before the Court of Pleas. They declined, and were accordingly committed to the Tower. The heather was ablaze at last.

De Foe who had been indulging in a little unofficial preaching at Tooting, handed over his congregation to a friend, the Reverend Joshua Oldfield; there was work waiting elsewhere. He perceived himself in a new, more secular, more exciting role. The country needed, with the utmost urgency, men who could set out, fearlessly and in terms capable of being understood by all, the state into which it was drifting under the hand of a mulishly stubborn Papist autocrat. Shrewd heads and wise tongues were demanded, as never before, to allay panic. . . . Or, if panic were the better spur to action, to guide it successfully. . . .

Whither?

The answer was as yet only a murmur. But it was a murmur heard from one end of England to the other.

On June 10th a Prince of Wales was born, and on the following Sunday London was officially ordered to celebrate the event. There must have been a grim undercurrent to those rejoicings.

On June 29th the Bishops were tried at Westminster Hall. The next day the jury brought in a verdict of "Not Guilty". English crowds in the streets tactlessly roared their approval. James, more tactlessly still, ordered Mass to be said on every man-o'-war. "The Priests were in danger of being thrown overboard," reports a chronicler. In September the King published yet another Declaration. He would inviolably preserve the Church of England. He was contented that the Roman Catholics should continue to be excluded from the House of Commons.

His contentment must have been brief, for two days later he received "certain intelligence that the Preparation of the Dutch"—concerning which Louis's ambassador at the Hague had already issued a warning—"were intended against England".

Events were now moving at increasing speed; the murmur was ceasing to be a murmur. But there were still intervals of diplomatic fencing. Now it was the turn of the Prince of Orange to issue a Proclamation.

The reasons for his intended visit to England and his father-in-law were, said William, "to facilitate the calling of a free Parliament, and to enquire into the birth of a Prince of Wales", an odd conjunction to form the basis of a friendly call.

That was on October 1st. On the 19th he set out to pay this visit, which was merely one of "facilitating and enquiry" —the tactics of the invader change very little during the centuries—with what to James must have seemed an excessive escort, fifty or more men of war, three hundred transports, with (to quote our same pernickety "Chronological Historian", Mr. Salmon) about 14,322 land forces on board. These forces included the Earls of Shrewsbury and Macclesfield, together with various other "Gentlemen of Quality". Also the Earl of Sunderland, Secretary of State, who was later discovered to have betrayed His Majesty's Councils to the Prince.

A storm delayed the actual sailing. It took place on November 1st. And on the 4th, the Prince's birthday as well as the anniversary of his marriage, the famous landing was made at Torbay. De Foe refers to the event in his paper, the *Review* (he made a point of doing so at each subsequent anniversary), as "a day made famous on various counts, and every one of them dear to Britons who love their country, value the Protestant interest, or have an aversion to tyranny and oppression. On this day William the Third was born; on this day he married the daughter of England; and on this day he rescued the nation from a bondage worse than that of Egypt—a bondage of soul as well as bodily service— slavery to the ambition and raging lust of a generation set on fire by pride, avarice, cruelty and blood".

Bold words indeed. But the last of the Stuart Kings was beyond punishing him for them.

The remainder of James's reign belongs to the ignominious tag-rag and bobtail of history. After issuing a spate of proclamations and pardons, he had assembled an army at Salisbury, but his own soldiers decorated themselves with orange ribbons, while the nobility who had once supported him deserted in an increasing stream to William. There was the usual sporadic rioting, and public excitement was suddenly intensified by the disappearance of James's younger daughter, Anne. There were rumours, among innumerable other rumours, that she had been murdered—by Papist allies of her papist father, of course—but they subsided with the publication of a letter in which she explained that she had just joined her brother-in-law, William. She, in other words, had become the most distinguished deserter of them all.

James was inevitably reduced to opening negotiations with his rival; William, in return, "sent proconsuls". On December 9th the Queen and the young Prince of Wales left for France; and on the following day the King attempted to follow them. Judge Jeffreys, caught, disguised and in hiding, in Wapping, was hustled to the Tower, and there, luckily for himself, died soon afterwards. In the City "the Mob demolished and plundered several Mass-houses and houses of the Roman Catholics, in particularly (sic) the Spanish Ambassador's."

James reached Feversham; there, unlucky to the last, "being drawn back by contrary winds, he was mistaken for a Jesuit and abused by the Rabble, none of his party taking any active steps to protect him". He returned, more or less under compulsion, and with heaven-knows-what plans seething in his buffalo-like mind, to Whitehall. There were "joyful acclamations" from his friends, but the arrival of the Prince's forces, and their prompt occupation of the strategical points of the City, chilled James's welcome. It was to be his last entry into the capital. Prince William politely but firmly instructed him to depart by midnight on December 17th, and under a guard of Dutch troops the last Stuart to reign in England allowed himself to be escorted to Rochester. On the 23rd he made a second attempt to sail for France. This time the weather was favourable.

The Revolution was a *fait accompli*.

"King James," remarks our chronicler, "reigned for three years, nine months and eleven days", in which period he succeeded in accumulating enough unpopularity to ensure the perpetual exile of himself and his descendants. The ghost of Charles the Martyr must have smiled bitterly, the ghost of Charles the Dissolute sardonically.

CHAPTER III

LITIGANT AND BANKRUPT

ONE WOULD have thought that, for a time at any rate, De Foe might have remained at home with his wife and young family, and attended to his equally youthful business. But by this time excitement in some form or another had become essential to him as air. Domesticity and trade were unlikely in the long run to stand much chance in competition with other unprofitable but enthralling diversions.

His civic responsibilities and privileges were not entirely overlooked. His father had been a member of the Butchers' Company, and though De Foe's business had no connection whatever with the sale of beasts, he was in January 1688 also admitted a member, "by patrimony", paying, in lieu of serving all offices, ten pounds fifteen shillings. He was now sufficiently established to lease not only the shop and warehouse in Cornhill, but a house at the then highly rural village of Tooting to which he and his family could retire in the summer.[1]

One feels that, on the whole, he was enjoying himself enormously; having the time of his life, indeed. With the spectacular triumph of Protestantism over Jacobean Papistry vanished multitudinous risks and dangers, though occasional harsh notes of dissent in the general chorus of congratulation made themselves heard, and certain untoward incidents interfered with his activities. On horseback, all his life De Foe's favourite mode of progression, he set out with other enthusiasts to greet the new ruler, known to be advancing at the head of his troops. At Windsor, however, disquieting

[1] According to Morden, there is no record that De Foe ever lived there regularly. There is a local tradition that he resided in Old Tooting Hall in 1688. Unfortunately the Hall was not built until 1784. It is, however, certain that he spent a good deal of his time in Tooting, and founded a nonconformist chapel in the parish. The Hall, later used as a workhouse, is now demolished.

De Foe often visited the near-by inn which then stood on the site of Bowling Green House, where William Pitt died on the 25th anniversary of his entry into Parliament.

news reached him. A party of Irish dragoons under Lord
Feversham, a die-hard supporter of James, had come into
collison with a mixed force of William's men on the outskirts of Reading, and were now roaming about the countryside murdering, robbing, raping and generally terrorizing
the inhabitants, prior to returning to their homeland, or, as
the inevitable alternative, being rounded up and hanged.
Bands of these freebooters had penetrated into Maidenhead
and Uxbridge and Colnbrook, but at this last point the
stiffening resistance of the outraged citizens daunted them;
the bands disintegrated further into individual criminals
concentrating upon individual crimes. As such, they became
even more terrifying, because more elusive, and there was
a general migration from the scattered villages to better
protected areas. Refugees arrived in scores at Kingston,
Hounslow and even distant Windsor with bloodcurdling
stories of the raiders' crimes. De Foe compares these to "the
undulations of the waters in a pond, when a flat stone is
cast upon the surface". A simile with the authentic De Foe
touch.

For a time he remained at Windsor, partly from prudence
—a virtue which he possessed to a considerable extent—
and partly because there was a vast number of interesting
events to occupy him. De Foe had indeed all the natural
qualifications of Our Special Correspondent. True, there was
no editor to credit him with his on-the-spot reports. But,
on the other hand, there was an even mightier autocrat,
even more highly placed, to work for, a Defender of the
Faith under whom an unfortunate but indefatigable writer
and organizer might find many years of honourable service
and be honourably rewarded.

It was rumoured that Maidenhead lay in ashes. De Foe
learned the news when he reached Slough, after having
made an early morning departure from Windsor. The same
fate, added his informants cheerfully, had overtaken Uxbridge and many other towns. Reading was still burning.
So, too, was Oakingham.

At this point De Foe, later to prove himself one of the
most superb rumour-mongers in English history, seems to
have become sceptical; the ubiquitous ruffianism even of
Irish dragoons without discipline or guidance had its limits.
He decided to drop his investigations for the time being,

and retraced his way to Henley. He entered the town a few hours before a detachment of Dutch troops marched in. From them he learnt of the escape of James, and of his being brought back to London. De Foe himself went back.

On December 18th, while Papist James was still waiting at Rochester for a wind that would be kind to blundering Royalty in a hurry to get to France, William made his state entry into the capital. De Foe, dressed handsomely, with innumerable orange-coloured ribbons decorating himself and his steed, joined in the procession.

Bells clanged, and the populace cheered—Protestant bells and Protestant cheers, of course. De Foe rejoiced as noisily as the rest. Rain and wind lashed the streets, but could not dampen the rejoicings. The double Coronation took place on February 13th. Unnumerable major and minor adjustments and promotions were made, but none in which the name of Daniel De Foe appeared. Fighting in Scotland and Ireland began, with intermittent successes so far as the natives were concerned, but on the whole registering a steady diminution of the chances of James's party becoming a menace to English freedom again.

On October 29th in the following year the Lord Mayor and Aldermen entertained their new King and Queen and all London at a magnificent banquet. All London included one of its newest freemen, Daniel De Foe. Among a company composed of young City aristocrats he rode, splendidly accoutred, under the command of the great Earl of Peterborough, to the Palace at Whitehall, from there to escort Their Majesties to the Guildhall.

One would like to assume that Mrs. Mary De Foe and her friends were standing in that crowd, proudly watching the procession clatter on its way. Perhaps they were.

He and his family might have been forgiven for thinking, or at any rate hoping, that this hour marked the turn of the tide. Unfortunately tides ebb as well as flow. He himself wrote years afterwards: "The English Tradesman is a kind of Phoenix, a Phoenix which rises out of its own ashes."[1]

And in spite of these hallmarks of prosperity there must have been a good many occasions when his seniors, particularly his father and his father-in-law, old Mr. Tuffley,

[1] *The Compleat English Tradesman.*

wagged their respectable heads disapprovingly. There were, for example, a number of lawsuits in which he figured, either as the plaintiff or the defendant. He was the latter in eight, brought by opponents between 1688 and 1694. In each of them he was charged with sharp practice amounting to fraud; whatever the verdict or the costs, the publicity involved was bound to have been of the wrong type.

The cases are interesting, if only because they indicate the extraordinarily varied nature of De Foe's business dealings. He seems to have been prepared to buy or sell anything upon which a profit might be made, second-hand ships included. In the latter half of 1688 De Foe disposed of one named *The Desire* to a sailor named Harrison. He himself, however, agreed to retain a quarter share, and to pay the same proportion in fitting her out. The preparations completed, she put to sea with Harrison as captain, and evading French privateers reached Lisbon. On the return journey Harrison's luck left him. An enemy man-o'-war captured the vessel; he himself was carried as a prisoner to Brest. At least so Harrison deposed afterwards before the Court of Chancery.

De Foe's story was very different. He stated (1) that he sold *The Desire* outright to Harrison, (2) that the money was never paid, (3) that he agreed to become part owner only because it had become clear that there was no chance of his obtaining the money, (4) that in any case Harrison had failed to draw up a valid and effective form of partnership, and finally (5) that so far from trading in Portugal, the said Harrison had illegally and traitorously been dealing with His Majesty's enemies, the French.

The depositions of Harrison, and subsequently of his widow (for he died in prison while the case was appearing before the Court of Chancery), were reinforced by the evidence of a shipwright, who stated, a trifle irrelevantly, that De Foe had sold the vessel for two hundred and sixty pounds, whereas she was worth only one hundred and fifty pounds, and that even when she had been fitted by De Foe, he—the shipwright—had been glad to leave her at the first opportunity. The dispute appears to have ended in some sort of compromise.

There was another shipping case on a larger and far more complicated scale during 1688, in which a ship's master with

the comfortably romantic name of Humphrey Ayles of
Redriffe sued De Foe for breach of agreement, the damages
claimed being one thousand five hundred pounds.

Ayles had agreed to sell the *Batchelor* to America with a
mixed cargo of merchandise and passengers, for which De
Foe was to be responsible. Ayles was to call at Boston and
New York, discharge part of his cargo, and afterwards sail
on to Maryland. At all three ports he was to collect any
goods that De Foe's factors might supply and then return
promptly to England. It sounds, on the face of it, a perfectly straightforward agreement; unluckily its signatories
were not equally straightforward.

Ayles did not reappear until he was long overdue, and
when he did the holds of the *Batchelor* were nearly empty.
He vigorously denied any negligence or any unnecessary
delay; adverse winds, together with the inability to obtain
anything more than seven hogsheads of tobacco, had been
to blame, and for this second reason De Foe's factor in
America was responsible. He swore that he had done all
that any master mariner could be expected to do, and
claimed one hundred and forty-four pounds for the delay in
Maryland. For three years the dispute dragged on and
finally ∙fizzled out. Probably both sides grew tired of
financing a case from which only the lawyers stood any
chance of making a profit.

A third story of De Foe's Cornhill days leaves his reputation, as Dr. Sutherland says, "a little dinted, perhaps, but
not seriously damaged". The plaintiff was a merchant of
York, and he charged De Foe with conspiring with "a
menial servant named Marsh".

Marsh had picked up a bill of exchange in his master's
chambers when the master himself was lying there dead.
The bill was for one hundred pounds, and De Foe bought it
from Marsh for sixty pounds—an excessive discount if the
deal were an honest one. The York merchant claimed the
balance of forty pounds. De Foe's defence was, as always,
attack. Marsh, so far from being a "meniall", was a gentleman of the Inner Temple, and an old,.trusted, and intimate
friend. The purchase of the bill had actually taken place
when its late owner was alive; moreover, De Foe had
repeatedly offered to pay the balance of forty pounds
outstanding.

The Court took him at his word, and ordered him to pay it, together with the legal costs of the Yorkshireman.

Two other cases may complete this melancholy list of De Foe's trading methods, which, growing steadily more elaborate and with an increasing bias towards the speculative-shady side, culminated eventually in the loss, not only of his own and his wife's fortune, but also of his reputation. Reading them in detail, one is left with the feeling that De Foe's character, under the strain of mounting financial losses, was deteriorating at a pace that was leading straight to gaol. And in those days, when the law regarded what is now looked upon as a mere lapse of integrity as serious enough for capital punishment, he might even have ended at Tyburn.

In 1691 De Foe became sufficiently interested in a public company to invest two hundred pounds and to accept the appointment of secretary and treasurer. The company had been formed to exploit the sales of an engine for diving, its inventor a Cornishman named Joseph Williams. De Foe, in his capacity as treasurer, was authorized to receive a levy of ten shillings per share for "putting the diving apparatus into practice", an odd enough levy in any case, made still odder by the fact that the inventor himself, as a considerable shareholder, had to pay De Foe seventy pounds for operating his own engine.

Williams paid this extra charge. But later—I am deliberately over-simplifying a case which must have given the lawyers glorious material for their bills of costs—he claimed that De Foe had jockeyed him into paying twice over. In that indictment he included another man, Thomas Williams, no relation, but a City goldsmith. The second Williams, unfortunately for De Foe, had been cited with him as one of the defendants in cheating the York merchant out of forty pounds on the bill of exchange. He must have cursed the day in which he ever became involved in De Foe's financial excursions.

De Foe's defence was that Joseph Williams (who naïvely protested that he was a simple-minded inventor, and in no way "skilled or conversant in the way of giving bills or notes", a statement that may well enough have been true), actually owed him a large sum; the fifty pounds that Williams gave him was merely to set off an equivalent sum already paid into the diving company's accounts.

The case, after the habit of De Foe's legal actions, petered out. The terms of its settlement remain unknown.

Finally, there was what Dr. Watson would certainly have called the Case of the Civet Cats, an affair which, apart from its unpleasant implications upon De Foe's honesty, was later on to provide his enemies with a jibe which as already stated he found particularly infuriating. They charged him with being a dealer in those pungently-scented animals in their natural state. He certainly was.

His business affairs were already in a precarious state when in the spring of 1692 he entered into an agreement with John Barksdale. Barksdale, a fellow-merchant in the City, had taken up the breeding of civet cats on a large scale. He kept no fewer than seventy cats in a special establishment at Newington. But for some reason or other the business ceased to be worth continuing. He wanted ready money. De Foe heard that the cat-farm was to be sold cheap, and realized its possibilities in connection with his scent business.

He bought it for the sum of eight hundred and fifty-two pounds fifteen shillings (one wonders what that odd fifteen shillings represented) agreeing to pay two hundred pounds down, another three hundred pounds in a month, and the balance within six months.

De Foe paid the first instalment. The rest he had to borrow. Samuel Stancliffe, with whom he had previously been in partnership, and who was already a creditor for one thousand pounds, lent him another four hundred. Apparently at the time he, surprisingly enough, did not know of the desperate state of De Foe's finances: when he discovered it, he first asked for his money back, and then, failing to get it, issued a writ. The cats were seized to satisfy it. But their estimated value by this time (October 1692) had dropped to four hundred and thirty-nine pounds seven shillings.

So far the story is merely one of an inveterate bargain-hunter, a feckless purchase, and a hard-headed creditor. But De Foe, as he had done on previous occasions, and as thousands of others with a gambler's temperament have done, diverted the whole of the loan to meet even more urgent debts. Barksdale, realizing that nothing beyond the original two hundred pounds was likely to be obtained from De Foe, assigned the Newington cats to Sir Thomas

Estcourt, a wealthy creditor. Of this De Foe was fully aware, for Barksdale had made him sign a document waiving all claim to them, a point of considerable importance.

Yet in that same month, when the cats were put up for sale—Sir Thomas's interest in the civet business being limited entirely to the satisfaction of a debt—De Foe, posing as the owner, deliberately set about finding another purchaser. It seems extraordinary that he should have succeeded in keeping the truth secret; even more extraordinary is that he succeeded in selling the cats, as the property of Stancliffe, to his own mother-in-law, Mrs. Joan Tuffley. She paid the amount of the second valuation—four hundred and thirty nine pounds seven shillings and ninepence—and in addition, another one hundred and fifty pounds for the animals' upkeep between the date of her bogus purchase, October 17th, and the end of the following March.

On the 27th of that month the blow fell. Sir Thomas, who until then seems to have forgotten the very existence of the Newington cat-farm, an odd lapse for a successful London merchant, sent his servants to take possession of it. The gaff was blown. Mrs. Tuffley, who by a crowning touch of irony had bought the cats "in order that the profits should be for the good of the said Foe and his family", discovered that the said Foe had perpetrated a swindle which no amount of plausibility or charm could explain away. Sir Thomas's right to the animals was irrefutable. Just to what extent, if at all, Stancliffe benefited from the fraud is unknown. But there must have been bitter moments in the De Foe household; futile explanations, recriminations, tears, disownings.

What were the reactions of the simple, deeply religious Mary De Foe, still little more than a girl, to these incessant excursions and alarms; these threats, bluffings, ignominious lyings and evasions? Did she ever guess before she attached herself for life to the sardonic, witty, voluble genius and seasoned traveller that, so far from settling down in the safe and reputable harbour of City life, he would regard the shop in Cornhill as merely a port from which to set sail on a hundred adventures, in which there was little glory and, in the end, less profit? Did she envisage, even for a moment, an existence in which there would be no stability, since stability to Daniel was only one step from boredom, and boredom utterly unendurable?

And old Foe? What of his ambitions for his son? Of his own fortune from this period onward we know little. He moved from Moorgate to Throgmorton Street, but spent the last years of his long life—he was seventy-six when he died—in lodgings at the Bell Inn, in Broad Street, near by. There is a single letter by him in existence, a testimonial he wrote on behalf of a servant named Sarah Pierce, who had been for two years in his service. He should not have recommended her, he says, had not her conversation been "becoming the Gospel".

If at this stage of his career that gifted son descended to depths which afterwards he recalled with abasement, there are excuses. His own sanguine temperament, with that delight in risks for their own sakes which so often goes with sanguine temperaments, led him on. From trading-ships voyaging to Portugal or the Americas in the teeth of all the dangers of enemy capture, to civet cats whose contributions to the manufacture of perfume fetched forty shillings an ounce, these extraneous adventures of his had an Arabian Nights flavour of romance beside which a London trades-man's life must have seemed insipid and futile.

The war with France, though it certainly added to the general atmosphere of excitement, must have hit him hard. Prudent men with far more stable businesses than his saw them collapse. True, he might have accepted bankruptcy earlier. But a bankrupt at the end of the seventeenth century —and, for that matter, a century and a half later—was ignominiously at the mercy of his creditors. To confront them openly was to run the risk, practically the certainty, of going to gaol. Once behind prison doors, he might remain there for the rest of his life, a fate beyond contemplation for a man of De Foe's type, while his entire estate was dis-tributed among the men who sent him there.

On the other hand, if he absconded, he immediately placed himself in the position of a criminal, one whose offence was punishable by death.

With the law so harsh towards crimes whose committal was frequently due to mere foolishness, inexperience or ignorance, it was reasonably certain that some sort of compromise would be evolved. It was evolved. A debtor might find temporary sanctuary, and from there conduct negotiations with his creditors. De Foe, when eventually adjudged a bankrupt owing seventeen thousand pounds, did precisely that.

There were in London a number of such sanctuaries in which not only debtors but law-breakers of every type from murderers downwards could find refuge. Originating in the sanctuaries afforded by the Churches, they remained in existence until well into the eighteenth century. Fleet Street had its "Alsatia", mentioned in *The Fortunes of Nigel*, Southwark its Mint Street. "Fresh from the Mint comes forth the Man of Rhyme", comments the vitriolic Pope, "happy to catch me just at dinner-time!" Lincoln's Inn Fields (Whetstone Park), Holborn (Fullwood's Rents), the Strand (Milford Lane), all, with their individual traditions, customs and legends, harboured small, sordid communities of minor and major criminals. The Mint, nearly opposite St. George's Church, was almost the last, as it was the best-known, of these social sewers; no writ could be served there; the only representative of the law who might enter with impunity was, by an unwritten "rogue's agreement", the thief-taker. He, when a thief had reached what was considered a reasonable limit in picking pockets, snatching purses and so forth, might come and collect his man, and haul him away to a public hanging at Newgate, his belated repentance indicated by white ribbons round his cap, a prayer-book in one hand and an orange in the other, and a large bunch of flowers in his coat.

Into one of these warrens, only less horrible, because less cramped, than prison itself, De Foe disappeared. Later, it is rumoured, he succeeded in getting to Bristol by some means or other, and there used to emerge from his hiding-place on Sundays, when he would be free from the risk of arrest, to stroll about the city, bewigged and powdered and wearing his best clothes, with the sword of the aristocrat he emphatically was not swinging at his side. There, it is further said, they knew him as "the Sunday gentleman", a personage to be treated with respect and listened to admiringly in the taverns he honoured with his presence. In London, long-suffering Mrs. De Foe carried on with help from her friends, and waited.

One may regard this period as a peculiarly critical stage in De Foe's career. It could so easily have been the beginning of a social descent from which there was no recovery; the first stages of complete moral disintegration. But this man was no Richard Savage. The fibre of his nature ran in unconventional patterns, and had its weaknesses, but its lines were consistent, and it was tough. His ancestry, his early training and environment, never lost their influence; he had still a fundamental respect for the decencies, and for justice and honesty between man and man. There were to be other occasions in the next forty years when he found it prudent to efface himself, but here, at any rate, he did his best to earn the right to walk the streets again openly and unafraid.

He took the first step by—to use the conventional phrase—"compounding with his creditors". He promised to pay his debts in full if they would give him his freedom and a chance of working out his own salvation. And they were shrewd enough to agree. His sheer plausibility, always a magnificent if intangible asset, probably won over any sceptics that stood out.

He justified their faith to the extent of paying off twelve thousand pounds by 1705.

CHAPTER IV

TILEMAKER, POET AND GENTLEMAN

IT WAS part of the essential paradox of De Foe's character that, bankrupt and confronted with the necessity of beginning a career all over again, he seems to have abandoned any idea of making a fresh start as a small trader, and, gradually made wiser by experience, regaining the status of a merchant again, while at the same time retaining his unstinted admiration for the man who *was* a successful shopkeeper. Similarly, he who had learnt so much and lived so vividly during those early years he spent on the Continent had now a fixed aversion from leaving England. We are told that he received, among other offers, one of a lucrative post in Cadiz, where various merchants wished him to act as their agents. On the strength of his statement (excusing its rejection, that "Providence has other work for me to do") one biographer[1] says that De Foe believed that he was permanently under the guidance of a benevolent and wise spirit. Judging from the number of adventures and misadventures in which De Foe succeeded in entangling himself in the course of the next forty years, I am strongly of the opinion that he preferred following his own inclinations, to the exclusion of supernatural or any other advice. It also seems reasonable to assume that his dislike for Continental travel might have been, at any rate, partly due to the family which he would have had to leave unprotected in England.

Whatever the reason, fortunately for both him and posterity he stayed in England and turned towards his English friends for help.

It is, I think, a remarkable tribute to his personality that in spite of several lawsuits involving the wrong sort of publicity, to say nothing of a resounding bankruptcy, he found people willing to come to the rescue. The fact that he was a freeman of the City must have been a useful asset, but his other assets were few and equally intangible.

[1]Dottin.

It would probably be safe to attribute his financial troubles more to his excess of natural gifts than to insufficiency of capital.

A man so versatile, and at the same time so contradictory in temperament, is certain to acquire many friends, and equally certainly many enemies. De Foe's friends came to the rescue in his many periods of adversity; his enemies invariably attacked him when he was on his feet again. For to be on his feet was, with De Foe, practically synonymous with violent and aggressive activity.

His wife still had faith in him, though by now practically the whole of her dowry must have been exhausted. She and others, probably more influential, did their best to come to some arrangement with his creditors which would leave De Foe at liberty to regain his position in the world of commerce, and would free him from the gibe of being "the Sunday gentleman", who dared to walk abroad only on the Sabbath, because on that day he could not be arrested for debt and cast into prison.

Precisely who those creditors were is unknown. In any case they had sense enough to see that De Foe at liberty and at work—and whatever his faults, idleness was never among them—offered a far better chance of their recovering their money than De Foe deteriorating in bitterness and futility behind stone walls.

So in the end he was given his freedom—on conditions. Soon afterwards he received an offer, both honourable and remunerative, of an appointment in Cadiz as representative of certain wine merchants.

He turned it down. The same Providence that had other work for him to do had, he insisted, implanted a secret aversion in his mind from quitting England. It was an early if not his first allusion to an invisible monitor whom he regarded as his heaven-directed guide.

This familiar or daemon, in line with the Socratic tradition, was to play a considerable part in his career, and for that reason occupies a considerable space in the pages of his biographers. "To this subject we shall often recur as this book proceeds, and in the section that deals with magic deal with it exhaustively," says Mr. Wright.

Personally I am inclined to think that there is a tendency to take De Foe's monitor rather too seriously. His intimacy and familiarity with the Scriptures seems an obvious explanation of much of his semi-mystical experiences. He prayed to God "in his solitudes, and with great fervency"; his sins and mistakes had aftermaths of fierce and—if one may say it—over-dramatized repentance; the brand snatched so many times from the burning was but an ancestor of the revivalist's penitent; his spiritual experiences the experiences of the same.

Monsieur Dottin says that De Foe "made it always a point of honour to follow those quick and often irrational impulses that swayed his will". Quick they were, no doubt, but not irrational. The decision to remain in England, for example, strikes me as the perfectly natural reaction to the double alteration of his reputation and financial position. On the one hand, he who had so lately been a reputable merchant was now a bankrupt, with many creditors and at least as many enemies. On the other hand, he was already known as a speaker with a future. As long ago as 1688 he had succeeded in fusing the Dissenters, both Independent and Presbyterian, in Tooting, into one united congregation, and had preached to them in the chapel he founded. And his wit and irony made him *persona grata* in the coffee-house and at Dissenters' clubs and Whig gatherings.

But he had one legitimate grievance added to the disgrace of his bankruptcy. A Bankrupt's Bill had lately been passed by the House of Commons under which merchants who had suffered injury through the war with France were, on producing proof of such injury, to be indemnified. It came before the Lords in February 1694 and was thrown out. The anonymous author of a pamphlet, *Observations on the Bankrupt Bill*, includes the name of De Foe among insolvents who might have benefited. "If they could have set bounds to their desires and not been too protesting," he comments acidly, "they might not have had occasion to claim the benefit of such a law." A law, unfortunately for De Foe, it never became.

De Foe's activities during the last years of the century were so diverse and blended that it is practically impossible to deal with them in strict chronological order. Additional complications are involved when his writings are examined for information that may be used to amplify what we know, or to fill up biographical gaps. De Foe, in common with all writers, made liberal use of incidents in his own life in work which either proclaims itself fiction or—in this case conspicuously—is fiction merely based on fact, but deliberately exhibited as entirely factual. The last was, indeed, De Foe's favourite approach to his reader.

"Here," he says in effect, "I have a story to tell you, a story of something that really happened," and proceeds to exercise his unique capacity for converting fact tinged with fiction into a completely convincing first-hand narrative. To use such material as an addition and support to any dependable biography is an obvious temptation; it is also to invite every kind of challenge on the part of the critic, as well as scepticism on the part of the critical and well-informed reader. The same applies equally to any attempt to deduce the genuineness or otherwise of De Foe's opinions upon marriage, commercial honesty and life in general from the stream of advice and admonitions given in his books. The tongue of the author was not necessarily always in his cheek. But one suspects it of being there fairly frequently.

(If only he had left us an autobiography, or, better still, a diary, covering those years!)

For a time he lived at Mickleham. At another period he had a house at Hackney, where several of his children, including Sophia, his youngest and best-loved daughter, were born. And here it may be said that, whatever his other parental deficiencies may have been, he saw to it that his children were well educated.

His post-bankruptcy occupations reflect both his versatility and popularity. They include the managership of a brick-and-tile factory at Tilbury, and the posts of a lottery supervisor and of commissioner under the Glass Act. Whatever leisure these appointments left him he spent in writing those pamphlets and books upon which, apart from *Robinson Crusoe*, his reputation rests to-day.

The story of his brick-and-tile adventure is veiled, not to say enveloped, in uncertainty. From a Chancery suit, brought against him in 1694—where would De Foe's biographers be without the steady guiding lights of his lawsuits! —it appears that he had for some years previously been in possession of certain clayey acres of land near Tilbury. His rights to occupy it were almost certainly derived from some other member of the family, for a branch lived at Shadwell and owned property there and in West Tilbury, adjoining.[1] De Foe called himself "Secretary" (his bankruptcy may have had something to do with this), but was actually managing director. He decided to develop the property as a brick-and-tile works, and there were sound reasons for the decision. London was undergoing the treble process of being rebuilt, replanned and enlarged, and there was an inexhaustible demand for bricks and their more ornamental accessories. Furthermore, Tilbury, near the capital, could successfully challenge any foreign competition, Dutch competition in particular.

From the first he employed English labour—a hundred families were on his payroll.[2]

But it was an uphill task. The bricks imported from Holland were a pleasant red in colour, due to the fact that they were incompletely burnt; the Tilbury bricks were any shade between grey and white, far more durable, but also, unfortunately, far less popular. On the credit side was the fact that De Foe knew some of the right people, and a tender of his for supplying bricks for the new Greenwich hospital was accepted.[3] Other problems were caused by the shortage of labour, and he was reduced to attempting to hire some of the beggars who infested the countryside.

Their retort was that begging paid better and entailed less work than brick-laying. The workmen he did succeed in enrolling loafed over their work, systematically spent from

[1] The West Tilbury parish register contains these entries: " 1605 Edmund Foe, married man, was buried here ye 28 March. 1621 Robert Smith, of Welleborne in Wiltshire . . . and Katherine Foe daughter of Edmund Foe (deceased) and Lucie, his wife, were married here on February 13."

[2] The exact site, until lately unknown, has now been located in front of the fort guarding the harbour entrance, on the north bank of the river.
Ninety years ago Mr. William Lee, one of De Foe's most ardent biographers, went down to Tilbury to discover whether the excavations involved in the railway then being constructed there had revealed any of De Foe's brickwork. It sounds, on the face of it, a forlorn hope, but it proved nothing of the kind. " Large quantities of bricks and tiles had been excavated," he reports. The narrowness of the bricks, and the peculiar forms of the tobacco pipes found mixed with both (bricks and tiles), excited some little wonderment among the labourers. " These," announced the author, dramatically, " were made 160 years since by the same man that made Robinson Crusoe! " Whereupon " Every eye brightened, every tongue was ready to ask and give information, and porters, inspectors and stationmaster gathered round me, wondering at what was deemed an important historical revelation."
Happy Mr. Lee!

[3] There still exists in Kensington Gardens a small structure which is said to have been built of De Foe's bricks.

Saturday night until Monday morning squandering their entire week's wages—from sixteen shillings to a pound—and in consequence wore nothing but filthy rags and went bare-footed.

Doubtless De Foe, though just, was a strict taskmaster; doubtless he had to be if he was to clear his name and pay off his creditors. The thing could only be done by keeping his expenses as low as possible and maintaining his profits. His enemies, from whose jealous and vindictive scrutiny he was never free, accused him of sweating his workmen. Unlike the Egyptians, they sneered, he did not demand that bricks should be made without straw; like the Jews he required bricks without paying his labourers.

De Foe, metaphorically (and probably literally) on horseback again, let them sneer. Other "projects" besides brick-making on the Tilbury marshes were materializing, other business had begun to present itself, to swell his income and reduce his liabilities.

The links between himself and the Court had their repercussions elsewhere. In May 1695 a tax was imposed on glass. Thomas Dalby, a friend of De Foe's, was instructed to appoint a commissioner to collect the money. De Foe, returning from one of his innumerable business journeys, learnt that Dalby had nominated him for the post. He retained it until, almost exactly four years later, the tax was repealed. It was more popular with the commissioners than with the glass-makers.

In the same year he was involved in a project of a very different type.

Although three earlier public lotteries had been officially declared illegal, the increasing difficulty of raising money for essential Government services made the temptation of tapping what must have seemed an almost limitless source of revenue altogether too strong. The Act of 1692 remained unrepealed, but it could be, and was, conveniently disregarded. Public lotteries, on the wildest, most extravagant scale, were initiated, bringing in their train every social evil that can afflict humanity suddenly seized by the conviction that the greatest happiness lies in the largest fortune obtained by a minimum of exertion. Which evils under that same conviction continued well into the eighteenth century.

De Foe twice accepted the position of a manager trustee, the first time being in October 1695, when his duty was to supervise a lottery in which the price of a ticket was a sovereign and the chief prize was fifty thousand pounds. Five months latter he supervised another in which the tickets cost only half a guinea each. Was there rather a wry smile on that mobile mouth of his when he accepted the post? Did he wonder for a moment what his Dissenting family and his Dissenting ancestry would have said to it? Or did the stimulating, all-excusing word "adventure", the name applied by every purchaser of a lottery-ticket, excuse such flagrant gambling?

The year 1695 has yet a third reason for being memorable in De Foe's life.

In connection with the first of the two lotteries there appeared officially, for the first time, his surname with the "De" as a prefix.[1] The switch-over was not, however, immediately complete, perhaps because he found it convenient to retain the simple "Foe" for business purposes. Why did he make the change at all? The simplest explanation is probably the correct one. He was going up in the world, or, to be more exact, moving from one world in which there were very definite social limitations into another, infinitely more intriguing, infinitely more to his taste, in which there were no limitations at all. Whatever his original patronymic, whether he was descended, as has been suggested, from a Defau, a derivative from the Latin "fagis", a beech, or whether his family came originally from Flanders or from Spain, it is probable that the vanity that formed so incongruous a part of his nature made him decide that two syllables were more indicative of a gentlemanly descent than one. Nine years afterwards he completed his elevation by having the new name legally reinforced by a coat of arms beneath which was the motto, derived from Juvenal, "Laudator et Alget".

His début in print had been made as long ago as 1683.

"No other author," says Monsieur Dottin, "has tried the patience and sagacity of the biographer so much as has De Foe. Most of the time he wrote under cover of anonymity, and discretion prompted him to conceal wherever possible his participation in the political literature of his time."

[1] The actual spelling is " Mr. Daniel De Foe ".

The statement is over-sweeping. There were fairly numerous occasions when he made no effort whatever to conceal his participation, and others in which it would have been, in any case, a futile waste of his powers of dissimulation to try to do so.

I am, however, glad to acknowledge my debt to Monsieur Dottin for his carefully edited list of De Foe's works. Between Chambers's compilation of 1786 and his own, published in 1928, the number of books and pamphlets, mainly the latter, which might legitimately be attributed to De Foe had risen from one hundred and seventy four to three hundred and seventy, varying in size from single sheets to full-length books.

De Foe's first effort, *An Appeal to Honour and Justice* a tract against the Turks, was written when he was only twenty-three; no copy of the original 1683 edition is known. His second[1] was another pamphlet, a single quarto sheet dated April 4th, 1687, *A Letter containing some Reflections on his Majesty's* [James's] *Declaration of Liberty of Conscience.*

The third item may be quoted, if only as a specimen of the length to which old-time book-titles explained and expanded. It ran: *A new Discovery of an old Intrigue. A Satyr levell'd at Treachery and Ambition; calculated to the Nativity of the Rapparee Plott, and the Modesty of the Jacobite Clergy. Designed by way of Conviction to the* 117 *Petitioners, and for the Benefit of those that study the City Mathematicks.*

A New Discovery was in the form of a poem running to about seven hundred lines, occupying thirty-six quarto pages, a truly formidable first effort in verse. De Foe reprinted it in 1705 in the second volume of his collected works.

Something may be said here concerning De Foe's poetry in general.

In point of fact, he never wrote more than a few lines worth calling poetry. One might go further, and say that his prose on occasion reached poetical heights that his versifying never did. His gifts, astonishingly varied as they were, never enabled him to soar into the regions that his great blind contemporary reached, or where Shelley moved and breathed as effortlessly as his own skylark. De Foe was, in

---

[1] Listed as his first by Thomas Wright, who apparently had not heard of the earlier work.

point of fact, at his most earthy and commonplace when the natural directness of his prose was paralysed by the limitations of rhyme and metre. I incline to think that he wrote in verse—and he wrote a good deal; about thirty of his accredited works are metrical—largely because it flattered his vanity to be regarded as a poet and as something more than a mere pamphleteer; because a gentleman and a wit, moving as an equal among other gentlemen and wits, should be able to prove himself capable of turning out, on occasion, a satire, an ode, an elegy. And his contemporaries accepted him as a poet, complete with inspiration. But so did other contemporaries accept respectively the Reverend Nahum Tate and Mr. Martin Tupper.

Perhaps his most marked affinity is to Pope, though Pope's wit has more edge to it and shows a keener appreciation of a climax. De Foe's verse (I quote Dottin) "is never melodious; it is generally laboured and often inaccurate". And, one might add, constantly descending from a kind of slick banality to mere doggerel:

> " Mischances sometimes are a Nation's good
> Rightly improved and nicely Understood."

Later in the same year of *A New Discovery* came the *Ode to the Athenian Society*.

After that there seems to have been a gap in his desire to express himself in verse. But in 1696 Dr. Samuel Annesley, his old and much revered schoolmaster, died, and De Foe wrote an elegy of two hundred and sixty-one lines to his memory. It contains passages not wholly unworthy, and many strongly reminiscent, of *The Deserted Village*.

> " If e'er his duty forced him to contend
> Calmness was all his temper; peace his end.
>
> His native candour, and familiar style
> Which did so oft his hearers' hours beguile."

The Athenian Society, the subject of an ode of seventy-one lines by De Foe, represents a phase of the author's determined, pathetic, and entirely praiseworthy attempt to acquire not only the physical but the cultural outfit of a gentleman.

According to Monsieur Dottin, he was at this point in his

career "straddling the topmost rungs of the ladder, smiling as he saw the star of an even greater ambition just within his grasp—or so it seemed to him". Without analysing a metaphor so complicated, not to say incoherent, one is safe in saying that De Foe was not at the top of any ladder, let alone precariously balanced upon two, in contemplation of the heavens. But he was still climbing, his ladder being, quite simply, one leading up to popularity and acceptance among the right people.

He and John Dunton, the old schoolfellow of his who had married Annesley's daughter, had maintained an unbroken friendship, and when Dunton set up as a bookseller the two men saw a good deal of one another. Dunton was a literary-minded scavenger of a when-found-make-a-note-of type; he formed a perfect complement to De Foe, with his unending interest in the trivialities and oddities of human existence. In 1690 the two, with other friends, formed a club, one which would have both appealed to and exasperated Dr. Johnson. They called it the Athenian Society; its members had pretentions, more or less justified, to familiarity with the Classics, a familiarity that in De Foe's case was based on an extremely limited acquaintance, but nevertheless upon which he presumed till the end of his life. In 1691 *The Athenian Gazette*, later, *The Athenian Mercury*, came into exisence. For seven years it may be said to have lived up to the slogan of a popular weekly of our own time, "To interest, to elevate, to amuse". Dunton was the head of the editorial staff; De Foe —naturally—and Swift—a little surprisingly considering his detestation of De Foe,—were among the contributors. De Foe, who refers to his *Essay on Projects* as being "Athenian", whatever the precise implication of the adjective may have been, dealt with the "Answers to Correspondents". One imagines him getting a tremendous amount of enjoyment out of the business. The questions sent in were of every conceivable type—theological, philosophical, political, and scientific. But whatever the subject, they formed convenient pegs upon which to hang his own views, expressed in his own brand of racy English.

The contents of *The Athenian Gazette*, were sufficiently popular to be reprinted in 1703 under the title of *The Athenian Oracle*. The book had a dedication, incredibly fulsome, to "The Most Illustrious and Magnanimous Prince,

James, Duke, Marquis and Earl of Montrose, Lord Lieutenant and General Governor of her Majesties Kingdom of
Ireland," and begins: "The Supreme Governor of the World
having Constituted Your Grace a Patron of Learning as well
as of Arms; the Promotors of both think they have a natural
Title to your protection." It was signed S. W. (Samuel
Wesley). An address from the bookseller to the reader
follows. It says quaintly:

" The Original Volumes, which once met with good acceptance from men of Learning and Curiosity, are now out of Print;
and 'twas a great Pity a Project so Universal and so Informing,
shou'd Die and never be Reviv'd; especially seeing the Common-
wealth of Learning, wou'd be the greatest Sufferer in that case.
The World cannot expect that Twenty Volumes shou'd be
comprised in the narrow compass, for tho' the pen of the Learned
Society were now and then Luxuriant upon the affairs of Love
and other lesser Matters, yet there's a World of Curious Enquiries."

There is indeed.
Some of the questions asked—and answered—have a
perennial quality; one feels they have been asked of oracles
long before Athens existed; for example: "Whether a tender
Friendship between two persons of a different Sex can be
innocent." Others included, "Whether the Recoyle of a gun
be at the Firing in the Chamber, or before, or at the
immediate Departure of the Fire from the Muzzle. . . ."
"Three Wagers depended upon this question," adds the
correspondent sternly, "therefore the sooner you Answer,
the sooner we shall drink your health."
Another query, extending to nearly a column, begins:
"I'm a young gent, almost of age; I have for some time
past made honourable Love to a Lady——" Other anxious
enquirers want to know whether mermaids exist, whether it
is lawful to trade in Negroes; how one may Break a Habit of
Playing Cards; what Angels eat; and which is the happiest
Animal. (The answer to the last question was: "Man,
he is both the happiest and most miserable.") Scattered
through the volume is also a considerable quantity of verse.
In 1698 appeared a pamphlet, inspired by an extraordinarily ill-advised action on the part of the Lord Mayor of
London, Sir Humphrey Edwin, himself a Dissenter. After

attending service on September 27th, 1697, he went, in his robes, and accompanied by his swordbearer, to his meeting-house, Pinners' Hall. The heather was on fire with a vengeance. The High Church Party (nicknamed the "High-Flyers" by their enemies, and as such referred to hereafter) were furious; the Dissenters even more so. De Foe flung a bomb-shell of his own unique brand into the conflagration: *An Enquiry into the Occasional Conformity of the Dissenters into Cases of Preferment. With a Preface to the Lord Mayor, Occasioned by his carrying a Sword to a Conventicle.*

His argument was that "Occasional" Conformity was a sin, and that for a Dissenter to receive the Sacrament merely as a qualification for the honour and privilege of the Lord Mayor's office was "a playing at Bo-peep with God Almighty".

"An upright man," said De Foe, "has only one religion. He cannot prostitute his conscience for worldly advantage."

In the same year he published his first prose work of real importance—an *Essay on Projects*. It ran to over three hundred pages, and the first edition was rapidly exhausted. (Unluckily for the over-optimistic publisher, a second edition could not be disposed of, and he reissued it under a different title in 1702.) The book was handicapped by an uninspired title, and dealt with serious matters. And De Foe, in common with innumerable other seventeenth-century pamphleteers with an itch to reform their highly unsatisfactory home-land, found plenty to write seriously about. But unlike the majority of them, he was incapable of dullness.

The book, dedicated to his old friend and patron Thomas Dalby, subsequently knighted, had been printed in the previous year; it had actually been written during the weeks he had been hiding from his creditors in Bristol and else-where subsequent to his bankruptcy. "Project"[1] and "projectors" were favourite words of his. It would hardly be an exaggeration, indeed, to say that "projects", in one form or another, ran like a continuous pattern throughout his active life. Among other things the essay dealt with plans for the improvement of roads—and who should be better qualified to speak of them than De Foe, who had ridden along so many miles of them, and who from first to last

---

[1] The *Oxford Dictionary* defines the word, as used by De Foe, as " a mental conception, idea or notion."

traversed the country seventeen times! For all main roads within ten miles of the City he suggested a breadth of forty feet, with trenches on either side eight feet broad and six deep, in which the water would be carried away. A permanent staff of trained roadmen would keep them in order.

But that was merely a section in his encyclopaedia of practical reforms. Others included:

A tax on incomes.

Pensions.

The institution of a royal or, alternatively, national bank.

A commission of enquiry into bankruptcy. (Here, of course, he was treading on the thinnest of thin ice!)

The segregation of the fraudulent debtor from the honest but unfortunate.

The establishment of a society "for encouraging polite learning, for refining the English language, and for preventing barbarisms of manners "—in short, an English edition of the present-day French Academy.

Insurance against Fire and Shipwreck. (Insurance companies were just coming into existence.)

An asylum for mentally defective people and idiots—" a Particular Rent-charge upon the great Family of Mankind." (He suggests a tax on authors' earnings as part of this scheme.) At that time the feeble-minded were herded with the insane, in conditions too vile for description.

Friendly Societies.

Finally, the essay deals with the Education of Women. Here he showed a farsightedness, an astonishing grasp of psychology, and an innate chivalry which, as another biographer pointed out, is paralleled in his age only by Steele. For the education of men and women in the seventeenth century De Foe has nothing but contempt. The value of wider and fuller knowledge he regards as incalculable. He would have both sexes taught, as well as music and dancing, modern languages, such as French and Italian, and history. The effects he emphasized by contrasting the well-taught woman, "furnished with the additional accomplishments of knowledge and behaviour", with a beautiful but uneducated one, who will probably be "turbulent, clamorous, noisy, nasty and the Devil". . . . A woman's ornaments and beauty, unsupported by education, are, he says, "a cheat in Nature, like the false tradesman who puts the best of his goods uppermost, that the buyer may think the rest are of the same goodness".

There was another quarto pamphlet, *Lex Talionis, or an Enquiry into the most proper ways to prevent the Persecution of the Protestants in France*, the editorship only of which he was concerned with, and probably not all of that.

De Foe, the successful brick-and-tile manufacturer, was paying off his creditors. But, simultaneously, his world was expanding, stretching enchantingly far beyond the Tilbury marshes. He had become a writer, a man whose pen could set London talking and thinking, a personage whom older, richer men were proud to meet. He could afford to ignore his enemies or to castigate them, as he chose.

More incredible still, he had achieved the entrée into the Royal circle. He was presented to the Queen, and was with her in something of the capacity of an honorary horticultural adviser when she gave orders for the laying out of Kensington Gardens, and at Hampton Court. It is hardly to be wondered at if his head should be turned a little.

He retrieved—how natural!—his horses; to them he added the carriage which was essential to him as a gentleman occupying a commissioner's post. He received invitations from other gentlemen: in 1697, for example, he spent a summer holiday at Steyning, in Sussex, as the guest of the wealthy Sir John Fagg. In November of the same year he took part in the procession that welcomed King William back from a visit to his native Holland. He was a regular attendant at the races, first established by the late King Charles at Newmarket, where in the distant days of that King he had frequently seen the Duke of Monmouth.

There was, indeed, a steadily increasing circle of diversions. De Foe was sampling the life of a stratum of society which, until these feverish days of prosperity came, had been made up of his patrons, the "entry", from whom his Dissenter's training no less than his poverty had separated him. He still spent, necessarily, a considerable part of his time in London, but not very much of it with his family; dining and wining with the gay intelligentsia at fashionable taverns left him with little leisure for domesticity. He built himself a small country house at Tilbury; from there he went sailing in a boat he had also bought.

This new devotion to the fashionable world had its

ironic side. He, the passionately earnest Dissenter whose prose was so largely derived from the Scriptures, descended to the composition of light amorous versifying. His rhyming dallyings with the immoralities, after the style of Rochester, did not last very long, probably did no particular harm, and certainly added nothing to his literary reputation.

And his wife, his children?

One's sympathies go out to Mary De Foe. To his absences from home, which she might have condoned, if not excused, her husband now added complications, and one complication in particular, for which she could have found no excuses at all. Either to escape her reproaches, or those of his shocked acquaintances, he took rooms in various parts of the City, varying them so frequently that even his coachman could not be sure of his whereabouts.

Finally, to demonstrate his complete conversion into a person of quality, he established in the house at Tilbury a mistress, an oyster-woman named Norton, who bore him a son.[1]

What is conspicuous in this cheap and silly emulation is not so much its snobbery—there have been many bigger snobs in the literary profession—but its *naïveté*. It is a reversion to adolescence of which a man of De Foe's mental equipment should have been incapable, and which in anyone else he would have chastised pitilessly. He ought, in short, to have known better.

The moralist has one consolation. The Rochesterian lapse did not last long.

The Poor Man's Plea, a quarto pamphlet of thirty-one pages, appeared on March 31st, 1698. A second edition was printed on May 24th; a third appeared in 1700. Its "arguments" are those of the average middle-class respectable citizen, that backbone of England loosely defined to-day as the Man in the Street. The "plea" itself is for the more impartial administration of the law. It is the pen of the earlier, unspoilt De Foe who writes:

"These are all cobweb laws, in which the small flies are catched while the great ones break through. . . . The man with a goldbug ring and gay clothes may swear before the Justice or at the Justice, may reel home through the open streets and no man take any notice of it, but if a poor man get drunk or swear an oath he must to the stocks without remedy."

[1] See page 272.

An echo, but an honest echo, of a greater man's:

"That in the captain is but a choleric word which in the soldier is flat blasphemy."

The war had ended in 1697 with the Peace of Ryswick. It was an armistice, a breathing space between rounds, rather than a peace. But between the circumstances of the contestants there was this basic difference. Louis was powerful enough to impose his will on the French people, sovereign of a servile state, the State itself. William was handicapped not merely by being a king dependent upon his Parliament for supplies and upon his people at large for his Parliament, but by being a stranger, an alien, a king on sufferance, only reigning at all because his predecessor had been too unpopular to be tolerated, and still regarded by many with the deep-seated suspicion traditionally extended by Britons to every "furriner".

If ever a sovereign needed support William did. If ever a subject was prepared to give that support De Foe was. Here were matters on a far bigger scale than the rightness or wrongness of a Lord Mayor attending a Nonconformist gathering in civic robes. Here were occasions for his pen, bright with possibilities of rewards beyond his dreams.

The Peace had been followed by a definite movement to disband the army. John Trenchard, one-time commissioner for forfeited estates in Ireland, and later financially independent M.P. for Taunton and a political writer of considerable importance, had published (1697) *An Argument showing that a Standing Army was inconsistent with a free Government*. He was, like De Foe, "a Whig in the wider sympathies"—so popular, in fact, that his enemies accused him of being not a Whig but a republican. Also, like De Foe, he was ruthless in his attacks on the High Church Party. He and a close friend named Gordon collaborated in producing *The Independent Whig*.

Trenchard was not alone in his views concerning standing armies, nor the only one to hurry into print in support of those views. But though De Foe and Trenchard had so many qualities in common, De Foe took the longer, shrewder, less idealistic view. He replied in a short essay, *some Reflections on a Pamphlet* (Trenchard's) and in the following year, that of William's accession, expanded his views in another tract, *An Argument showing that a Standing Army, with the Consent of Parliament, is not inconsistent with free Government and is absolutely destructive of the Constitution of the English Monarchy.*

The essence of this "Argument" lies, of course, in the guileless qualification "with the consent of Parliament". These five words converted the controversy from an affair of a King in opposition to a Government to a purely Parliamentary one, an affair of Whigs versus Tories, with, ultimately, the votes of the people themselves as the deciding factor.

This has been termed "De Foe's first great tract". I would rather state that here for the first time he exhibited the qualities which, developed more fully in later years, gave him the right to rank among writers—his mastery of his own language as a vehicle of expression, his pellucid common sense, his capacity for constructive criticism, his wit, his good humour, his plausibility. . . . Perhaps, most of all, plausibility was his greatest asset.

All London read the pamphlet, and in the end was cajoled into acquiescing to Parliament taking the burden of maintaining the standing Army. The King accepted half a loaf as better than military starvation, and De Foe found himself on the pleasant and delusive outskirts of fame.

In February 1700 he wrote an elaborate "Satyr", his second, of fourteen folio pages, called *The Pacificator.* He himself says in an unusual burst of modesty that "It is not distinguished by any merit that would render it unpopular upon the fleeting occasion". I agree with the author, though one biographer (Lee) considers it one of De Foe's best productions in verse. The thesis of the poem is an imaginary war between authors—contemporaries of De Foe—who are Wits and "Men of Sense".

> " *Wit,* like a hasty Flood, may overrun us
> And too much *Sense* has oftentimes undone us.
> *Wit* is a Flux, a looseness of the Brain
> And *Sense-abstract* has too much Pride to reign.
> *Wit* is a King without a Parliament,
> And *Sense* a Democratick Government.
> *Wit* without *Sense* is like the laughing *Evil,*
> And *Sense* unmixed with *Fancy* is the *Devil.*"

He then proceeds to suggest a general literary armistice in a series of rhymed personalities of the type calculated to divert the family circle at Christmas-time, but from which Wit, alias Fancy, strikes me as being conspicuously absent.

> " That each may choose the part he can do well
> And let the Strife be only to excel.
> To their own Province let them all confine
> Doctors to Heal, to Preaching the Divine.
> *Dryden* to Tragedy—let *Creech* translate—
> *Darfrey* make Ballads—Psalms and Hymns for Tate.
> Let *Prior* Flatter Kings in Panegyrick—
> *Ratcliff*, Burlesque—and *Wycherley* by Lyrick.
> Let *Congreve* write the Comick—*Foe*, Lampoon,
> *Weseley* the Banter—*Milbourn* the Buffoon;
> And the Transgressing Muse receive the Fate
> Of Contumacy, Excommunicate.

Viewed impartially, De Foe's position when the seventeenth century ended and the eighteenth began was that of an active, incredibly active, man of affairs, who, after an unhappy beginning in trade, had by sheer hard work and intelligence re-established himself. There was every reason in the world why he should concentrate upon the business of making that position impregnable. His wife had borne him eight children, six of whom had survived. The success of his Tilbury brick-and-tile factory and several lesser ventures had given him back the luxuries that he regarded as part, by right, of his background; none knew better than he the risks of trying to combine commerce, dull though at times it might be, and clogging to the soul, with the gay but unprofitable life that sparkled its invitation in the coffee-houses. In *The Compleat English Tradesman* he wrote ruefully:

" A Wit turned Tradesman! What an incongruous Part of Nature is there brought together, consisting of direct contraries ! No Apron Strings will hold him. . . . Instead of Journal and Ledger, he runs away to his *Virgil* and *Horace* ; his Journal Entries are all Pindaricks, and his Ledger all Heroicks ; he is truly dramatick from one end to the other, through the whole scene of his Trade; and as the first Part is all Comedy, so the last two Acts are all made up with Tragedy; a Statute of Bankruptcy is his *Exeunt Omnes*, and he generally speaks the Epilogue in the *Fleet Prison* or the *Mint*."

Facts which could hardly be more admirably summarized, paralleled by Pope's

> " The clerk, fordoomed his father's will to cross,
>   Who pens a stanza when he should engross."

Shrewd words! But the temptation was too strong, the magnet too powerful. If De Foe had been at heart a tradesman, if in commerce he had found and accepted his true vocation, if these exhilarating excursions into politics and pamphleteering had been no more than a side-line, an entertaining hobby, the Tilbury adventure might have in course of years developed into a solid business of the type which passes in honour and dignity from father to son.

Its life, however, was to be brief.

De Foe had been a loyal subject and supporter of Charles II. He had no illusions concerning Charles's nonchalant and frequent lapses from the moral code; he accepted them as the prerogative of all Royalty. And when the King died, the King who was, at any rate, broadminded and farsighted and had a sense of humour and an appreciation of the unconventional, he mourned him genuinely, as, indeed, did the vast majority of his subjects. England felt, generally speaking, that it could have better spared a better man. James, his younger brother and successor, had demonstrated that at least in one respect he was a better man—and the country endured him for three years, and then expelled him in favour of his daughter and son-in-law. And with the arrival of William, De Foe realized that here, at long last, he had found a sovereign at whose feet he could lay unstintedly his loyalty and affection and devotion, devotion that went far beyond hat-waving and cheering and prancing on horseback in his most decorative clothes at the head of royal processions. That day at Henley, when he had first contacted the invading Dutchman and his escort marked, I think, the real turning-point, the moment when De Foe accepted his mission.

CHAPTER V

WILLIAM AND *THE TRUE-BORN ENGLISHMAN*

THE DIFFICULTIES entangling the King gave De Foe opportunities of proving his value. He could write lucidly; he could also speak convincingly because he genuinely believed in the arguments he put forward and because he did not lose his temper. Apart from occasional lapses into indiscretion, he had, one might say, every qualification demanded of the ideal public relations officer.

William's standing army had been reduced to the preposterous total of seven thousand men. The country in the elections of 1698 had sent a disquietingly large number of Tories to Parliament, gentlemen who detested the idea of any further foreign entanglements or of any further war with France. Louis the Fourteenth might scheme—but let him scheme!

Louis did. The King of Spain, a childless imbecile, died, the last of his line, in 1700. All Europe had been aware that the end was near, and that the Spanish throne would, like an African chieftainship in past days, fall to the first prince quick enough and strong enough to hold it. William had done his best to damp down in advance the inflammable possibilities of the situation by persuading Louis to agree to a Treaty of Partition. The Electoral Prince of Bavaria was a leading figure in this, and his unexpected death led to another Treaty—signed also by Louis, but signed, as William grimly suspected, with his tongue in his cheek. England disliked both treaties; she was in the mood to dislike any treaty.

It was in October that Charles II of Spain died, and French honesty was put to the test. Charles had left his throne to Louis's grandson, the Duke of Anjou, which meant that Spain would be united to France as Italy was already, and the three countries, for all practical purposes, be fused into one nation. Unless, of course, Louis stood by his treaty with William.

The question was soon answered. Louis acknowledged his grandson King of Spain.

William, who for years had been doing his patient, uninspired and dogged best to bring his own newly acquired country into a state capable of limiting, or at any rate neutralizing, the octopus-like development of its chief enemy, saw clearly that the time for peaceful negotiations was at an end. England, the England that had invited his sovereignty, but had never warmed to him, never understood him, would have to be united and brace herself afresh for the risks, the dislocation, and, above all, the cost of another campaign on the further side of the Channel.

But the country remained absolutely unconvinced. It neither wanted another war with France nor believed that another war was inevitable. De Foe's pen came into action. His pamphlet in support of standing armies was only two years old; he reinforced it with two fresh pamphlets.

The first appeared on November 15th. It was, so to speak, a double-barrelled affair, its title running, *The Two Great Questions Consider'd.*

"I. What the French King will Do with Respect to the Spanish Monarchy." "II. What Measures the English ought to Take."

A preface, written while the pamphlet was actually being printed, provided an answer to the first question. "Letters from France announce that the King of France has saluted his grandson, the Duke of Anjou, as King of Spain."

Eight days after the pamphlet's appearance an anonymous writer accused De Foe point-blank of place-hunting.

On December 2nd De Foe issued a Supplement, *The Two Great Questions further Consider'd.*

In November 1700 the old question of Occasional Nonconformity came to a head. As before, the extremists on both sides were agitated because a Dissenting Lord Mayor, Sir Thomas Abney, received the Sacrament according to the Church of England upon the induction to office. The High Church supporters had scathing comments to make upon a Nonconformist conforming and "venturing damnation to play at long spoon and custard" for a transitory twelve-month.

De Foe, for once technically in agreement with them, reprinted his tract on *Occasional Conformity*. But with two differences. He wrote a new preface addressed to the celebrated John Howe. Howe was a broadminded cleric who, in spite of suffering severely under the penalties inflicted on Dissenting preachers, was entirely willing for members of his flock in Silver Street, off Cheapside, to worship occasionally at their parish churches. He had headed the deputation of Nonconformist ministers who presented an address of congratulation and loyalty to William upon his accession. Abney, the second Lord Mayor to set the heather alight, was one of his congregation.

De Foe's revised preface was written in the hope of obtaining from so influential a minister some expression of approval or disapproval of the practice—in short, *a ballon d'essai*. Unluckily, the winds of chance blew the *ballon* in the wrong direction. The Reverend Mr. Howe, now seventy and in poor health, was neither flattered nor placated. His retort was a thoroughly bad-tempered one. On January 24th, 1701, De Foe blandly retaliated in *A Letter to Mr. How* (sic) *by way of Reply to his Observations on the Preface to the Enquiry into the Occasional Conformity of Dissenters in Case of Preferment*—possibly the longest title to a letter on record, and strongly reminiscent of the House that Jack Built. "Sincerity," said De Foe therein, a trifle unctuously, "is the Glory of a Christian; the Native Lustre of an honest Heart is impossible to be hid; 'twill shine through all his life in one action or another, in spite of scandal."

To which pious sentiments the Reverend Mr. Howe did not condescend to reply. He remained unplacated. De Foe, though he failed to realize it, had with the issue of these pamphlets forfeited his high status in Nonconformist circles. His very name was taboo among the elect. They believed that he had joined the ranks of the enemy, or, even worse, that he had become an unreliable opportunist. "When a Nonconformist minister saw fit to quote from De Foe's work," says Paul Dottin, "he always studiously avoided mentioning the name of the author."

In the same month, December 1700, De Foe, with an obvious eye on the approaching election, wrote *The Six Distinguishing Characters of a Parliament Man*, addressed to the People of England. This appeared on January 4th, 1701, the "characters", otherwise characteristics, being loyalty, piety, common sense, maturity, honesty and morality—a mixed bag in twenty-two quarto pages. Five days later came *The Danger of the Protestant Religion considered from the Present Prospect of a Religious War in Europe.* Here, in thirty-two pages, also quarto, De Foe advocated, firstly, an alliance with Austria, and, secondly, a defensive union of all Protestant countries and States. The pamphlet was published in January. Then, still in January, came *Considerations upon Corrupt Elections of Members to serve in Parliament.*

All these were what might be termed straightforward pamphleteering, with Religion, War and Politics linked as a triple theme. But that single month included something entirely outside the ordinary pamphleteer's orbit, seventy-one pages of subtle and scathing irony in verse—*The Trueborn Englishman.*

Two men in conjunction may be said to have inspired this, the most popular work of De Foe's to date.

One was his idol, King William, whose popularity among his subjects, superficial from the beginning, ebbed slowly, steadily and undramatically throughout the reign which has been sneeringly labelled "the most prosaic in English history". Against the charges most flung at him he had no defence whatever. He was a born foreigner, and so in the eyes of his subjects remained. His case was, to a certain extent, paralleled by that of the Prince Consort. But with this vital difference: Albert never had the culminating ill-fortune of co-reigning with his wife.

The imminence of a fresh war with France, and the consequent necessity for an adequate army to fight such a war, coming at a time when Englishmen of all classes wanted no wars with anybody, set the ever-smouldering resentment against the King glowing angrily. And among those who fed the fire was De Foe's second inspiration, John Tutchin, the schoolboy companion of De Foe who so narrowly escaped Judge Jeffreys's savage sentence for his part in Monmouth's rebellion. Tutchin was another of those remarkable people who gravitated into De Foe's life story, and who really demand a full-length biography on their own account. Approximately De Foe's age,[1] he is said by a detractor to have been expelled from school for theft. In 1685 he published *Poems on Several Occasions*, together with a

[1] The date of Tutchin's birth, followed by a query, is given in the *Dictionary of National Biography* as 1661.

pastoral entitled *The Unfortunate Shepherd* and *A Discourse on Life*—an ominous literary beginning for a young man of twenty-four. Possibly his military adventures at Sedgmoor and subsequent capture had something to do with it. Five years afterwards he wrote *An Heroick Poem upon the late Expedition of His Majesty to rescue England from Popery, Tyranny and Arbitrary Government*, and in 1692 was rewarded with a clerkship in the victualling office worth forty pounds a year. In 1693 he charged the Commissioners with robbing the Crown of vast sums of money. He may have been right, but failed to prove his charges, and was not unnaturally dismissed.

On August 1st, 1700, Tutchin, living up to the tradition that a man with a grievance is a man damned, published a poem called *Foreigners*. Therein he attacked the Dutch in general and the King in particular. He was arrested nine days later. De Foe's reaction to this attack by his one-time friend upon William, that model for all monarchy, was as violent as might have been expected. The poem he referred to as "A vile, abhorred pamphlet, in very ill verse". And his retaliatory gesture was *The True-born Englishman*.

It has a preface, the only portion in prose, followed by an introduction beginning:

> " Speak, Satyr, for there's none can tell like these
> Whether 'tis Folly, Pride or Knavery
> That makes this discontented Land appear
> Less happy now in Times of Peace than War."

And Satyr speaks accordingly. (The early eighteenth century was indeed a period in which she was particularly strident and vociferous.)

Part One opens with the familiar couplets:

> " Wherever God erects a House of Prayer
> The Devil always builds a chapel there.
> And 'twill be found upon examination
> The latter has the largest congregation.
> His laws are easy, and his gentle sway
> Makes it exceeding pleasant to obey.
> The list of his Vice-regents and Commanders
> Outdoes your Caesars or your Alexanders.
> Through all the World they spread his vast Command
> And death's eternal Empire is maintained."

After which, the author fairly gets into his stride. He gives a list of the Satanic regents placed in each country— Pride in Spain; Drunkenness ("the darling favourite of Hell") in Germany; Ungoverned Passion in France; Folly in Russia; Fury in Denmark; Fraud in Scotland; and so on. But—

> " England, unknown, as yet unpeopled lay
> Happy had she remained so to this day!"

It was not to be.

> " Her open harbours and her fertile plain. . . .
> To every barbarous nation have betrayed her,
> Who conquer her as oft as they invade her."

Which cheerful conceit, historically less than a half-truth, he elaborated as only De Foe could elaborate.

> " Thus from a mixture of all kinds began
> That heterogenous thing, an Englishman."

Eventually he reaches his climax. The recent ejection of the last of the Stuarts, who

> " If he did this subjects rights invade,
> Then he was punished only, not betrayed.
> And punishing of Kings is no such crime,
> But Englishmen have done it many a time."

is followed by the arrival of William, and here De Foe's heroick couplets cease to be satirick, and become very heroick indeed. Also extremely chaotick.

> " Thus England groaned, but a man's voice was heard
> And great Nassau to rescue her appeared.
> Called by the universal voice of Fate
> God and the people's legal magistrate.
> Ye Heavens regard! Almighty Jove, look down!
> And view the injured monarch on the throne.
> On their ungrateful heads due vengeance take
> Who sought his aid, and then his part forsake!"

One surmises that the injured monarch was duly appreciative of all these sprawling metaphors; there is no doubt at all that his subjects were. His Majesty did in fact send for the author to congratulate him in person. Nine editions of *The True-born Englishman*, selling at a shilling a copy, appeared within a year of publication. And its popularity continued. Nevertheless De Foe, like Dickens over a century later, paid the penalty. According to his own statement, eighty-thousand additional copies, badly printed on worse paper, were issued by unscrupulous publishers at a penny or so apiece in the three following years, and he lost over one thousand pounds.

An interesting point may be raised here, in the early stages of De Foe's career as a writer. In the absence of copyright laws, any author whose work was considered sufficiently popular to make pirating worth while was liable to be so victimised. In De Foe's case piratical action was further simplified by the fact that these pamphlets, in common with many later ones, were published anonymously, though the world at large was aware of the writer's identity. A further point, unconnected with copyright, was that much of what he wrote was challenging enough and popular enough to be worth attacking.

On the other hand, this bare-faced thieving was a magnificent advertisement. And no one knew better than he the value of publicity. His lines were quoted, recited, and chuckled over by his friends; his enemies retorted in other pamphlets, far less witty, far more scurrilous. They called him, among other things, an ill-bird that defiled its own nest, the spawn of both nations, and a loathsome thing shaped like a toad, with spots and scabs. De Foe, accepting the showman's axiom that "every knock's a boost", let them say what they pleased. His reputation as a satirist, a wit and a poet was at last universally accepted. He had arrived.

It would be pleasant to ring down the curtain for a little on that glittering and satisfying scene. But the penalties of neglecting his business, dabbling in politics, and taking short cuts to add to his capital were already accumulating.

He borrowed money from a goldsmith to pay the duty on a large quantity of imported Spanish wine, and the goldsmith was tactless enough to insist on keeping the tuns in his cellar until the loan was repaid. The sale of the wine was held up through technical difficulties, interest on the loan mounted up, the wine itself deteriorated, and finally the goldsmith sold the entire consignment by auction. In that single deal De Foe lost over six hundred pounds. Later, he was to fall a victim to swindlers, who, equipped with forged letters of recommendation, robbed him of valuable stock. And there was the war with France, dragging on and on. . . .

De Foe at this juncture in his career exhibits a remarkable and complex study.

Enormously painstaking over details while daring to the point of recklessness, he was, from a purely material point of view, a travelled, active, ambitious man with a liking which might almost be called a passion, and which lasted all his life, for dressing with the rich elaboration of a gentleman of the time. He was at the same time a student of human nature and, in pursuit of such study, prepared and anxious to mix with every level of society; a philosopher; and finally, a politician of advanced views with capacity for expressing these views that must many times have suggested to others as well as to himself that in politics lay his true sphere.

The True-born Englishman was sprung upon an appreciative world in January 1701. Between his subsequent meeting with William and that fatal February day in the following year De Foe achieved a position in the King's counsels which is an extraordinary tribute to the two qualities in which so many professional statesmen fall short— his shrewdness and his tact.

The bond which rapidly developed between De Foe and the King was, on the face of it, as remarkable as it was intimate. Their origins had no point in common. Their nationalities were different. William was ten years older, and in any case their social levels were such that in no normal circumstances could they meet on equal terms, nor had they contacts upon which anything other than a formal sovereign-and-subject attitude would arise. Yet between this dour and reserved Dutch prince and the ex-wine dealer, son of a London tallow-chandler, and lately a bankrupt hiding from his creditors, an unshakable friendship arose. The most probable explanation is that in De Foe William found a man not merely with similar religious and political views and theories, but one who formed an almost ideal barometer of middle-class England's reactions. For the middle-class man of those days had no effective contact with the King, nor with the peers spiritual and temporal and the members of the Commons who framed the laws.

On De Foe's part that friendship soon deepened into sheer hero-worship. On every November 4th his *Review* would contain a eulogistic article on *The Great Day of England's Glory*. And after the King's untimely death he wrote:

> " A Guard of glorious Light formed His Ascent,
> And wond'ring, Stars adored him as He went."

probably the first and last specimen of lyrical nonsense which he did not pen with his tongue in his cheek.

But De Foe was far more than a mere political barometer of the middle classes. He had theories, sound and otherwise, but on the whole remarkably sound, because based on common sense and experience, which he wanted to see converted into practical experiments. With the King himself willing to give audience and immediate consideration, all the wearisome and disheartening disillusion and disappointment involved in appealing to the highest authority through a succession of lower authorities, and of circumventing all the artifices of entrenched bureaucracy, were eliminated.

To the King he went direct with his plans for carrying on the new War. They included the transference of the seat of war from Europe to the enemy's South American possessions—a plan Elizabethan in its boldness. Chili was to be first attacked, while a base was to be created in Havana. Later Guiana was to be captured.

Lest these grandiose plans should be regarded as mere visions, De Foe, always practical, prepared and exhibited charts and topographical details.

William listened and studied the supporting documents. My Lords Portland and Albemarle, his two most trusted advisers, found De Foe plausible and—what was far more important—convincing. The new Parliament, elected in February, might and did include an inconvenient influx of Tories, but the country at large, slow and reluctant in grasping the significance of events though it might be (and made still more slow and reluctant by its King's unhappy inability to sway any project by personal magnetism), was at last beginning to realise that the arch-plotter Louis was an enemy whose elimination was the only alternative to its own extinction as a power. De Foe had done his best to kill the sneer that the King was a foreigner; the King himself had demonstrated that he was a brave, clear-headed and patriotic substitute for the sovereign of Scots origin who had been ignominiously hustled into exile.

All his life De Foe took risks as a gambler takes them. Now he was wagering on his personal popularity and on his peculiarly confidential relationship with the King. Their association is so much bound up with contemporary politics that it is extraordinarily difficult to detach activities which are a legitimate part of his biography from a general history of his period.

He had already crossed that nebulous, highly dangerous frontier which separates the partisan from the secret co-operator. By natural stages he had progressed from writing pamphlets for his party and in support of a King who, in De Foe's eyes, possessed every quality a King should possess, to the post of unofficial adviser to that King, and thence to a trusted reporter on the gyrations of the weathercock of public opinion. At this point he might have halted, and, openly supported and openly opposed, have frankly confessed himself a political agitator in the interests of the Whig cause in general and of William, high chief among Whigs, in particular.

But that role would have been altogether too crude, too alien to his secretive genius. He became, instead, a private investigator, a secret-service agent or, to use the shorter, uglier English word employed by his enemies, a spy. Thereafter he made it his duty to mix among gatherings, particularly gathering of "old Whigs", Whigs of the die-hard type, among whom William was still a dangerous interloper or, alternatively, an inconvenient meddler in English traditions and customs, and subsequently to send reports concerning those who had better be "put into those posts in which they may seem to be employed, and therefore . . . divide the party"—an eighteenth-century equivalent to "Divide and Conquer".

The work brought to the surface all De Foe's unspectacular thoroughness; unfortunately it also brought to the surface his vanity. In his naïve pride in his job, he boasted of his intimacy with the King, and of the confidence which William had in his judgments.

The incident of the Five Men of Kent involved him in trouble which a wiser, more reticent public servant would certainly have avoided.

The new House of Commons was, colloquially speaking, "uppish" as well as merely difficult. It sat behind closed doors. Its decisions were leisurely and autocratic. It disagreed with, and indeed defied, the House of Lords, and even went so far as to impeach various Whig peers of whose previous activities as ministers it did not approve.

Under the deepening shadow of war the country was becoming increasingly uneasy. Kent, the nearest and most likely point for any invasion, was not merely uneasy, but alarmed and indignant. On April 29th a petition was drawn up and signed by the squires, magistrates, grand jurymen and other people of consequence in the county. It did "most humbly implore this Honourable House to have regard to the voice of the People, that our Religion and Safety may be provided for, and"—a delightfully ironic anti-climax—"your loyal addresses may be turned into Bills of Supply".

Five men, headed by one named Colepeper, carried this eminently reasonable document up to London, and on May 7th, in spite of determined opposition, presented it. And although they had every legal right, to say nothing of moral right, behind their action, the same five men of Kent found themselves flung into prison by an outraged and extremely ill-advised House of Commons, whose authority they were charged with "insolently and seditiously attempting to overthrow".

To be fair, however, there was some justification for this high-handed resentment. The Tories regarded the presentation of the petition not as a genuine *cri de coeur* from apprehensive Kentishmen, but as an ingenious political manœuvre on the part of the Whig supporters of the King, with De Foe lurking, not too mysteriously, in the background. Which was precisely what it was.

A week passed. Then De Foe made a dramatic personal appearance in the House.[1] Accompanied by an armed escort

---

[1] There is a legend that he was disguised as a woman, but in view of the formality of his entry, to say nothing of his escort, this seems highly improbable.

of sixteen gentlemen, he advanced upon Harley, the Speaker (to whom later, ironically enough, he was to act as trusted assistant), and handed him a letter, this being written by himself, though for some inscrutable reason in a disguised hand. With the letter went a Memorial, the full title of which was, "A Memorial from the Gentlemen, Freeholders and Inhabitants of the Counties of ——, in (sic) behalf of Themselves and many thousands of the good People of England". It was signed intimidatingly, "Our Name is Legion, and we are Many More".

It was a remarkable manifesto even for De Foe. Fifteen grievances of "loyal Englishmen" were set down, against a Parliament labelled, among other things, corrupt, tyrannical, insolent, traitorous, negligent, unlawful, debauched and scandalous. It reminded this highly adjectival assembly that they were not masters of England, "nor above incurring the resentments of the people whom they had been elected to serve".

Which People, the Memorial intimated, did, among other things, "REQUIRE and DEMAND that all Public Debt be discharged immediately, and that persons illegally imprisoned be immediately freed, including the Gentlemen of Kent who had presented the Petition and had been so scandalously used".

Drastic medicine indeed for a Parliament which may have forgotten, after the habit of democratic Parliaments, the source of its existence!

De Foe's accompanying letter challenged Harley to distribute the Memorial among his fellow-members.

The Commons' reaction to the Memorial can only be described as craven. One member named Howe stated publicly that he went in fear of his life. Others, less dramatically, made feeble protests and slipped away into the country.

As for De Foe, there is little doubt that he enjoyed the whole melodramatic business enormously. He knew, had known from the beginning, that so far from being a spontaneous outburst of freedom-loving Britons against a tyrannical Government, the Memorial was largely the seizure by the Government's astutest opponents of a heaven-sent opportunity created by an error in tactics.

The error was hurriedly and clumsily cancelled, and the

five victims were set free with the rising of the House. Their release was publicised and stressed by a public banquet given them at Mercers' Hall prior to their triumphal return to their Kentish homes. De Foe, of course, figured as a prominent guest at the banquet. One lyrical reporter compares him to Jove at an assembly of the Gods, and adds that "one might have read the downfall of Parliaments in his very countenance".

Jove's prototype appeared again, inevitably on horseback, amongst those who cheered them on their way.

In its blend of genuine indignation and astute opportunism the whole affair was typical of De Foe, whose cool and ingenious brain so often and so incongruously found itself in active partnership with his easily inflamed emotions.

The double excitement over the petition and "Legions" thunderbolt died down. De Foe was, of course, a marked man; the role must by now have become familiar, and one to which he took no objection. On December 7th Marlborough, on behalf of his country, signed a treaty with the United Provinces and Austria, the Treaty of the Grand Alliance. On the 13th Louis made a blunder unworthy of his sagacity and experience and on a scale which makes it historical. James II, dying, in exile, had begged Louis to acknowledge his eldest son as the rightful King of England. Louis, moved by pity or malice, or both, did so.

In England the news had an effect which anyone with the faintest comprehension of national psychology would have foreseen—white-hot indignation resulting in the instant fusion of both political parties. William dissolved Parliament; when the House met again after the elections the pre-war element was predominant. The whole country was alert, electrified by the fact that at last it was confronted by a definite and open challenge to decide its own destiny, its own freedom, its very existence.

It was only the head of the nation whose energies were ebbing.

William had never been a robust man. To that, as much as to the natural sombreness of his disposition, may probably be attributed his lack of the warmer emotions—the chief cause of his unpopularity. Throughout his comparatively short reign he had suffered from overstrain as well as from overwork, complicated by chronic asthma. On February

20th in the following year he was hunting near Hampton Court, then in Royal occupation. He was urging Sorrel, his mare, to a gallop when she stumbled into a molehill, and flung him to the ground. His collar-bone was broken. The accident was not very serious, but in his feeble state of health the shock was. Fever supervened. On March 8th his subjects heard that he was dead.

He had been a widower since 1694, when Queen Mary, something between an enigma and a nonentity, had died of smallpox. For over seven years, a lonely alien in spirit to the last, he alone had held such brittle and uncertain power as England permits her sovereigns. Now, at fifty-two, he had surrendered it. Our Kings, with a single, obvious exception, had for centuries learned to die in their beds. But they had not yet learned to die of old age.

To De Foe the blow was a double one. He had lost a close friend; a unique intimacy had been violently ended. And he was committed to a twilight period of uncertainty until the new sovereign's personality and opinions had given him a chance of assessing and planning his own political future. In that twilight would lie the opportunities of his and William's many enemies.

The eighteenth century has been termed the century of taste. By to-day's standards it was in many respects one of extraordinarily bad, not to say execrable, taste. Jacobite partisans openly joined High-flyers, High Church men, in toasting Sorrel, who had caused his master's death:

> " Illustrious Steed, to whom a place is given
> Above the Lion, Bull or Bear in Heaven,"

as well as "The Little Gentleman in Black Velvet", who was responsible for the hole into which Sorrel stumbled.

De Foe, in *The Mock Mourners*, a sixpenny pamphlet written in May, castigates in rhyme those whose spite even Death could not check. . . . But there was other work for his pen.

From the King's accession, De Foe had been his loyal subject and fervid supporter, a fact of which he prudently made certain William should from the first be fully aware.

For, as Professor Sutherland has pointed out, the King stood for everything that De Foe most passionately believed in. He was literally, and not in theory only, the Defender of the Faith, the Protestant Faith, and the Faith of the Dissenters. He stood for logical toleration and moderation. He supported the union of England and Scotland. He saw, as De Foe's own clear eyes saw, that the future of England lay in the development of English trade. And he was as inexorable in his determination as he was patient in his planning to limit the further expansion of French territory and French influence. In Louis XIV he had a fitting opponent.

CHAPTER VI

THE SHORTEST WAY, AND THE PILLORY

THE POSITION of a man whose life was guided largely by his religious and political affiliations was, in those incongruous times, when laxity and intolerance went hand in hand, an uncomfortable one. He could be High Church and Tory, or High Church and Whig, and hold public office, though whether or not it was high public office depended largely on the personal attitude and power of the monarch. He could be a Tory or a Whig, and an occasional Dissenter, and still hold office. But to be not only a notorious and active Whig but an uncompromising Dissenter into the bargain was a direct challenge to Fate.

De Foe busied himself in the early days of Anne's reign with a miscellaneous collection of pamphlets. In June he attacked the High Church party in *A New Test of the Church of England's Loyalty, or Whiggish Loyalty and Church Loyalty compared*. He also wrote *Reformation of Manners*, a satyr; *Good Advice to the Ladies, showing that as the World goes and is like to go, the best way for them is to keep Unmarried*; and *The Spanish Descent*, all these being in verse, and the last a scathing commentary on the recent failure of an English fleet. The new Queen had, under pressure of public opinion, now in a very highly belligerent mood, declared war on France and Spain, and fourteen thousand men under the Duke of Ormonde and Sir George Rooke had been dispatched to Cadiz. They sailed home again without even effecting a landing. (It is only fair to both De Foe and Rooke to add that on the return journey the fleet had captured a number of Spanish galleons laden with bullion, and that De Foe praises the Admiral for it.)

If Mary was enigmatical, her younger sister's mentality presented no problems at all. In our meagre list of Queens regnant she stands out as the simplest, one might almost say the most childlike, character. Only the stolid and affable stupidity of the Lutheran Prince George of Denmark, whom she married, exceeded her own mental narrowness. But there was, at any rate, one subject upon which she was both clear-headed and firm. She was a High-flyer. Not for her any compromises, any laxity in favour of Nonconformists. And indissolubly linked with her High Church rigidity was her Toryism. Whig ministers were removed; when the fanatical Dr. Sacheverall began an agitation against the Dissenters, proclaiming that no one could be a true son of the Church of England who did not lift up the banner of the Church against the Dissenters, she gave it her support. The old cry "The Church is in danger" was raised once more, and with it the old problem of occasional Nonconformity.

But the Whig peers still blocked the path to any repressive legislation.

De Foe found the temptation to rush into the fray irresistible. He brought out another edition of *An Enquiry into Occasional Nonconformity*. A month later, he followed this with *The Shortest Way with Dissenters; or Proposals for the Establishment of the Church.*

Its thirty pages embodied what was, in effect, a colossal and ironic practical joke. Unluckily for De Foe, it not merely fell flat, but—far worse—was taken seriously. And such jokes have a boomerang tendency to return and smite the joker. His facetiousness had for once completely overwhelmed his natural shrewdness and sense of proportion.

With the De Foe tongue in the De Foe cheek he lashed the Dissenters without pity, and referred to the Established Church in terms of reverence and adulation. Churchmen of all types and classes were deceived. "Those whose temper fell in with the times hugged and embraced it, applauded the proposals, filled their mouths with the arguments." An eminent cleric in the country wrote to a friend in London, "I join with the author in all that he says, and have such a value for the book that, next to the Holy Bible and Sacred Comments, I take it for the most valuable piece I have. I pray God put it into Her Majesty's heart to put what is there proposed in execution."

Almost any paragraph from *The Shortest Way* will convey the vigour and dash of De Foe's greatest and most disastrous "satyr".

"If one severe law were made, and punctually executed, that whoever was found in a conventicle should be banished the

Nation, and the Preacher be hanged, we should soon see one end of the tale ; they all come to church, and one age would make us all one again.

"If men sin against God, affront His ordinances, rebel against His Church, and disobey the precepts of their superiors, let them suffer as such capital crimes deserve ; so will religion flourish, and this divided nation be once again united.

"The humour of the Dissenters has so increased among the people that they hold the Church in defiance, and the House of God is an abomination among them. Nay, they have brought up posterity in such prepossessed aversions to our holy religion that the ignorant mob think we are all idolaters and worshippers of Baal . . ."

He must have known that he was running risks. But it does not seem to have occurred to him how tremendous they were. Though his name did not appear on the pamphlet, he must also have realized that sooner or later, probably sooner, its authorship would become known. Vanity, perhaps joined with belief that the aura attached to a man until so lately the King's confidant still afforded protection, may have assured him that, whatever the upshot of his joke, there was little to fear.

Whatever his beliefs, his psychology proved completely at fault; both sides believed the pamphlet to be a genuine, if over-violent piece of High Church propaganda. The Dissenters themselves regarded it as an attack by a dangerous and fanatical opponent. But when De Foe, a trifle scared by the reactions evoked by his elaborate tomfoolery, issued *A Brief Explanation of a late Pamphlet*, and, putting it crudely, blew the gaff, the result was cataclysmal. The Whig politicians were amused, but they were the only people who were. The High-flyers were naturally thrown into frenzies of fury. Ridicule cast on the established religion was bad enough, but to that offence had been added the inflammatory effect of the pamphlet upon those arch-enemies of Church and Crown, the Dissenters, who (it was argued), assuming an attack on their privileges to be imminent, might very well proceed to rioting. The pamphlet, in short, constituted a definite danger to the public peace.

The Dissenters also refused to be in the least placated by the explanation. For some time past they had regarded De Foe as one to be suspected, an asset whose value was highly problematical. The man was altogether too clever to be trusted. De Foe habitually insisted that he had sacrificed himself on his fellow-Nonconformists' behalf: the Non-conformists themselves would have been glad of a less embarrassing offering.

On January 3rd, 1703, the blow fell. The Earl of Notting-ham,[1] one of the Queen's Secretaries of State, a High Churchman whom the reckless satirist had nicknamed "Don Dismal", issued a warrant for De Foe's arrest. It charged him with "High Crimes and Misdemeanours". Warning of this almost certainly reached De Foe, for, as on a previous crisis in his career, he vanished into hiding. Only a few intimate friends knew of his whereabouts; these included the faithful Mary, who visited him at intervals with the current news. Incidentally, others, not mentioned by name, were included in the charge. It may be presumed, though the fact is not certain, that the "others" referred to the printer and publishers, as they would certainly have been involved in a similar prosecution to-day. In any case, they were arrested.

On January 9th De Foe wrote a long letter to Nottingham. Its extraordinarily abject tone is an indication of the depths to which his volatile spirits had sunk.

"I had long since surrendered to Her Majesty's Clemency had not the menaces of your Lordship's Offer possessed me with such Ideas of Her Majesty's and your Lordship's resentment as were too terrible . . . My Lord, a Body unfit to bear the hardships of a Prison and a Mind impatient of Confinement have been the only reasons of withdrawing myself. And, my Lord, the cries of a numerous ruin'd Family, the prospect of a long Banishment from my Native country and the Hopes of Her Majesty's Mercy move me to throw myself at Her Majesty's Feet. I beseech your Lordship to assure Her Majesty that I am free from any seditious Design . . . With this, the lowest submission, I entreat Her Majesty's pardon for this Mistake, from which I am ready to make any Public Acknowledgment."

The letter concluded with a flicker of the old De Foe instinct for bargaining. He offered to serve for a year or longer as a volunteer in the Royal Cavalry in the Low

[1] The translator of Monsieur Dottin's *Life of Foe* refers to him repeatedly by a quaint oversight, as " the Count of Nottingham ".

Countries, or, if completely pardoned, was even prepared to raise an entire troop and place himself at its head.

A second question may be asked: what had reduced him to a condition of terrified grovelling? The answer here is simple. As a Londoner, he had full knowledge of existence in prison, and of its alternative, the pillory. Conditions three centuries ago were such that without the mitigations which only large-scale bribery could obtain, a sentence of any length was frequently equivalent to death, or, if not death, permanently ruined health. . . . As for the pillory, De Foe knew all the hideous implications of that, too.

Mary De Foe herself brought the letter to Nottingham but the Dismal Don merely tried to bribe her to reveal her husband's hidingplace. In extenuation, it should be said that Nottingham was actually attacking bigger game than De Foe, who was not merely deep in the Whig secrets but was indirectly linked with Robert Harley, the Whig speaker.

On January 10th, one day later, the following appeared in the *London Gazette:*

"Whereas Daniel De Foe, *alias* De Fooe, is charged with writing a scandalous and seditious pamphlet entitled 'The Shortest Way With Dissenters'. He is a middle-sized, spare man, about forty years old, of a brown complexion, and dark-brown coloured hair; a hooked nose, a sharp chin, grey eyes, and a large mole near his mouth; was born in London, and was for many years a hose-factor in Freeman's Yard in Cornhill, and now is the owner of the Brick and Pantile Works near Tilbury Fort in Essex, Whoever shall discover the said De Foe to one of Her Majesty's Principal Secretaries of State, or to any of Her Majesty's Justices of the Peace, so that he may be apprehended, shall have a reward of £50 which Her Majesty has ordered immediately to be paid upon such discovery."

What humbler, more intimate enemy was responsible for supplying my Lord Nottingham with these details, and so furnishing later centuries with the only verbal portrait in existence of our greatest journalist?

On January 14th Nottingham sent an officer of the Court to Croome, publisher of *The Shortest Way*, with instructions to seize the manuscript and every available copy of the pamphlet. And on February 24th it was burned, by order of the Commons, in the public square of New Place by the common hangman. By now both printer and publisher were in prison. But not the author—yet.

Still in hiding, he was also still active. Giving up any idea of moving Nottingham by a personal appeal, he reverted to print. *A Brief Explanation of a late Pamphlet entitled "The Shortest Way with Dissenters"* he referred to (with, one imagines very slender expectation of being believed) as merely a "Banter" upon the High Church party. He spoke, incidentally, and with sorrow, of the Dissenters who had so cruelly misunderstood him. He hoped the anger of the Government would be allayed.

It was a forlorn hope, and he must have known it. Grim Dutch William would have saved him, but the stout red-faced lady now occupying his throne had no tolerance for jesters who sneered at the Established Church. And De Foe's less highly-placed enemies were many. One of these offered to forgo the reward for the mere pleasure of tracking him down and handing him over to the authorities; another, a colonel, undertook to hang him, also gratis, when the capture had actually been made. There were even retaliatory pamphlets, among them *The Fox with his Firebrand Unkennel'd* (presumably a reference to Aesop's Fable), and a parody, *The Shortest Way with Whores and Rogues*, whose truculent author wanted to fight, being "one that neither loves nor fears you, and, were it lawful, would meet you any day with a brighter weapon than a pen!"

A brave challenge, especially as the challenger must have been fairly certain that no opportunity for putting it into effect would arise.

De Foe succeeded in remaining in hiding, though with increasing risks, until April. In that month he wrote a long letter to a friend named Paterson, one who in the past had acted as a sort of political liaison-officer between De Foe and Harley. Its tenor can be judged by a short extract:

"Gaols, pillories and suchlike, with which I have been so much threatened, have convinced me that I want passive courage, and I shall never for the future think myself injured if I am called a coward."

Paterson, in spite of the urgency of the appeal, did not actually contact Harley at once, but waited until the following month, by which time De Foe himself was already in custody. Harley not merely came to the rescue; he found employment for De Foe, and later became his chief friend and patron.

On May 20th the authorities, "acting upon information received", appeared at the Spitalfields house of a French weaver, arrested De Foe, and conveyed him to Newgate. They took possession also of his manuscripts, but returned them later.

Again an anonymous informer had supplied the necessary information. In the Calendar of Treasury Papers for 1702–17 appears this letter, dated May 25th, 1703, from Nottingham to the Lord High Treasurer.

"The Person who discovered De Foe for whom a Reward of £50 was promised in the *Gazette* sent to me for his Money, but does not care to appear himself. If, therefore, your Lordship will order that sum to be paid to Mr. Armstrong, I will see that the Person shall have it who discovered the said De Fooe, and upon whose information he was apprehended."

It will be noted that Nottingham was still in some doubt about the spelling of the prisoner's name.

De Foe was remanded in custody until July 7th. In the interval he appears to have recovered his mental equilibrium, for he busied himself in the preparation of the first volume of *A True Collection of the Writings of the Author of the "True-born Englishman"*, thus shrewdly putting his most popular book in the foreground. The "Collection" is of special interest because it has as a frontispiece the author's portrait, (already mentioned) engraved by a Dutchman, M. V. de Guicht, or Vanderguicht, from a painting by Jeremiah Taverner.[1]

The portrait may have been an excellent likeness, though it is difficult to visualize in it the description given in the *Gazette*. (But possibly the comparison between a Royal Academy painting and the subject's passport details might be equally unflattering.) Hazlitt characterized the impression of the whole countenance as being "rather a striking than a pleasing one". It is surmounted by a magnificent wig; the subject is wearing a "a richly-laced cravat and

[1] A portrait painter, states Redgrave's *Dictionary of Artists of the English School*, who flourished in the first half of the eighteenth century. Redgrave adds inaccurately, "He was the author of several plays". Actually the dramatist was Jeremiah's son, William, of whom the *Dictionary of National Biography* has a good deal to say, while disregarding the artist.

a fine loose flowing coat". And below, equally impressive, is his coat of arms.

Once in Newgate, existence, paradoxically enough, became tolerable; more than tolerable, in fact, since on the one hand his resilient spirit soon recovered itself, and he began to feel more optimistic concerning the future, while on the other hand the actual conditions of his confinement were incomparably better than those of less fortunate prisoners. It is quite possible that, wallowing in his new humility, he had, for the time being, overlooked his own political value as a man in possession of important and highly inconvenient secrets. It was probably for this reason he was separated from the ordinary prison riff-raff, though at the same time he had endless opportunities of studying them, rather in the position of a temporary and distinguished visitor on the safe side of the bars.

He was indeed lucky.

The Great Fire almost destroyed Newgate. But it had risen again from the ashes under an administration still as insensitive and soul-destroying as its own stone walls. Its gateway overlooked Snow Hill, in whose gutters the offal of Smithfield flowed or stagnated. The entire system of management was based on extortion. To the headkeeper (who had to bribe heavily to obtain the post) came all profits, legitimate sometimes, but commonly infamous. Each of his satellites, from the senior jailer downwards, made what he could when and where he could, according to his rank and opportunities.

A vivid description of Newgate's horrors is given in Mr. Dickson Carr's *The Murder of Sir Edmund Berry Godfrey;*

"First, first, there is the lodge at the gateway.

"Here you are clapped in irons, as a matter of course, until you pay 'easement'. If you are clearly penniless and without friends, they will either knock off the manacles or keep them on, according to the humour of the moment. But in any case you will go into the underground Condemned Hole, where you may repose if your nose suffers you to rest—until you have paid half-a-crown to get out."

A well-to-do prisoner was lodged in the Master side, where he paid fourteen shillings and tenpence on entrance, eighteen pence for coals, and a shilling to be spent among the prisoners. Beds in the Long Room were extra, and sheets were another extra.

"But most go to the Common Side, where there is din that never ceases, and men and women are herded indiscriminately, and the physical filth is surpassed only by the filth of the language, and the limbs of quartered men lying in an open cupboard waiting for the final horror of their disposal may be seen."

De Foe heard of, though he did not see, all these things; his memory seized and held them; and in *Moll Flanders* he found space to describe them.

The days passed in reading and writing. Friends visited him. His enemies did not; they could not, said the Rev. Mr. Howe, to whom he wrote, even forgive him, though God might.

Comparisons have been made, more or less inevitably, between the imprisonment of De Foe in Newgate and John Bunyan in Bedford Jail a generation earlier. In each case the most obvious fact is that prison life intensified the dominant qualities inherent in the man; in De Foe's case the political, in Bunyan's the spiritual. They were condemned to isolation and silence, and in isolation and silence their geniuses flourished.

On July 16th, ten days before his trial, De Foe published a sequel to his *Reformation of Manners*. It was called *More Reformation; a Satyr upon Himself*. Unfortunately, neither poem brought much grist to a mill that was becoming increasingly short of grist. His unfortunate wife and family were nearing complete destitution. The neglected brick-and-tile factory at Tilbury was floundering in bankruptcy. A lawsuit concerning casks of beer added to the complications; for liquor supplied to De Foe's workmen, Chapman, the publican, claimed fifty-three pounds six shillings. De Foe issued a defence which is still preserved. He might have ended the whole thing if, as he was convinced he would be, he had been set free at the Assizes.

But he was not set free.

His trial occupied three days—July 7th, 8th and 9th. From the first it was, to coin a phrase, a tissue of misfortune. The Advocate General, Sir Simon Harcourt, later to reach eminence as Lord Chancellor, exhibited a violence reminiscent of Judge Jeffreys. ("You are paving your way with the skulls of Churchmen," was one of his comments.) He tried to bully the prisoner into an open admission of being the author of *The Shortest Way*. But De Foe refused to be trapped.

His own counsel was William Colepeper, chairman of the Quarter Sessions of Maidstone and the eldest son of Sir Thomas Colepeper of Hollingbourne. Colepeper was conspicuous as the leader of the Five Gentlemen of Kent when the celebrated petition had been presented to the Speaker two years earlier. To quote from his frigid little biography in the *Dictionary of National Biography*, he "intermeddled with poetry", being the author of *An Heroick Poem upon the King*, another (without the adjective) *To the Lady Duty*, and a third *To the Reverend John Brandreth*. But he also intermeddled as a political candidate. In the General Election of 1702 he polled thirty votes out of thirty-five in his own division and one thousand six hundred and twenty-five elsewhere, but was not elected owing to opposition canvassing by Sir G. Rooke,[1] Lord High Admiral of England. Shortly afterwards, following Colepeper's indiscreet comments on the Admiral being at Bath instead of being with the Fleet, a gang in Rooke's pay were bribed to attack Colepeper. The latter promptly brought an action against Drew, Merram and Britton, in that they did "maliciously . . . confederate and conspire to beat, wound, and evilly treat the said William Colepeper". Captain Nathaniel Denew was also involved, being charged with "lying in wait of his malice and forethought and assault premeditated, with threatening, sprightful and approbrious words, then and there daringly, wickedly and maliciously and vehemently urged provoked and stirred up the said Wm. Colepeper to fight with him a mortal duel"

The lawyers ran no risks of understatement in indictments drawn up in Queen Anne's day!

Altogether twenty-eight "lurid ruffians" were involved, including Denew, promoted to Lieutenant Colonel, and a Mr. Knatchbull, who had been rewarded with a place of eight hundred pounds per annum, both since their crimes. Rooke was their immediate patron; but behind him, it was suspected—more than suspected—loomed the sinister figure of Don Dismal, soon to fall from office. Denew was convicted and fined two hundred marks[2]; another, Richard Britton, also convicted, was fined a hundred pounds.

De Foe recorded the whole affair in *A True State of the*

---

[1] Spelt Rook in the *Dictionary of National Biography*.
[2] From the Conquest onwards, thirteen and fourpence. Its legal use as indicating the amount of a fine lingered until 1770.

Difference between Sir George Rooke, Kt. and William Colepeper Esq., in a folio pamphlet of forty-four pages which was published on August 22nd, 1704.

To revert to De Foe's trial.

The shameless bullying of Harcourt had its effect. Colepeper became so convinced that his case was hopeless that he urged De Foe to plead guilty and to throw himself on the Queen's clemency. Reluctantly De Foe did so—only to realize his mistake. He was doing precisely what his enemies hoped. Clemency there was none. He was sentenced to pay two hundred marks, to stand three times in the pillory in a public place, to remain in Newgate during the Queen's pleasure, and, upon his release, to obtain guarantees for his good conduct for seven years.

De Foe was stunned. They took him back to his cell, there at his leisure to think over the prospect. The fate of a man in the pillory depended entirely upon his popularity—or the reverse—with passing fellow-citizens. Completely helpless, he might be greeted by sympathizers, or pelted with garbage, filth or even more terrible missiles until he became unconscious, or actually died.

Colepeper did his honest best to make amends for an honest blunder in tactics. He travelled to Windsor, where the Queen was, and presented a petition on De Foe's behalf. His only reward was an attack with a cane from a Tory who recognized him.

But later there arose a new glimmer of hope. William Penn, the pious but unfortunate Quaker who is credited with having given his name to one of the American States, happened at that time to be staying in London. In May he presented Anne with an address on behalf of himself and his fellow-Quakers, thanking her for her maintenance of the Toleration Act. From Kensington Palace he and a companion went to visit Newgate with the double object of trying to alleviate the misery there, and winning over some of the less hardened inmates to Christianity, if not to Quakerism.

He saw De Foe and heard his story, the sequel being that on July 16th he informed Godolphin that the prisoner was prepared to give, on oath, a list of his accomplices, provided "he may be excused from the punishment of the pillory".

Anne was not particularly impressed. But she was willing to please Penn to the extent of referring the case to the Lords of the Committee. Nottingham waited, grimly sure of the result. On July 27th he was able to inform Captain Richardson, the officer in charge of prisoners remanded to Newgate, that the final decision had gone against the prisoner.

On the 29th De Foe spent the first of his three days in the pillory. It was erected in Cornhill in front of the Royal Exchange, the two others being in Cheapside and at Temple Bar.

Once again the resilience of his nature asserted itself.

One biographer[1] has attributed the prisoner's "beatified optimism" solely to De Foe's unconquerable belief "that the steps of any man whose intentions are good are ordered by the Lord", and that "in no record of a human being that one knows of was the hand of the Deity more manifest". Possibly. But it is as well to bear in mind that throughout his life De Foe's character exhibited a mixture of the energetic, astute, practical, not always scrupulous man with an eye on the main chance, and of the equally energetic, astute and practical labourer on behalf of the religious and political creeds of his fathers—the net result being the production of an immense amount of extremely mixed literature.

De Foe might not always succeed in gauging the temper of his countrymen. But he gauged it unerringly now. Just before the fatal 29th he plunged into verse again with a *Hymn to the Pillory*. It began:

> "Hail, hieroglyphic state Machine
> Contrived to punish Fancy in
> Men that are Men in thee can feel no pain
> And all thy Insignificants disdain."

After a list of some of the eminent occupiers of his position, he went on to say of himself:

> "Tell 'em the men that placed him here
> Are scandals to the times,
> Are at a loss to find his guilt
> And can't commit his crimes.

Concerning the pillory itself,

> "Thou art the state-trap of the Law
> But neither canst keep knaves nor honest men in awe
> These are too hardened in offence
> And those upheld by innocence."

[1] Thomas Wright.

By some means or other he succeeded not only in getting the hymn printed, but in circulating it among the crowds that choked the streets adjoining the Royal Exchange on the morning of his punishment. To the London mob, always so mutable, so unpredictable, in its reactions, must have come a sudden realization that the helpless, tormented, middle-aged figure before them stood for something that was fundamentally English in its unconquerable and invariable reaction against tyranny. They flung no rotten eggs, no decayed vegetables, no fish-entrails, but hung flowers round the grotesque contraption that held him prisoner, and drank his health, and nicknamed him "Supervisor of the City pavements", and when the time for release at last arrived, "halloo'd him down from his wooden punishment as if he had been a Cicero that had made an excellent oration in it".

It must have been exasperating to his enemies. They, too, circulated lampoons, *The True-born Hugonot: A Pleasant Dialogue between the Pillory and Daniel De Foe: The Dissenting Hypocrite*. And in later years Pope, in one of his bursts of petty spite, wrote "Earless on high stood unabashed De Foe", knowing it to be a lie, since De Foe's ears were never cropped.

De Foe's was the triumph. Unfortunately it was brief; the unspectacular, indefinite ignominy of Newgate still awaited him. And after Newgate? A destitute wife and seven children, a ruined business, and innumerable implacable enemies with Nottingham at their head.

There were other things as well to take into account. De Foe himself was changing. His religious outlook was as it had always been, but politically he was mellowing. He was a Whig, but one no longer prepared to damn every shade of Toryism and every man who professed to believe in any of them. Such a change is common enough, and in De Foe's case, though its convenience soon became apparent, there is no reason to doubt its genuineness.

The dyed-in-the-wool Tories had, of course, no use whatever for "an infamous stigmatized incendiary, one who lives by Defamation and who, by writing to the level and Capacity of the Mob is become a bold, impetuous Demagogue, and the admired Oracle of the deluded People". That a man who should have been degraded and finally extinguished after a three-day trial had retaliated by a three-day triumph —that was unforgivable.

PART THREE

HARLEY & CO.

CHAPTER I

RELEASE, AND THE *REVIEW*

AT THIS point Robert Harley, later to be created Earl of Oxford and Earl Mortimer, begins to play a prominent part in De Foe's career.

Harley, a year younger than De Foe, took a prominent part in the 1688 Revolution, and entered Parliament a year later. Like De Foe, he was by birth a Whig and Dissenter; unlike him, he added a genius for public business, together with an infinite capacity for standing with a foot in both camps until such time as he judged it safe to risk assuming the leadership of the Tories, and ultimately of the High Church party.

The links between De Foe and Harley were, in a way, far more complicated than they were between him and his idol, William. Harley and De Foe were socially nearer, while throughout their association Harley deliberately kept De Foe financially dependent.

Both men were born schemers—Harley with his aristocratic background and vast knowledge of procedure, De Foe with more intuition and daring. It was when De Foe's intuitions clashed with the principles he professed, and for the time being those professions went to the wall, that his most fervid supporters found it hardest to support him, and the contumely of his enemies had most justification. His mind worked subtly at a period when there were no halftones where politics and religion were concerned. A man was a villain (or hero) if he were a Tory and a Churchman, and a hero (or villain) if he were a Whig and a Dissenter. But in any case he was a villain or a hero.

The keystone of Harley's policy was moderation. He was

a servant of the Crown before the days when the entire function of Government was exercised by whichever party chanced to be in power. The Cabinet in Anne's time was in effect a coalition, with the majority party predominating. That, in turn, meant opportunities for scheming, for intrigue, for individual rises and falls. Harley was a "moderate" man, but his moderation was purely tactical and had no connections with his ambitions. As for De Foe—"I have always thought that the only true fundamental maxim of Politicks that will ever make this Nation happy is this, that the Government ought to be of no party at all". Moderation could no further go—politically.

With his financial position as desperate as it was, why should not a broad-minded Whig serve another broad-minded Whig, even if their religious views, originally identical, were now at variance?

De Foe's original offer of service had fallen flat. But events were moving fast in those summer days of 1703.

Nottingham, of course, was fully alive to the inconvenient possibilities that might arise when De Foe was released. Any alliance between a pamphleteer of such calibre and Nottingham's inveterate enemy would be a nuisance, if not a danger. So far he had been unable to discover any link between them, but so long as De Foe was in prison there remained a chance of intimidating him into confession. To Newgate, then, the Dismal Don went, accompanied by Harcourt, the Attorney General. A ruthless cross-questioning ensued. But even with the prospect of immediate and unconditional freedom dangled before him, De Foe refused to admit that he had at any time had the least acquaintance with Harley "other than by fame or by sight, as we know men of quality by seeing them on public occasions".

He may have been speaking the literal truth, though there is no doubt that, directly or indirectly, Harley had been surreptitiously encouraging his anti-Tory activities. Nottingham and Harcourt departed, after drawing absolutely blank. When the ordeal was over De Foe wrote to Harley saying that he was at the end of his tether.

De Foe had other, more welcome visitors, including two peers and the indefatigable Colepeper and his four companion gentlemen of Kent. But John Howe and other Dissenting Ministers refused to come.

De Foe contacted Harley before the trial. But Harley had not responded: he was in no hurry. Later, however, he met the Lord Treasurer Godolphin and discussed De Foe. Godolphin agreed that the man might prove useful. After this interview Harley sent a note to De Foe. It was ironically cool, utterly non-committal "Pray ask that gentleman what I can do for him."

De Foe's answer was drawn from the Bible. He reminded Harley of the blind man's reply when Christ said, "What wilt thou that I should do unto thee?" "Lord, that I might receive my sight."

Harley then lapsed into enigmatical silence again. But he was not inactive. He sent small sums from time to time to help the De Foe family, and on September 20th he wrote to Godolphin. If the Government intended to avail themselves of the services of De Foe, it was high time to act. Already the prisoner's friends were discussing not only the best way of raising the money to pay the prisoner's fine, but another petition to the Queen to obtain his release.

Godolphin agreed. Harley then suggested that the fine should be cancelled; also that it should be emphasized that any pardon given him at the same time was due entirely to the generosity of Her Majesty. "This," ended the far-sighted Harley, "may perhaps engage him better than any *after* rewards, and keep him more in the power of an obligation."

Godolphin again concurred. The next step was obviously to engage the sympathies of Anne.

Godolphin had an uphill task, a far more difficult one than if De Foe's offences had been merely political. On many, one might say most, matters the Queen could be relied upon to exhibit either a casual complacency or a childlike variability of outlook which made her both a victim and an exasperation to her ministers. But upon one subject, the established Anglican Church, she was, as already mentioned, a woman of clear-cut and unswerving views. And it was the Anglican Church which, she had been told, De Foe had attacked.

At first she refused to discuss the matter at all; then she blamed Nottingham for any excess of punishment that De Foe had endured. Godolphin abandoned the prisoner's claim to royal clemency, and held forth on the sufferings of the prisoner's innocent family. Here he found himself on safer and more profitable ground, and took adroit advantage of it. He appealed to the Queen's pity and, by implication, lowered still further her opinion of Nottingham, at whose harsh and dominating hands she herself had suffered considerably.

Anne melted. She helped Mary De Foe generously from her own purse, and issued an order to Godolphin to pay the prisoner's fine, as well as the costs involved. On September 26th the triumphant Godolphin was able to write to Harley that he—Harley—had only to issue the order, and De Foe would be free.

Harley, however, had still work to do before the word was spoken. Sureties for De Foe's future good behaviour had to be found. And in any case a few more weeks in the privacy of prison would play their part in obliterating the whole unfortunate incident.

He was, however, human enough to let the prisoner know that the order of release was definitely on the way.

At the beginning of November Harley wrote to Godolphin: all was ready, and after five months in Newgate, the mere thought of which had reduced him to something like hysteria, De Foe was released to enjoy the fresh air and sunlight again, and to meet his family and friends.

His gratitude was as genuine as it was exuberant. There is still extant the letter he wrote to Harley on November 9th, in which, typically, he compares himself to the one leper in ten who gave thanks. Harley's reply is unknown, but the "one leper" was given to understand that a fit appreciation of Her Majesty's clemency could be shown in only one way— by unstinted devotion to Her Majesty's Ministers in such manner as those Ministers dictated.

Before this could happen, the ruinous complications of his own private affairs had to be straightened out.

He was turned forty. His Tilbury venture had ended in ruin. How much, beyond a source of income, it had ever been to him was questionable. My personal view is that outside the journalistic and pamphleteering world which he had made peculiarly his own, most of his financial excursions were experimental. He learnt what they could teach him, and, having learnt it, tired of them, and, tiring of them, let them slide to extinction with no particular regrets.

Over the brick-and-tile business he stated that he had lost three thousand five hundred pounds. "Violence, injury and barbarous treatment demolished me and my undertakings," he explained, and then, descending as usual to practical details, enlarged on his difficulties in obtaining workmen of the right type.

"I affirm from my own knowledge," says De Foe, "when I have wanted a man for labouring work, and offered nine shillings a week to strolling fellow at my door, they have frequently told me to my face that they could get more a-begging."

He informed Harley that at least a thousand pounds would be needed to placate his creditors. Harley's response can only be guessed, but that he gave De Foe some assistance is reasonably certain.

De Foe had been extremely busy with his pen during his imprisonment. Apart from his *Hymn to the Pillory* he wrote nearly twenty pamphlets, mostly between the summer of 1703 and that of 1704, as well as the beginning of *Jure Divino*.

But his most important publication was his story of the Great Storm. It occurred in the last week of December 1703, and was worth recording.

At four o'clock on Wednesday, the 24th, an unusual wind arose, becoming steadily more violent as the day wore on; De Foe on his way home narrowly escaped death from a falling wall. The gale raged all that night and throughout the following day. On Friday it rose yet higher, and the streets became heaped with wreckage from roofs and walls. At ten o'clock that night De Foe, gathered with his terrified family in his small brick-built house in the City, noted the abnormal level of the mercury in the barometer; it was, in fact, so low that he thought one of the children must have been tampering with it. Suddenly, a little later, there was yet another increase in the gale, and the whole house shuddered. It was obviously unsafe; but as to leave its shelter was certain death, the family remained where they were.

Followed periods of comparative lull, during which exhausted and terrified Londoners told themselves that the worst was over; then the wind would rise once more, and amid a chorus of thunder and driving rain add further to the general confusion. It was not until Wednesday afternoon that it became obvious that the storm was really subsiding, and that citizens might risk leaving their homes and face the problem of getting back to normal living.

It was an ironic postscript to De Foe's Tilbury adventure that, had the factory been still in his possession, he could have made a fortune from the sudden and almost limitless demands for tiles, the price of which rocketed from a guinea a thousand to six to seven pounds.

As a practical alternative he decided to write an account of the storm. A publisher, John Nutt, was found; a notice was inserted in a number of journals asking for personal experiences—for the area of the storm extended far beyond London—and De Foe himself set out on a tour of investigation, chiefly in Kent.

There are several points of particular interest connected with that excursion. De Foe had been only a few weeks free to travel beyond the ghastly limitations of the prison yard. He was, for the moment, at loose ends. With every faculty acutely sharpened to outside impressions, he had every inducement to employ those faculties. And finally, though it is improbable that he realized it, the story of the Great Storm formed his first deliberate essay in descriptive reporting—work in which his extraordinary genius found its finest opportunities.

He approached the business with his usual thoroughness. The title alone was formidable:

The STORM, or a COLLECTION of the most Remarkable Casualties and DISASTERS which happened in the Late Dreadful Tempest, both by SEA and LAND.

"The Lord hath His way in the whirlwind, and in the Storm, and Clouds are the dust of his Feet. Nah. 1. 3."

The Preface was signed, "The Ages' Humble Servant"; the first chapter dealt with "the Natural causes and Original (sic) of winds", and referred learnedly to the Arcana of Oeconomy, as well as to Aristotle, Seneca, the Stoics, Mr. Hobbs and Descartes. Chapter 2 included a table of degrees of winds, starting "Stark calm, calm weather", and ending "A fret of wind, a storm, a tempest".

The conclusion, rather startlingly, is in verse. The author calls it "An Essay". Politics and religion are included

My Lord

July. 16. 1708

I had Gone on farther to Reply to This Most Insolent Memoriall, But y̍ the Subject of y̍ Review being before This book came Out Pricted upon y̍ Same Article. viz. The Danger of y̍ Church. I Shall handle it apart

I Think it my Duty to Lay it before yo̍ L'Ship as it is, and have Sent Six of Them, Not That I Think it worth yo̍ L'Ships Recommending, but That, if yo̍ L'Ship Pleafe to Concern yo̍ Self for me so far, yo̍ Own hand May Make This Empty Returne to The (to me Unknown) Benefactors of whose Goodness to me yo̍ Lordship was Pleas'd to be a Medium, and w̍th I have no other Way to Acknowlege

If I knew how to Ask my L'd Treasurer Pardon, Either for y̍ Weaknefs of my Defence in his Cafe, or y̍ Rudenefs of a Dedicaçon without a Name, I Should be Glad to do it, But I am too Obfcure and Remote to do it Perfonally and y̍ Same Reason That obliges me Not to Sign y̍ Dedicaçon Obliges me Not to do it Publickly

The Writing This book I hear is Charg'd upon D'r Drake, I can Not forbear Afsuring yo̍ L'Ship, That however he Might be The Drudge or rather Amanuenfis in y̍ Work — his Master The Duke of Bucks is as plainly Pictur'd to me w̍th his Pen — his hand Correcting Dictating and Instructing as if I had been of y̍ Club w̍th Them

I Ask yo̍ L'Ships Pardon for This freedome and am yo̍ L'Ships Most Humble and Obed̍t Serv̍t DeFoe

LETTER DATED JULY 16TH, 1708 WRITTEN FROM
SCOTLAND BY DE FOE TO GODOLPHIN

among what is, in fact, some of the poorest doggerel he ever published.

The Storm appeared, an octavo book of 300 pages, priced at three and sixpence, on July 17th in the following year.

Harley, of course, read this; indeed, it is not too much to assume that the metrical anti-climax, with its attacks on the Tories and High-flyers, was added with a special eye on that statesman's reactions.

De Foe, on leaving prison, went to Bury St. Edmunds to recuperate. There he installed himself in what a house agent would term a highly superior residence. It was called "Cupola House", for the excellent reason that a cupola surmounted it.

Having introduced himself to the local body of Dissenters, he published a poem, written in prison, *An Elegy on the Author of the " True-born Englishman "*—a self-pitying piece of doggerel, interesting because it gives us our only hint of the terms upon which he was released.

"Had the scribbling world been pleased to leave me where they found me," he comments acidly in the preface, "I had left the world and Newgate both together, and as I am metaphorically dead, had been effectively so as to satires and pamphlets. 'Tis really something hard that, after all the mortification they think they have put upon a poor abdicated author in their scurrilous street-ribaldry and bear-garden usage . . . they cannot yet be quiet."

"Memento Mori here I stand," he lamented,
"With silent lips but speaking hand.
A walking Shadow of a Poet,
But bound to hold my tongue and never show it.
A monument of Injury
A sacrifice to legal tyranny."

On the other hand, the lines may have been written as a final answer to certain inconveniently frequent questions, and deliberately intended to be not only vague but inaccurate.

At Bury St. Edmunds itself he wrote also a *Hymn to Victory*, a poem in praise of the Duke of Marlborough, and a prose pamphlet called *The Protestant Jesuit Unmask'd*.

His stay at Bury was short. Dyer, the news editor, started a rumour that he had fled to escape his enemies; Fox, the bookseller, added that he had failed to surrender to his bail. Stephen, a state messenger, carried the vendetta a stage further and announced that he held a warrant for the released prisoner's arrest. De Foe met all this malice head-on by coming up to Town to see Harley personally.

He was assured that he had nothing to fear.

His holiday at Bury should have been continued. But the strain of again facing a small but bitterly hostile clique of enemies proved too much for him. Soon after his return to London in October he collapsed, and for two months he was on the sick list. That his illness was serious may be judged from the fact that he announced that the publication of his paper, the *Review*, would cease with the end of the first yearly volume.

But here his friends, and not his enemies, took a hand. They protested, they solicited; an anonymous benefactor sent him a large sum to distribute at his own discretion among the poor; and reincarnated as *A Review of the Affairs of France, with Observations on Home Affairs*, it appeared three times weekly instead of twice.[1]

Precisely how the idea of the *Review* originated is uncertain.

According to its editor, it had its birth in his cell in Newgate. That De Foe, free again not only from prison, but from crippling financial entanglements, should write regularly on behalf of his rescuers and their party seems an obvious and natural redirection of his talents. Considering that—to use a Fleet Street cliché—he had been born with ink in his veins, the real wonder is that the editorship of a journal of some type or other should have been delayed until he was middle-aged.

But even in the seventeenth-century a considerable sum was required to float a paper. Harley furnished funds once more, though nominally the *Review* was independent politically. Its full title was *A Weekly Review of the Affairs of France Purg'd from the Errors and Partiality of News-Writers and Petty Statesmen of all Sides*, and the first number appeared on February 19th, 1704. Originally a small eight-page penny weekly, it soon halved the number of its pages and appeared on Tuesdays and Thursdays. About a year later still it appeared on Saturday as well.

[1] Mr. Wright makes the common error of referring to it as becoming "tri-weekly", which would mean appearing every third week.

Its object, stated the editor, was to prevent various "uncertain accounts, and the partial reflections of our street scribblers". The "street-scribblers" were already very thoroughly entrenched. They had been busy for over eighty years, since *News from Spayne* appeared in 1620 with the single and disloyal object of exposing James I. The *London Gazette* of 1667 was a comparatively late comer. The historian's chief difficulty is to differentiate between pamphlets, and special numbers (or editions) of legitimate journals.

From the psychological angle the *Review* is peculiarly interesting. De Foe was serving Harley as faithfully as he had served William, though without that quality of personal singlemindedness and devotion which had died with the Dutch king. Harley stood for moderation, though moderation now in the Tory camp. De Foe, also standing for moderation, was in the Whig camp.

Yet in spite of this ill-fitting harness, he contrived both to travel at his own pace and at the same time to satisfy Harley, the reason being that the two men were mutually dependent, and never mutually antagonistic. Apart from Harley's genuine respect for De Foe's abilities, and De Foe's equally genuine sense of obligation, each had every inducement to keep on good terms with the other. To that end, they achieved a gentleman's agreement which was honourably observed, and which might well serve as a charter for proprietors and editors to-day.

From time to time Harley would tentatively put forward his views. De Foe would endorse them in the *Review* in his own inimitable way if he approved of them; if he could not approve, he remained silent and refrained from attack. Harley in his dealings with De Foe exercised throughout a masterly restraint, listening to what his brilliant subordinate had to say, and keeping in the background the fact that he *was* a subordinate, though now and again there would be gentle reminders that De Foe had a good deal to be grateful for. At intervals there would be money gifts. But never to excess— a mere fifty or a hundred guineas to reinforce that gratitude.

When De Foe was charged by his enemies with deserting from the Whig to the Tory cause he retorted:

"Why am I still harassed by merciless and malicious men? Why pursued to all extremities by law for old accounts? . . .

"Certainly had I been employed or hired [by which he really meant bribed] by those people that own the service, time would have set their servant free from the little and implacable malice of litigious persecution. . . ."

The complications involved in what would to-day be called the make-up of the *Review* itself were endless. There was, for example, "News of the Scandal Club", a humorous, or at any rate irresponsible section which was maintained up to the thirtieth number, and then discontinued through lack of space. It reappeared in a twice-weekly pamphlet that De Foe called the *Little Review*, which in turn perished after twenty issues, though not until it had brought its editor into collision with his old ally, Dunton, whose *Monthly Oracle* was still continuing the traditions of *The Athenian Oracle*. Dunton charged De Foe with plagiarizing the style, if not the actual contents of the older paper. Had De Foe been living to-day, he would probably have retorted that there was no copyright in ideas, and that competition was healthy.

He had other journalistic opposition, and made other journalistic enemies, apart from the official *London Gazette*. They included *The Daily Courant*, the sole "daily" then in existence, with the incredibly meagre circulation of eight hundred copies an issue, and *The Post Man* and *The Post Boy*, twin Tory publications appearing thrice weekly.

Yet if all these periodicals, De Foe's included, had not been mere implements of political propaganda, there should have been plenty of room for the *Review* which was, properly speaking, no newspaper at all, but literally what its title indicated. The publication which it most nearly paralleled was *The Observator*, published by Tutchin, already referred to, whose connection with Monmouth's rebellion had led to a sentence so brutal by Jeffreys that he had begged for death as an alternative. The twice-weekly dialogues between "Observator" and "Countryman" represented a new form of imparting entertainment and information which appealed by its novelty to readers who liked their current literature in a simple question-and-answer form.

Tutchin's end was tragic. He had received many threats of violence from his political enemies; he defied them successfully until, in the autumn of 1707, he was attacked by a hired gang of ruffians and beaten up so terribly that he died of his injuries.

Charles Leslie, the die-hard Tory who edited *The Rehearsal*, was another enemy. De Foe, easily the wittiest, shrewdest hitter of them all, struck out blithely right and left, and enjoyed himself enormously. There were times when his prophecies proved fantastically mistaken—the heartening news of Ramillies arrived in London on the very day that his *Review* was announcing that any further victories would be in Spain. But his readers continued to believe in him.

The sales of the *Review* itself would appear absurdly limited by present standards. But each copy, circulating among the coffeehouse intelligentsia of the day, was read and re-read. (The paper reached a state of popularity which necessitated the reprinting of some of its articles as special editions). As De Foe wrote the whole paper himself, not only were the traditional difficulties common among owner, editor and contributor non-existent, but its style as well as its contents was a mirror of his own temperament, the result being that his articles tended to suggest that they had originally been written as sermons, while his attitude, irrespective of subject, combined a magnificent detachment with Christian humility, a blend which his enemies labelled insolence and found utterly infuriating. "He studies to provoke in the most affronting manner he can think of!" snarled one exasperated critic; "and then he cries 'Peace and Union, Gentlemen, and lay aside your heats!'"

The very title was something of a joke. De Foe had called his paper *A Review of the Affairs of France*, not from any particular interest in that country, but because, firstly, he wanted to emphasize the risks arising from English complacency and, secondly, he wanted an excuse to attack Louis and everything he stood for.

His supporters were permanently in a state of pleasurable suspense; they never knew what subject or what line of argument he was going to take up. Sententious and pontifical he might be at times, but he appealed to the social level he knew so intimately, that of the middle-class citizen, and the middle-class citizen and his family appreciated and trusted him. He told home truths with a Dissenter's uncompromising directness, one particular *bête noir* being the immorality of the London theatres.

The *Review* became the most-read journal in London. That it should have influenced later journals, the *Tatler*, the *Spectator*, is inevitable. And throughout its career, which ended in 1713, the contents of its eight volumes were the sole work of a single mind and a single pair of hands. Reporter, leader-writer, editor, business manager, De Foe was them all, while at the same time he was turning out a spate of pamphlets and books on every conceivable subject—the unmasking of Protestant Jesuits, a general History of Trade; a poem to the Duke of Marlborough, the grievances of the Scots; all written in the clearest, most cogent English; all briskly and good-humouredly conscientious and convincing.

But in spite of his journalistic popularity, De Foe's career at this time rather suggests a man staggering boldly but unhappily from one patch of quicksand to another, safety and tranquillity always a little beyond his attainment. Political enemies alone he could have dealt with, but it was another matter when his creditors joined them in an unfair and infernal coalition. In addition, there was always Harley to watch; the bland but inexorable employer whom he could never in any sense of the word afford to offend; Harley, whose velvet scabbard had an unforgettable sword of steel.

In May 1704 Harley had supplanted Nottingham as Secretary of State. The *Review* was then only three months old, an age at which one would have expected it to demand the entire energy and attention of its editor. Yet Harley had no hesitation in suggesting a further responsibility, nor De Foe in accepting it. It was work that, for the first time, justified his enemies' charges of spying. He was to make enquiries; to interview and report upon men of whom the Administration ought to beware. He was also to establish relationships with editors of papers opposed to the Government. Finally, he was given permission to act as an *agent provocateur*, to write articles attacking Harley, so dissipating suspicion, and paving the way to obtaining lists of those who were financing the opposition papers.

A bitter capitulation indeed for De Foe, the rigid Non-conformist who so easily might have become a Dissenting preacher! Yet something may be said in extenuation. Such infiltrations were a commonplace in the crude rough-and-tumble of seventeenth-century politics. He had already, in Dutch William's day, been branded as a spy, as one who ran with the fox and hunted with the hounds. The line between acting as a secret agent and a political organizer was at best a shadowy one. . . . And there was, always, in the background, the steady pressure of his creditors and the claims of a wife and family.

He had indeed no objection to carrying on these activities abroad; it is indeed probable that he would have preferred to. He had in anticipation already paid an unofficial visit of enquiry to Hanover. Alternatively, he was prepared to attach himself to Marlborough's staff in the Low Countries. As a reward for these extra risks, he suggested a place in the auditor's office. "Matters of Account," De Foe assured Harley, "are always my particular element."

But in spite of De Foe's hint, he was sent neither to Hanover nor to Holland, but remained in England, supported by an unofficial pension paid out of Harley's own pocket.

CHAPTER II

POLITICAL ORGANIZER

DE FOE'S circle of influential acquaintances widened. Among them were Godolphin, the Lord Treasurer, and later Lord Halifax. At rather long last—perhaps it was purely instinctive—De Foe seems to have realized the necessity of making himself useful to as many powerful people as possible. At the same time the old reckless De Foe who took risks and damned the consequences was still in existence; the veneer of caution and gentle speech his new job imposed was at times dangerously thin. He published, in April 1704, an attack on the Commons, *Legion's Humble Address to the Lords*, a single folio sheet. It did not give the author's name, but his enemies were good guessers. If Harley had not intervened, there is very little doubt that De Foe would have found himself in the pillory again.

In November 1704, De Foe fell foul of Sir Humphrey Mackworth, who was introducing a Bill which proposed "to establish in every parish a parochial state-aided factory in which the destitute poor should be employed".

The plan, plausible enough, and, indeed, unusually progressive for the period, exasperated De Foe, who was temperamentally a passionate individualist and from experience as an employer a firm opponent of any such interference by the State in the inexorable operation of the laws of supply and demand. He retaliated with one of those pamphlets which, collectively, have placed him among our earliest, if not necessarily greatest, economists. He laid down certain axioms: that there was in England more labour than hands to perform it; that there was a want of people, not of employment; that no man of sound limbs and sense need be poor for want of work; that all workhouses for employing the poor, as they then employed them, served merely to ruin families. If Sir Humphrey's plan were logically extended, wool (for example) would be manufactured in the place where it was sheared, the result being that "everybody will make their own clothes, and the trade which now lives by running through a multitude of hands will then go through so few that thousands of families will want employment".

Finally, De Foe emphasized, it was a regulation of the poor that was needed, not merely setting them to work, in other words, unemployment is a matter of social adjustment rather than of legislation. What we do need laws for, he says, is to make the people sober, industrious and thrifty. He particularly stresses sobriety:

"I once paid six or seven men together on a Saturday night, the least ten shillings, and some thirty shillings for work, and have seen them go with it directly to the alehouse, lie there till Monday, spend every penny and run into debt to boot, without giving a farthing to their families. From hence come poverty, parish charges and beggary."

If De Foe's arguments are not wholly sound and conclusive, the clear-cut English in which they are expressed is beyond criticism.

He remained in London throughout the winter, a very busy if not a very happy man. He published a second volume of the collected edition of his pamphlets, and in five weeks, February 22nd to March 27th, wrote half a dozen fresh ones, including another attack on the High-flyers in connection with the new Bill for the Prevention of Occasional Conformity, an alleged account of the Men in the Moon, and an elaboration of this called *The Consolidator, or Memories of Sunday Transactions translated from the Lunar*—an elaborate, rather heavy-handed satire which included Dryden and Swift among its victims. The whole conception is strongly akin to *Gullivers Travels*, which it is supposed to have inspired. There were yet further elaborations of the lunar theme; it is a valid charge against De Foe that, having hit upon an original idea, he was often too reluctant to abandon it.

A pamphlet concerning the treatment of a clergyman named Gill deserves mention. Gill had abandoned the use of the Liturgy but, for legitimate reasons too involved to be dealt with here, refused to surrender his living. The rector of his parish had, however, another cruder weapon. As a

Justice of the Peace, he charged Gill with being "an idle vagabond", and impressed him as a soldier. De Foe rushed to the rescue. The opposition retaliated by attacking Gill's private character, which appears to have been far from impeccable. And Gill proved himself unworthy of being championed; he made no attempt to vindicate himself.

On April 5th De Foe wrote the first of three letters to Lord Halifax.

Charles Montagu, the first Earl, was one of the great figures of the period. Aristocrat, poet and statesman, he has the double distinction of establishing, or helping to establish, both the Bank of England and the National Debt. He was Premier in 1697, out of office during Queen Anne's twelve-year reign, and an object of respect amounting to adulation among the contemporary intelligentsia, excluding those acidulous two—Pope and Swift.

But the chief interest in De Foe's letter of April 5th lies in its reference to his brother, who had brought a communication from Halifax.

"The proposal your Lordship was pleased to make by my brother, the bearer, is exceeding pleasant to me to perform. But my misfortune is that the bearer, whose head is not that way"—surely one of the most delicate insinuations of stupidity on record!—"has given me so imperfect an account that makes me your Lordship's most humble petitioner for some hints to ground my observations upon."

Later, De Foe offered to serve Halifax, and was paid by him, anonymously, a considerable amount of money for services rendered.

With a general election imminent, De Foe published on April 30th his *Advice to all Parties*—advice which had peace as its main theme, and was in essence a religious tract, if one excludes a typical slash in passing at Popery, concerning which he writes,

"Those who do not understand it hate it by tradition; and I believe there are a hundred thousand plain country fellows in England who would spend their blood against Popery, that do not know whether it be a man or a horse."

In June he left London on business which normally he would have found immensely congenial. He was making his début as a political organizer. But the trouble over *Legion's Address* delayed him, and it was not until August that, with Christopher Hurst, a custom-house employee and an old friend, as second-in-command, he began a tour of the Eastern Counties, his instructions from Harley being firstly to discover from the most typical and most influential people, principally in the largest towns, how public opinion was shaping; and, secondly, to do what he could in the way of tactful propaganda.

His enemies were, as ever, on his track. This time it was through no fault of De Foe's. An officer of the Guards called at his house soon after his departure, found the bird flown, and forthwith announced that he had come with a warrant to arrest De Foe, and he was to be taken at any price. Who was at the bottom of the plot is unknown, but Mrs. De Foe countered it by writing to her husband, and De Foe returned at once to refute the charge. He succeeded in settling the matter in a couple of days, and also dealt adequately with an obscure individual named Toke who had, on behalf of his Tory employees, challenged him to a duel. Once more he started, and had got as far as Bury St. Edmunds when he received a message from Harley that Sir George Rooke had ordered his arrest. Harley added, however, that De Foe had nothing to worry about, after which he was able to begin his tour through Suffolk and Essex in earnest.

He had plenty to do on Harley's behalf before the General Election. But he also had matters of his own to attend to. The *Review* was the most convenient weapon with which to attack his enemies: it had been so ever since its inception. In it he now found an opportunity of blazing forth as the indignant citizen upon whom the vilest trickery had been practised while travelling in the provinces upon his own honest business—a masterly example of the truth, but not the whole truth.

Incidentally, his enemies at about this time invented an additional exasperation. He had grown used to his works being pirated; now they inverted the process and attached his name to writings he had not even seen. In his *Elegy on the Author of the True-born Englishman* he wrote bitterly:

> "I bear the scandal of their crimes
> My name's the hackney title of the times.
> Hymn, song, lampoon, ballad and pasquinade
> My recent memory invade.
> My muse must be the whole of poetry
> And all Apollo's bastards laid to me!"

The Elections were held in the following spring. De Foe made Coventry his headquarters; its central position gave it certain advantages, but even more important was the fact that, for reasons persistent to this day, feelings there ran particularly high, the Tories being in the majority. The 1705 election there was scandalous beyond the conception of the staid and conscientious elector of to-day. The system of registration was incredibly lax and casual, and the High-flying magistrates complacently made it still more so. Only Hogarth could have done justice to the scenes before and after the Election. De Foe watched it all with a sardonic eye that missed nothing; he reported to Harley, emphasized Coventry's scandals as being symptomatic of all England's if the country fell under Tory domination, and blazed fiercely away in the *Review*.

Under additional financial pressure from the absent Mrs. De Foe, he obtained permission to continue the good work in the west.

With his friend Hurst he left London, galloping the first twenty miles of his journey. He had, incidentally, arranged to have his letters addressed to him as "Alexander Goldsmith".[1]

He reached Dorchester, where he received a shock at seeing an Anglican priest and a Nonconformist minister amiably drinking tea together. A little later began a series of unpleasant and unpredictable complications. He had arranged that certain friends should receive his correspondence and retain it until his arrival, and the friend at Weymouth happened to be a Captain Turner. But by the sheerest bad luck a selection of De Foe's letters were handed over to another Captain Turner, a sailor. He, opening these, was considerably alarmed as well as mystified by finding some of them in

---

[1] Wright assumes that De Foe actually made the journey alone, and that Christopher Hurt (*sic*) was merely the name under which he travelled.

cipher. Eventually the right Turner received them, and in due course De Foe.

The matter, however, did not end there. The Mayor of Weymouth saw the correspondence, and coming across a mention of a current rumour that the Queen had broken her Coronation oath—in what manner and on what occasion was unspecified—decided that his town had suddenly become the focus of a band of conspirators. He interviewed all those who had been in contact with De Foe, incontinently arrested them on a charge of planning "a phanatick plot and bloody design to persuade folks to a peaceable rebellion", whatever that may be, and brought them up before the judge at the Dorchester Assizes, then sitting.

The charges were all dismissed, and the over-officious Mayor properly snubbed. De Foe continued the journey to Exeter, his headquarters, unaware that the story of Weymouth had preceded him, and that dark hints were in circulation concerning a dangerous spy said to be roaming the countryside. He went on to Bideford; thence, in blazing summer weather, to Crediton, where he halted a few days. The Exeter Tories spread the news that the infamous De Foe had fled arrest. Hugh Stafford, a Crediton judge, issued a warrant for his arrest and sent to the house of the local minister, where De Foe was lodging, to put it into execution. He was too late, however; the wanted man was well on the way to Launceston. Stafford issued copies of the warrant broadcast, and at Bideford De Foe was actually brought before a judge. Once more, however, his enemies were unlucky; the judge was a personal friend and acted as his protector.

De Foe wrote bitterly to Harley. He was, he said with justice, being tracked from place to place like a wild beast. Furthermore, he was desperately short of money. Meanwhile, he continued to observe and record, and to distribute tracts in the interests of peace, his patron, Whiggery, and Dissent.

But "far other things" his heart still continued to prize. The tradesman, the speculator, the exploiter of chance opportunities, still remained in the foreground. At Dartmouth, for example, his restless eyes noted a shoal of small fish in the harbour, and he hurried to inform the fishermen, and later bought for three-halfpence enough fish to make a large meal. (One would have thought they might have given them to him for nothing.)

He went on to Plymouth, where on the night he arrived a terrific storm destroyed ten ships lately returned from Barbados with valuable cargoes. From Devonshire he left with little regret for Bath, which, for no particular reason except its smell, he appears to have liked even less. "It is more like a prison than a place of diversion," he wrote. At this stage Hurst had to return to London. Nevertheless, De Foe was not to continue his journey alone. Davis, his brother-in-law, had arranged to join him there. He filled in a few days of waiting by exploring the neighbourhood. Davis returned with appreciative greetings from Harley and, what was more to the point, further financial help.

Their journey home was pleasant, for Davis was a man with a sprightly and inventive mind, an ideal travelling companion. The route itself was varied. Instead of going straight to London, De Foe, probably influenced as much by the sunny perfection of the autumn weather and the dryness of the roads as by political considerations, turned eastward to make some further enquiries, and to discuss the situation with the Whig agents he had appointed.

He reached London on November 6th, 1705, after covering eleven hundred miles on horseback.

The trip had been an adventure after his own heart. Even his private affairs had benefited. He had had unique opportunities for publicizing the *Review*; he had also brought off a small but successful speculation in wool. But he was forty-five, and in his day a man of forty-five was elderly; his family, seen so intermittently, were growing up, and he wanted a rest.

A rest, in De Foe's case, meant only one thing, a safe and reasonably lucrative Government post. Yet though he was to live to be over seventy that ambition was never to be fulfilled. It was the one request that Harley, for all his appreciation, did not grant.

His enemies, now that he was in the arena again, intensified their attacks. Politics, like necessity, refuses to recognize any normal conventions. He was subjected to an extraordinary variety of assaults. Copies of the *Review* would be stolen from coffee-houses, or bought in bulk merely to be destroyed. His books were pirated. He received thirty letters threatening his life. To these he retorted sarcastically in the *Review*.

"The mean, despicable author of this paper is not worth your attempting his correction at any price; gaols, fetters and gibbets are odd, melancholy things; for a gentleman to dangle out of the world in a string has something so ugly, so awkward and so disagreeable about it, that you cannot think of it without some regret."

And he continued to move about unarmed, carrying only "a little stick, not strong enough to correct a dog".

Creditors, some of them in connection with debts of nearly twenty years' standing, some even unaware that they were being involved, were cited or persuaded to allow themselves to be cited in bringing forward impossible claims.

Harley, detached, kindly, smooth of tongue, ruthless when opposed, was his bulwark, his breakwater against the unceasing waves of malice. (Yet there must have been moments when he wondered whether De Foe was worth it.)

The winter passed. De Foe greeted the New Year (1706) with a *Hymn to Peace, Occasioned by the Two Houses giving an Address to the Queen*. It was the sort of thing he—and, one might add, any later rhymster in the Pope tradition—could turn out fluently and effectively, and for precisely that reason was soon, and rightly, forgotten.

". . . Storms of men" he wrote.
"Voracious and unsatisfied as death
  Spoil in their hands, and poison in their breath,
  With rage of devils, hunt me down,
  And to abet my peace, destroy their own."

The man's real genius displayed itself soon afterwards in an entirely different direction—*A True Revelation of the Apparition of one Mrs. Veal, the next day after her death, to one Mrs. Bargrave at Canterbury, the 8th of September 1705, which Apparition recommends the Perusal of Drelincourt's Book of Consolations against the Fears of Death*.

The history of that little volume has external interests which link themselves to practically all De Foe's more important works.

Mrs. Veal was for many years regarded as the supreme small-scale example of De Foe's capacity for blending facts with the sheerest inventions. But, as Dr. Sutherland points out, we now know that it is virtually a direct report of a supernatural experience which, on September 8th, 1705, a real Mrs. Bargrave of Canterbury did, according to her own account, really experience. De Foe, born reporter as he was, went down to get at the truth of the matter, and on returning to London recorded the story.

Over a century later Sir Walter Scott, admiring but entirely sceptical, put forward an explanation of the origin of *Mrs. Veal*.[1]

An enterprising bookseller had ventured to print a considerable edition of *The Christian's Defence against the Fear of Death*, a work by the Rev. Charles Drelincourt, minister of the Calvinist Church in Paris. The book, a complete failure, lay dead stock on the hands of the publishers. In this emergency, the bookseller applied to De Foe to assist him.

"De Foe's genius and audacity devised a plan which, for assurance and ingenuity, defied even the powers of 'Mr. Puff', in *The Critic*, for who but himself would have thought of summoning a ghost from the grave to bear witness in favour of a halting book of divinity.

"The effect was most wonderful. *Drelincourt on Death* took an unequalled run. The copies had hung on the bookseller's hands as heavy as lead bullets.[2] They now traversed the town in every direction, like the same.

In short, the object of Mrs. Veal's apparition was perfectly attained."

One might speculate indefinitely upon the probabilities of De Foe approaching Drelincourt's publisher or the publisher approaching De Foe, before the expedition to Canterbury was made. But the financial adjustments, if any, are hardly likely to have amounted to more than a few shillings. *Drelincourt On Death*, although maintaining its popularity, so curiously (or ingeniously) stimulated in 1706, until the end of the century, is now little more than a regular occupant of a dealer's sixpenny shelf. Mrs. Veal's apparition remains a classic example of how to invest the supernatural with complete credibility.

[1] See Vol. 6 of *The Miscellaneous Prose Works of Sir W. Scott*, 1887.
[2] This is nonsense. Sir Walter, had he taken the trouble, might have discovered that Drelincourt's book was already in its third edition.

CONCLUDING PAGE OF A LETTER DATED MAY 12TH, 1737
FROM DANIEL DE FOE JUNR. TO HIS COUSIN

De Foe begins with the statement that Mrs. Bargrave is an intimate friend whom he has known for twenty years; a woman of a very cheerful disposition, "notwithstanding the ill-usage of a very wicked husband". Mrs. Veal, on the other hand, was a maiden gentlewoman—the "Mrs." was an extra-legal compliment bestowed so commonly in the eighteenth century, and, indeed, much later—of about thirty years of age. She was handicapped by intermittent fits which caused her to "go off from her discourse to some impertinence", and was supported by a fond brother, who, incidentally, did his best to laugh the story of the apparition out of countenance.

The narrative itself is simple. At noon on that September day Mrs. Bargrave was sitting alone in her house, meditating on her hard lot, when there was a knock at the door. Entered Mrs. Veal, wearing, surprisingly enough, a riding habit. Mrs. Bargrave greeted her; they nearly kissed, but not quite. Mrs. Veal said that she was going on a journey, and added that she had given her brother the slip to pay the visit. After which they went into "another room within the first"; Mrs. Veal sat down in the elbow-chair her hostess had just vacated, and the two women chatted on various subjects, the comfort derived from the Rev. Mr. Drelincourt's book being among them. Other books were also mentioned, including some verses called *Friendship in Perfection*. Mrs. Bargrave had read them, and, as Mrs. Veal had not, she offered to lend the visitor a copy she had made. The conversation continued for nearly two hours. Towards the end Mrs. Veal said she intended to write to her brother, telling him how to dispose of her rings and certain sums of money. This statement had followed an enquiry: "Mrs. Bargrave, do you think I am mightily impaired by my fit?" Mrs. Bargrave had answered, in effect, "Not at all", but had nevertheless had an uneasy feeling that a fit might be coming on. She accordingly placed herself in a chair in front of Mrs. Veal to keep her from falling to the ground in case a fit did arrive, tactfully chatting as she did so about the beauty of Mrs. Veal's dress, which was of "scowered silk newly made up".

Soon after this Mrs. Veal made enquiries concerning Mrs. Bargrave's daughter. The girl was at a neighbour's, and Mrs. Bargrave got up and went to look for her. She came back to find her visitor already on the doorstep. The journey, said Mrs. Veal as she departed, would not begin until Monday; till then she was staying with her cousin, Captain Watson, and hoped to see Mrs. Bargrave there.

Monday arrived. Mrs. Bargrave, having heard nothing, sent a girl to the Captain's. But Mrs. Veal was not there; she had, in fact, died at the precise moment that her apparition had called on Mrs. Bargrave. De Foe concludes:

"The thing has very much affected me. . . . And why we cannot dispute matter of fact, because we cannot solve things of which we have no certain or demonstrative notions, seems strange to me. Mrs. Bargrave's authority and sincerity alone would have been undoubted in any other case."

So much for the story. And a very good story it was— and is.

How much De Foe made out of it, apart from any contribution from Drelincourt's publisher, is unknown; his payment for an ordinary pamphlet of similar length was rarely more than a couple of guineas.

In July De Foe published *Jure Divino*, a satirical poem upon which he had been working intermittently ever since his release from Newgate. It ran to ten thousand verses and filled three hundred and fifty folio pages; it satirized the theory of the Divine Right of Kings, glorified Marlborough and some of the Whig politicians, and increased the detestation with which De Foe's enemies regarded him. He himself regarded *Jure Divino* as something of a masterpiece; posterity has unhesitatingly labelled it doggerel and consigned it to oblivion. Its chief interest to-day is the light its publication throws upon the rascality of seventeenth-century publishers. Benjamin Bragg had been responsible for the production not only of *Mrs. Veal* but of *The Consolidator* and *The Experiment* in 1705. Now, bribing a dishonest printer, he accumulated sheets enough to bring out a competitive edition at five shillings at the same time that De Foe's copy, with his portrait as frontispiece, appeared at twelve shillings.

It was an act of gross treachery which Bragg, when charged, met with the defiant statement that no one had a right to publish anything except through a bookseller, and that as a matter of principle he would continue to pirate any works not so published.

Poetic justice, however, followed. De Foe lost none of his original subscribers, while lesser pirates printed off copies which they sold at a halfpenny a section—there were twelve in all—with a further offer to stitch these together for an extra sixpence.

CALEDONIAN INTERLUDE

THERE was urgent work of a different nature awaiting him. The Union of England and Scotland, Dutch William's ambition, came up for reconsideration, and English commissions were sent north to investigate and report. Harley decided to send De Foe unofficially to Scotland with the same object.

He left early in September 1706 with a glow in his heart, for before his departure he had been given the honour of kissing the Queen's hand and the assurance that, if he managed the business successfully, he would receive a permanent Government pension. His connection with Harley was becoming steadily more intimate; its roots were going deeper and deeper. One has only to study the instructions under which he acted during this tour to realize that his work combined the tactful diplomacy of an ambassador, the persuasiveness of a political orator, and the subtlety of a trained secret-service agent—all in the person of one who ostensibly was an honest, patriotic, simpleminded Englishman travelling north on purely private business.

No role could have suited De Foe better. There was, however, just one small modification he would have appreciated. His expenses were to be paid out of Harley's private purse. He would have been happier if they had been met by the Government.

He started out in early September on what was to prove one of the most complicated and interesting tours of his life. Indulging in that lifelong passion for fine clothes which was one of his incongruous characteristics, he dressed himself as a gentleman of position, and let it be known that he was travelling to Scotland merely on a matter of private business. He reverted to his previous alias of Goldsmith, and took a confusingly indirect route.

He arrived at Newcastle, *via* Nottingham, on the thirtieth, and went straight to John Bell, the postmaster. This visit was vitally important. Harley had arranged for Bell to supply De Foe not only with funds but with the equally essential horses. Actually one of the two horses had an accident, and he was compelled to linger in Bell's society for several days until another was bought. In that time the postmaster somehow found out who "Goldsmith" really was. It must have been one of the most thrilling discoveries of his life.

Mid-October saw De Foe in Edinburgh.

He did not like the Scots; he never pretended to like them. (It would be almost safe to say that he was too English to like anyone who was not.) He called them "a hardened, refractory, terrible people", and "a fermented and implacable nation", and emphasized the insult by maintaining an attitude of cool and kindly condescension. He even went further, and wrote a poem in praise of the country (though not of its inhabitants)—a "panegyrick" which must have been in the nature of a last straw.

Once arrived in Scotland, he decided to abandon "Alexander Goldsmith" and to revert frankly to his own name. But there the frankness ended. He assumed the role of a gentleman with capital to invest, the investment varying with his mood and his company. He intended to build ships. He intended, in partnership with an unnamed peer, to start a glass factory. He intended to develop salt-mines. He intended simply to buy an estate upon which he could settle with his wife and seven children. . . . He produced other programmes calculated to impress other credulous people in other cities; in Glasgow he became a fish merchant; in Aberdeen a wool merchant; in Perth a draper. No doubt there were moments during these discussions when he found himself skating over very thin ice indeed. But experience had given De Foe a singularly wide range of commercial knowledge. And he had always been an expert skater.

There were two parties in the north, implacably and eternally in opposition—the Clans, who were furiously opposed to any kind of Union and any terms of peace whatever with the country which had hustled their own royal countryman from the throne, and the Presbyterians, who were blood-brothers in religion to De Foe himself. Of the innumerable Highlanders who had invaded Edinburgh De Foe wrote:

"They are formidable fellows, and I only wish Her Majesty had 25,000 of them in Spain. . . . They are all gentlemen and insolent to the last degree. But certainly the absurdity is ridiculous to see a man in his mountain habit, armed with a broad sword, target, pistol, or perhaps two, at his girdle a dagger, and a staff, walking down the street as upright and haughty as if he were a lord . . . and withal driving a cow!"

The Chief of the English commission was the Duke of Queensberry, with whom, in the course of his work on behalf of the English Government, De Foe was bound sooner or later to come into official contact. That such contact was unofficial as well is rather pathetically indicated by his sale to the Duke in April 1707 of four volumes of his works and a "consol"[1] for two pounds twelve shillings. The bill for these items, in the handwriting of De Foe and bearing his signature, the Duke's, and that of Mr. Alves, who appears to have been the intermediary, is now in the possession of Mr. Alexander Leslie, of Glasgow.

The weeks slipped past. Edinburgh seethed with excited partisans. The Duke of Queensberry was execrated by mobs whose patriotism was further stimulated by the slogans and free gins of agitators. They hurled, according to De Foe, "stones, dirt and curses" at his Grace who was, however, luckier than Sir Patrick Johnson, another Unionist, whose house they attacked with sledgehammers.

On the opposite side was the Duke of Hamilton, whose coach was followed with blessings and prayers.

De Foe viewed these demonstrations with his usual ironic detachment. Detachment, however, did not save him. On the last day of October the violence of the mob reached a climax. He had been kept in his room with a cold and had been further advised to stay there. Sheer curiosity overcame his judgment. He called a coach, and, his cold notwithstanding, set out to visit a friend and find out what was happening.

[1] Defined in a dictionary of 1706 by Phillips (a nephew of Milton) as " A Kind of Bracket or Shouldering-piece that juts out and serves to support a cornice, or to bear up figures, Busts, Vessels and other Ornaments of a like Nature ".

He was recognized as "an English dog" and followed. He was lucky enough to reach the friend's house in safety, and sensible enough to stay there until darkness fell, before returning eventually to his room. The crowd tracked him there, but mistook the floor on which he was lodging, and the "great stone" they hurled smashed the wrong windows— those, in fact, of an entirely unoffending Scot.

Eventually the situation became so serious that the Lord Provost had to call out a battalion of the Guards. "And so," says De Foe, relating the events of this highly exciting evening to Harley, "the tumult ended."

Not so his personal perplexities, however. The pose of an amiable southerner looking out for investments in glass factories or salt works could not be sustained indefinitely: he had to invent new reasons for the length of his visit. Such improvizations were his forte; to quote Professor Sutherland: "De Foe's lies were generally successful because they were plausible; and they were plausible because he half believed in them himself."

To which might be added, "and because he told them with such whole-hearted enthusiasm".

He announced that he was writing a History of the Union, and was busy, as every good historian should be, in verifying his references. On another occasion he explained that he was writing a new and original version of the Psalms, a feat which would require at least a couple of years' immolation in college. He also mentioned a mythical weaving factory he proposed to establish. Those were his dignified and gentlemanly excuses for dallying; what was less gentlemanly —but far nearer the truth—was his story that he was an undischarged bankrupt seeking sanctuary from his creditors in Scotland. The last invention had, at any rate, this advantage; shrewd Scotsmen found it easy to believe. It was impossible to imagine a southerner confessing to such a story unless it were true.

Basking in the sunshine of comparative affluence, he was in no hurry to end all these complicated deceptions. Yet now and again there were shadows. One fell across his path at the end of November, when he heard from his wife saying that she had received no money whatever from Harley for the last ten days. (The urgency of her letter throws a curious light on the narrow financial margin of the De Foe family.)

De Foe at once wrote to Harley, who apologized and put the matter right.

In the following month De Foe's father died.

One would have liked to know the emotional relationship between old James Foe, tallow-chandler, butcher, and member of the Butchers' Company, staunch and uncompromising Dissenter, and model citizen and husband and parent, and his brilliant, unpredictable son during those later years. James was seventy-six when he died; the convulsions of the Restoration and the nightmares of the Plague and the Fire had become history. His horizon, one suspects, had narrowed, as old men's horizons do, to the little world of his children and grandchildren; Sidney Smith's exhortation to "take short views of life" is as sound for old age as it is for depression.

For some years he had been living in Throgmorton Street, but for the last three had lodged at "The Bell" in Broad Street near by.

In his will, executed on March 20th, 1705, and in which Daniel was appointed sole executor, James Foe set out his injunctions in considerable detail. His funeral was not to cost more than twenty pounds. To his granddaughter Elizabeth he left another twenty pounds; to a Mr. John Marsh yet another. To his cousin, John Richards, he left the money the said John Richards owed him before November 1st, 1704. His grandson, Benjamin Foe, received a gold watch, a second grandson, Francis Bartham, a silver one. A granddaughter, Ann Davis, was left a bed, a chest of drawers, and other furniture. A hundred pounds went to his grandson, Daniel De Foe junior, when he came of age. The rest of his estate went to the five sisters of this grandson, to be divided among them by their father, the executor.

There was a final significant clause which specified that if the executor or his wife should by any accident stand in need of any part of the legacy for "the subsidence, education or clothing of the said children", then De Foe or his wife might make use of it for such purposes, and the money be regarded as being part of the legacy.

It is surmised that somewhere about this time Daniel, De Foe's eldest son, married. Of his wife, nothing is known beyond the fact that her name was Dorothy, that she bore a son, the third Daniel of his line, and died before 1720.

De Foe received news of the old man's death on Christmas Eve. He did not—he could not—return for the funeral: there was far too much still to be done in Scotland.

Throughout the time he spent there he worked with an energy that seemed inexhaustible, though actually he was to pay heavily later on. He wrote Harley innumerable letters, formal and informal, advisory and cautionary, as well as reporting everything worth reporting. If Harley had a corps of lesser spies, as he undoubtedly had, who kept watching eyes on the movements of the super-spy, De Foe, too, had his satellites. "'Tis the easiest thing in the world," he wrote cheerfully, "to hire people here to betray their friends," and compares his role to that of Cardinal Richelieu.

In addition to all this, he was steadily churning out pamphlets supporting the Union and anything else that happened to appear of importance, and finally keeping the *Review* supplied with copy.

"It does not seem to have occurred to De Foe," writes Mr. Edmund Blunden in *Votive Tablets*, "that he was an extraordinarily busy man." Mr. Blunden errs; it did occur to him.

In a letter to Harley dated February 2nd, 1707, he wrote:

"Denying yourself regular and needful hours of rest will disorder the best constitution in the world. I speak from my own immediate experiences who, having despised sleep, hours and rules, have broken in upon a perfectly established health, which no distresses, disasters, jails, or melancholy could ever hurt before."

His work in Scotland continued. The first, and most vital Article in the Union was carried by a majority of thirty-three votes out of a total of one hundred and ninety-nine, the date being, as he noted, the anniversary of William's landing, November 4th. Anyone imagining, however, that this happy coincidence would lead to an armistice between De Foe and his enemies would imagine a vain thing. He fell foul of the Reverend James Webster of the Tolbooth Church who, at first supporting the Union, ended by attacking both it and the English Dissenters in general. In that January of 1707 De Foe retaliated with what he termed "the utmost tenderness and civility", which was nevertheless sufficiently infuriating to drive Mr. Webster to a fiery reply. De Foe hit back with *A Short View of the Present State of the Protestant Religion.*

After which he wrote, doubtless with his satirical tongue in his cheek, *Caledonia: a Poem in Honour of Scotland.*

The Act of Ratification was passed on January 18th, and on March 6th the Queen gave her formal assent to the Union. The news reached Edinburgh four days later. De Foe took advantage of the general goodwill and congratulations to put in a personal plea to Harley:

"While I write this, the guns are firing from the Castle, and my man brings me up the Queen's speech. Now let me depart from hence, for mine eyes have seen the conclusion . . ."

Then, contradicting himself, he adds:

"I confess I believe I might be serviceable here a long time hence. But everybody is gone up to solicit their own fortunes, and some to be rewarded for what I have done—while I, who am depending on your concern for me and Her Majesty's goodness am wholly unsolicitous in that affair."

In point of fact, the early months of 1707 found him in one of those oases of general good luck all too rare in his life. He was mixing with the aristocrats and holding his own among the wittiest. The Duke of Queensberry entertained him at Drumlanrig Castle; he met Lord Buchan, Lord Belhaven—the latter an opponent of the Union—and other distinguished people. He was writing regularly for the *Review.* All was going so merrily that he even meditated upon settling permanently in Scotland. His enthusiasm for the country threatened at times to make him the one thing it is impossible to imagine De Foe becoming—a bore. "The fellow can talk of nothing but the Union," complained a friend, "and has grown mighty dull of late."

In February he attacked Lord Haversham, an old opponent, who had ungratefully cast slurs on the memory of William. De Foe compared the ingrate to dogs that bay the moon. "But the beauteous planet shines on," he wrote scathingly, "and suffers no eclipse from their rage."

But not all his literary activities were truculent. He found time to give shrewd advice to the Scots concerning their coal trade, their linen trade and their salt trade.

A week after the Treaty rejoicings had ended De Foe wrote again to Harley.

If he was becoming a trifle uneasy over his future, he did not say so; the ostensible reason for writing was merely to mention a bargain in claret that he had come across. Would Harley like to take advantage of the opportunity? Harley remained silent. De Foe could only accept the snub, and, probably sensing that affairs beyond his power to influence were happening in London, loyally set out from Edinburgh to visit other Scottish cities in which the advantage of the Union might still remain unappreciated.

As always when travelling, he found endless things to interest him. He studied the peasants—their habits, their work and their recreations, especially horse-racing. (Did he ever recall those Newmarket days, long past, when he watched the saturnine Charles and Monmouth, his ill-starred son, make their bets there?) The Highlands he left unvisited; mountain-climbing and the hardships involved had no attraction for him.[1]

But no diversions could drug his anxiety about the future. He wrote again and again to Harley who, to be just, was doing his best, though his own political life was ending. He was actually in negotiation with Godolphin with a view to rewarding De Foe with a Government appointment. And Godolphin had intimated that he was trying to secure De Foe's appointment as one of the new Custom House officers who would be needed for Scotland—an appropriate and probably congenial reward.

Literary history might have had to be differently written if De Foe had been rewarded with the post. Unfortunately a third party, Lowndes, Secretary to the Treasury, was involved. Godolphin believed that if Harley personally recommended De Foe, Lowndes might concur, and at this point Harley's fatal half-heartedness wrecked the scheme. He may have done something about it, but there is no evidence that he did very much. He had his own political worries, apart from which he must have realized the consequences of keeping so useful and so faithful a servant under his own thumb. . . . De Foe's letters, growing more and more anxious, remained unanswered.

[1] See page 79.

On July 19th De Foe bitterly records that he regards himself as totally forgotten. Might he not, at any rate, return to London?

Still silence.

On September 11th he wrote again, saying that he was now desperate and penniless. The letter is a pathetic document.

"While you supplied me. . . . I baulked no cases, I appeared in print when others dared not open their mouths, and without boasting, I ran as much risk of my life as a grenadier storming a counterscarp."

Harley may have judged it expedient to make no move at this point; it is even possible that he was genuinely touched. He replied in a letter which enclosed one from Godolphin. He was to receive "full satisfaction". This did not materialize, however, until the end of November, and took the form of a bill for one hundred pounds.

De Foe, elated, prepared to set out on his return journey. He did not leave immediately. He was still in Scotland in the middle of December, and he did not reach London again until the last day of the year. It was fifteen months since he had seen his family. But he belonged to the not very rare type of man who, while prepared to acknowledge the admirable qualities of his wife, and be genuinely proud of his offspring, finds other, less permanent features of his life more interesting. There was both money and time at his disposal; there were interesting spots to linger over en route, and he had any additional excuse he needed in the shortness of the days and the dangerous conditions of the roads.

The fact that his enemies were awaiting him would have been no deterrent. He attacked them, as nowadays he habitually attacked them, in the *Review*. He plunged into an orgy of recrimination and defiance; of charges and counter-charges. (He was accused, among other crimes, of knocking down a peasant girl, and cutting off her hair to make himself a wig.) He attacked Tyranny, Ignorance and Intolerance, none of whom could hit back; he also attacked the King of Sweden (Charles XII) for remaining inactive when his army might have turned the scale in Europe in favour of the Allies, and as a result narrowly escaped arrest on the complaints of the Lord Chief Justice and the ambassadors of Sweden and Muscovy.

Harley came to the rescue again and saved him.

The two following letters,[1] published for the first time, throw into pathetic vividness De Foe's circumstances at this period.

Tuesday night.

Sir

I have yours of the 8th Instant in which you desire a Meeting with me to Advise &c. on something you have to propose.

You can not take it ill, Sir. That being wholly a stranger to you And My Self a Person Not without Enemys, I make Some little stipulation before hand, after which I shall show all readyness to give you The best advice or assistance I can.

If, Sir, you please to Communicate in writing Anything of the business you Design to propose to me, by which I may judge whether I am able to render you any Service or noe.

Or if you please to Call as you Come to the Exchange at Waits Coffee House in Bell yard in Grace Church street and let the Mistress of the House know when and where you would meet, and but in the least give a knowledge of your Person, I will wait on you as you shall direct.

You will excuse my being thus Cautious, for which I shall give you very sufficient reasons when I see you.

Interim I am Sir,
your most Humble Servant
De Foe

(Addressed)
To

Mr. Tho. Bowrey
In Marine Square Near
Goodmans Fields

Sir

I wrott you a line Or Two last week in Answer to yours, and being wholly a stranger to you. Desired a Word or Two of your affair.

But I am so Well Satisfyed Since in your Character, That Hearing you have been Indisposed, I give you This trouble to let you kno' I shall be very ready to meet you where you please, in Order to do you Any Service I am Capable of—and if your Illness Continues So as to Make your Comeing Abroad Incon-

[1] From typescript copies in the Guildhall Library Muniment Room. MS. 3041/3.

venient, Tho' I have not a great Deal of Time to Spare, yet rather Than your business you have to propose should suffer by Delay, Il make no Difficulty to Wait on you at your House.

I am

Newington March 14. 1708   Sir

Your Very Humble Servant

DE FOE

CHAPTER IV

GODOLPHIN; SACHEVERELL; HARLEY RESURGENT

THEN, a bolt from a clear sky, fell utter disaster, disaster for which he had no responsibility whatever.

Harley, the eternal intriguer, had been over-subtle—or perhaps not subtle enough?—in stirring up differences among the members of his own party, the Whigs, and simultaneously dallying with the Opposition. He was at loggerheads with the Duke of Marlborough, whose influence over the obstinate, weak, stupid Anne was still considerable, in spite of the fact that his wife had been replaced by Abigail Masham, Harley's cousin and intimate friend. But it was not these things that wrecked his career. The Fates suddenly flung an unpredictable weight in the scales against him.

Harley's carelessness concerning private documents had given his private secretary opportunities to enter into treasonable correspondence with the French king. He was detected; on January 19th he was charged and tried, and subsequently executed. The repercussions of the scandal paralysed Harley's immediate future. Anne, under Marlborough's relentless pressure, could no longer give the Secretary of State her support. And without that his position had become impossible.

He resigned. And De Foe? Under the first shock, he assumed that his own humbler ambitions would be utterly frustrated. But he was unduly pessimistic. He assured Harley that he would never desert one to whom he owed so much; Harley replied, feelingly but a trifle vaguely, that Godolphin would employ him; "but what is for the public service and agreeably to your sentiments of things". He reminded him that it was actually the Queen whom he was serving, and concluded: "Pray apply yourself as you used to do . . . I shall not take it ill from you in the least."

In such words, to quote Professor Sutherland, a bankrupt magnate might dismiss a valet whom he could no longer afford to keep. De Foe, incidentally, was no longer socially comparable to a valet. In 1706 he had formally applied to the College of Heralds for permission to bear arms. Permission was granted; the arms emblazoned—Per chevron engrailed, gules and or, three Griffins passant, countercharged. The motto he chose, as already mentioned, was "Laudatur et alget". The name Foe was now legally and finally De Foe, and its owner finally and legally a gentleman.

Genius is always prone to exhibit strange and inexplicable facets. De Foe, greatest of all English journalists, shared with Shakespeare, greatest of all dramatists, the same passion for social recognition. In De Foe's case two motives, other than snobbery, may, singly or together, have moved him—a desire to be able to face in equal terms the aristocrats whom he met often in coffee-houses and other haunts of the intelligentsia; an appreciation of the fact that, to one who had suffered two bankruptcies, the pillory, and Newgate, a newly granted coat of arms would serve as a certificate of complete rehabilitation. As for the future, well, a man of spirit and adaptability can always afford to take risks.

He followed Harley's advice. As a result, the twin shadows of unemployment and poverty—he dreaded one as much as the other—were simultaneously lifted. It was now the turn of the Lord Treasurer, "Little Godolphin", to take charge of his fortunes. De Foe was reintroduced to the Queen, and again kissed hands, and was assured of "the continuance of an appointment Her Majesty had been pleased to make him in consideration of a former service he had done".

After which ceremony Godolphin, engineering a private conversation with De Foe, broke the news that he was being sent on another expedition to Scotland.

This time the object was different, and even more secret.

It had become known that a French fleet, under Admiral de Fourbin, was assembling at Dunkirk. It was feared that its object was to support an invasion of Scotland by the Pretender, these fears being reinforced by a notable increase of Jacobite activity.

De Foe was to investigate and report.

Godolphin was a small, timid, taciturn man, with the

qualities of a first-grade civil servant; industrious, honest and possessing a touch of genius—his only touch—where finance concerned. Our wittiest Stuart commented that Godolphin was "never in the way and never out of the way". His most human quality was a love of horse-racing. Within limitations, he liked and trusted De Foe who, in turn, respected, without admiring, his new master.

De Foe duly set out, his companion on this occasion again being Davis. The two reached Coventry; there Davis's horse developed a limp, and another was hired from a man named Mayo. Davis rode on this animal as far as Scotland, and, having decided to keep it, forwarded what he considered adequate money in payment. The horse-owner demanded more; eventually an agreement was reached. Three years later a pamphlet was issued called *The Hue and Cry after Daniel De Foe and his Coventry Beast*, accusing De Foe of "borrowing" the horse and conveniently forgetting to pay for it.

It was a preposterous jumble of lies and truth—De Foe in any case had nothing to do with the matter—and no later denials entirely obliterated the harm it did to his reputation.

In Edinburgh again in mid-February De Foe reported from time to time to Godolphin and the Earl of Sunderland. There was a brief, doubtless nostalgic, reversion to the old William and Mary days when the Duke of Queensberry invited him to Drumlanrig and there consulted him about improving the gardens. He also discovered traces of old lead-mining activities in the surrounding hills, and suggested developing them.

His more serious diversions included listening to a sermon which lasted for seven hours, and a trip to a dangerous pass.

The French fleet discreetly put back to port; the risks of invasion faded, and by the end of the year De Foe was able to return to England, home and—literally—beauty, for all his three unmarried daughters had developed into charming and accomplished young women. The family settled in a comfortable detached house at Stoke Newington, then a pleasant little country town, and not an overcrowded London dormitory.[1]

His next job was a tribute to his versatility. It concerned the arrival in England, and subsequent distribution of,

[1] See page 269.

between two and three thousand Palatines whose country had been ravaged by the armies of Louis XIV, and who had escaped to England. A number of these eighteenth-century "displaced persons" had, been settled in tents in the neighbourhood of Stoke Newington; probably their propinquity to De Foe suggested to the Government that he might find a solution. He did. He worked out a detailed plan for conveying them to the New Forest, and there letting them construct a satellite town of their own. (One is struck, again and again, by the extraordinary modernity of his approach to such matters.) But other matters claimed departmental attention, and the plan remained in the blueprint stage.

In August he was sent to Scotland again, his third visit, and remained there five months. As always, he found more than enough to interest him—the development of British trade, the value of the Firth of Forth as a war-base, the possibilities of the Highlands, the people themselves.

At the beginning of February 1710 he received news which sent him returning post-haste to London. Doctor Sacheverell was on the warpath again.

The two men were old and bitter enemies.

Henry Sacheverell, M.A. at twenty-one, Doctor of Divinity at thirty-four, was born in 1674. He combined, as De Foe combined, political and religious views in one emphatic whole, being a Tory High-flyer, as certain of the rightness of his views as De Foe, Whig Dissenter, was of his. Low churchmen and his political enemies he abused with equal violence, though his sledge-hammer methods lacked the good-humoured reasonableness of De Foe, whom he was genuinely earnest to convince. Furthermore, he had no sense of humour.

From De Foe's point of view, he was Enemy Number One and he attacked him in his *Shortest Way with Dissenters* and *Hymn from the Pillory*.

On August 15th Sacheverell preached an inflammatory assize sermon at Derby, and later published it: on November 5th he preached another, at St. Paul's, in the presence of Garrad, the Lord Mayor and the Aldermen, on "The perils of false brethren in the Church and State", in even more heated language, insomuch as it accused the Whig ministers as false friends and enemies of the Church, and referred to them as "wily volpones" (Godolphin's nickname was "The Fox").

A suggestion was made that the sermon should be officially published. The aldermen, very sensibly, turned down the proposal. But Sacheverell himself published it with a dedication, strongly suspected of being by permission, to the Lord Mayor.

Both Houses of Parliament were shocked, especially as only a month earlier they had passed a joint resolution to the effect that the Church was in a flourishing condition, and that saying otherwise was to exhibit oneself as an enemy to the Queen, the Church, and the Kingdom. On December 14th Sacheverell, in company with Clements, his printer, answered a summons to appear at the bar of the House of Commons in connection with "malicious, scandalous and seditious libels, highly reflecting upon Her Majesty and Her Government, the late happy Revolution and the Protestant Succession". Clements was let off. Sacheverell was impeached and remained in custody.

The impeachment was a far from unanimous affair, the voting being two hundred and thirty-two to one hundred and thirty-one. Godolphin voted with the majority, Harley with the minority. Later, Sacheverell was released on bail.

What followed between then and his trial, which lasted over a fortnight, forms a remarkable example of the reactions of public opinion. Excitement rose to a tremendous pitch; in the eyes of the mob the fiery doctor had suddenly become elevated to a public hero. Forty thousand copies of the St. Paul's sermon were sold. Prayers were desired for him in many London churches. Crowds stood for hours in front of his house, cheering and demanding his appearance. And when, on February 27th, the trial began, he was escorted by delirious crowds, yelling their good wishes and trying to grasp his hands. Elsewhere they demonstrated their devotion to him and the Established Religion by wrecking Dissenters' meeting-houses and singing appropriate songs. The Queen herself was involved, for on her way to hear privately the course of the trial, her coach was held up to a chorus of "God bless your Majesty and the Church. We hope your Majesty is for Doctor Sacheverell."

On March 22nd Sacheverell was found guilty by sixty-nine votes to fifty-two and suspended from preaching for three years.

The mob regarded this as a nominal sentence, and as practically equivalent to an acquittal. They rioted afresh accordingly.

What part had De Foe in all this?

A good deal. He used the pages of his *Review* to attack, with all the ridicule at his command, the country's new idol. Sacheverell's popularity, he insisted, was maintained only by the infatuation of a crowd of silly women, who

" Lay aside their tea and chocolate . . . and forming themselves into cabals, turn Privy Councillors, and settle the affairs of State. Having caught the contagion, they have little leisure to live, little time to eat and sleep, and none at all to pray. Even little girls and boys talk politics, Little Miss has Dr. Sacheverell's picture put into her prayer book, that God and the Doctor may take her up in the morning before breakfast. Tattling nonsense and slander is transferred to the males, and adjourned from the toilet to the coffee-houses and groom-porters . . . This new invasion of the politician's province is an eminent demonstration of the sympathetic influence of the clergy upon the sex, and the near affinity between the gown and the petticoat. . . . As soon as you punch the parson, he holds out his hand to the ladies for assistance, and they appear as one woman in his defence."

This was straightforward enough, though one can imagine it resulting in a fairly lively libel action if it had appeared in any public journal to-day. So, too, was his statement that the Doctor supported the Pope and the Devil, the two being practically synonymous in De Foe's vocabulary. But he followed up this attack by writing a letter to General Stanhope, a member of the Committee of Impeachment, in which he gave a list of boon companions who not only had drunk to excess with Sacheverell, but who swore to having seen him, kneeling, drink the Pretender's health, and heard him speak scandalously of Her Majesty.

He was running considerable risks, and must have known it, but balanced them against his rising popularity and success as a journalist. As well as his contributions to the *Review*, which he was steadily developing into an organ of first class importance—it now appeared three times a week, with a special edition for Scotland and a circulation extending to Ireland—he wrote various tracts, scathing or persuasive, but in either case as plausible as only he could make them. He also acquired *The Edinburgh Courant* and, of far-reaching importance, came to terms with Dyer, his old opponent of Shoe Lane.

Dyer might be termed De Foe's opposite number in the Tory ranks. He ran a newspaper which had the unique quality of having the contents of a single issue varied according to the type of person the editor considered likely to read it. De Foe suggested "a fair truce of honour", which truce consisted in each refraining from mentioning the other by name, whatever the political views expressed. Dyer agreed.

But De Foe's other enemies, encouraged by the fact that the tide was now flowing strong strongly in their favour, were less accommodating.

There was one matter concerning which he found himself in something of a cleft stick, and that was the conflict with France, which still dragged on. He realized, with a far-sightedness that went beyond his own century, and, indeed, later ones, that any war which not only brought the victor success but left the conquered state ruined, starving, and with nothing left to lose, was, from the practical economist's point of view, suicidal, and would in effect merely substitute one national tyranny for another. In the early part of 1710 the Allies, with the French at their mercy, made demands which Louis, for all his desire for peace, could not possibly accept.

Yet at that time De Foe had been supporting the Whigs in their refusal to make peace on anything like equitable terms —a policy the Tories endorsed.

Apart from Sacheverell's mob appeal and the old arguments for and against High Church or Nonconformity, the general unpopularity of the Whig party among all classes from the Queen downwards was such that nothing De Foe could write or say was likely to produce any real effect.

Hence, when the Sacheverell verdict was known, he found himself needing plenty of physical as well as moral courage. Both the Jacobites and the High-flyers unleashed their fury against their arch-enemy. They not only tried to kill the *Review*, they tried to kill its owner. Morphew, the printer, threw up his job in terror; another man named Baker replaced him. De Foe himself received fifteen letters threatening him with death. He gives an account of how he once entered a room occupied by five would-be assassins, who, however, turned cowards in the face of his daring. Three times he was actually attacked. He openly announced that he wore chain-mail under his coat when he walked abroad. But only during the hours of daylight. After dark he did not go out at all. He must have recalled the time when poor John Tutchin met his death under the blows of murderers' cudgels.

Sunderland, Marlborough's son-in-law, was dismissed. "Little Godolphin" followed him into the wilderness. Harley and his friends found themselves tasting power and office afresh. De Foe, his own party discredited, but his old friend—now definitely a Tory, though a lukewarm one with elastic principles—once again his patron, had to trim his sails to meet the new situation.

The switch-over occurred in the summer of 1710. Sunderland's fall had occurred in June. De Foe, apart from politics, had been worried because of the irregularity with which his salary had been paid, though in justice to Godolphin he did eventually receive what was owing. On July 17th De Foe had an interview with Harley. Details of what passed between the two men is guesswork, but the result was De Foe's re-employment. On August 8th Godolphin was ordered to resign, and did so. De Foe presented himself to the ex-Lord Treasurer to discuss the question of his own future. One biographer[1] stigmatizes this as "effrontery". The epithet seems to me altogether too severe; the action appears both tactful and politic. Godolphin reminded him, as Harley had done when he had fallen, that De Foe was the servant not of an individual but of the Government—any Government—under the Queen.

It seems incredible nowadays that this sweeping change in the high Ministers of State should have been made entirely by the sovereign, with no reference whatever to the people, and that the country should find itself governed by a predominantly Tory Cabinet with a predominantly Whig House of Commons. But Anne was suddenly exhibiting a belated independence allied to her native obstinacy, highly disconcerting to her intimates, including the dominating Marlboroughs, with whom she violently and finally quarrelled.

The office of Lord Treasurer remained for a time unfilled.

[1] Dottin.

Harley was appointed Chancellor of the Exchequer. De Foe wrote congratulating him. It was always with regret, he said, that he found himself obliged by circumstances to continue in the service of enemies—an interesting example of De Foe's sense of realism, since on at least three occasions he had been formally assured that he was in the service of only the Queen and the Queen's Government.

His attitude at this period is not difficult to understand; what is more difficult is to assess its genuineness. On the whole, one may agree with Professor Sutherland that he conducted his political life as if he were a permanent civil servant, at the same time reserving the right to side with whichever party suited his convenience. His political morals were, in point of fact, no better and no worse than a hundred other journalistic handymen of his time; it was merely that his eminence in his particular role made him more notorious, and, as such, more subjected to censure. By modern standards many of De Foe's chameleon-like changes may appear ignominious and indefensible. But he had always, as a final justification, the support of his wife and children at Stoke Newington to consider.

Harley's reply to his congratulations were thoroughly satisfactory; De Foe's services would again be brought to Her Majesty's notice. And his pension was safe. Whereupon De Foe, seizing the opportunity, referred to his secret bureau of political information, which was, as usual, running short of funds. And what about a tour in the provinces, to contradict reports that the new Government was Jacobite? But Harley had other plans. De Foe was, for the fourth time, to visit Scotland.

Prior to that, however, doubtless following on an official hint, if not definite instructions, he had turned the facile searchlight of his common sense on economics, a complicated and uninspiring subject, but one that was thrusting itself forward in the public mind. After the general delirium of the Sacheverell affair, the country had relapsed into a dangerous financial slump. On August 23rd De Foe published, at threepence, *An Essay on Public Credit; Being an Enquiry How the Public Credit comes to Depend upon the Change of Ministries or the Dissolution of Parliament; and whether it does so or no*, and in the course of October three more tracts, of which the last was *An Essay upon Loans*.

On October 21st, considerably later than he originally planned, owing to Harley's delaying tactics, he set out, on horseback as usual, for the north, where, incidentally, he had lately acquired a partnership in a weaving concern. He could not have been particularly happy. The election results had been shatteringly disappointing. The Tories now outnumbered the Whigs by two to one, and many newcomers were of the high-flying type which he particularly loathed. Added to which the new Parliament was demanding an advanced Tory policy. Harley's one hope was to keep the extremists in order with the help of the moderate party.

This time there were several variations in De Foe's journey. For one thing, he travelled alone. For another, he adopted a new French-sounding pseudonym—"Claude Guilot". His correspondence was, as before, in code. But trouble arose at Newcastle, owing to the postmaster, his old friend John Bell, having a fixed impression that De Foe was still in Godolphin's service, and working in the cause of the Whigs.

He made Edinburgh his headquarters until mid-November. A month later he was ready to return to London. Bad weather, however, held him up, and what Monsieur Dottin calls his "satiric verve" inspired him to fill up the time of waiting by publishing *Atlantis Major*, a pamphlet violently libelling a number of Jacobites who were also friends of Harley.

Harley read it, and was naturally indignant. De Foe was prepared, suspiciously prepared, with his defence. He had not written *Atlantis Major*, nor did he know who had written it. But he had heard of it from various persons whom he had encouraged to publish it, hoping that they might put the manuscript in his hands, in which case he would have been able to stop it appearing.

The story must have been one of the feeblest ever put forward by De Foe, expert prevaricator as he was. So, no doubt, the experienced Harley thought, though he accepted it.

De Foe started out for London again in the middle of January 1711. At Newcastle, stirred by a fresh attack of "satiric verve", he stayed long enough to publish a sort of Old Moore's Almanac called *The British Visions*, containing twelve prophecies for the year. It proved so profitable that its publication became a yearly event. The *Review* itself, unfortunately, was making heavy weather. It reflected, possibly more truthfully than its editor-proprietor realized, his own pliability of principles, or lack of them. It angered and alienated the Whigs, and gained nothing but the contempt of the Tories. De Foe was sneered at as a turncoat. He protested violently that he was nothing of the sort; that his paper had always been a supporter of moderate views. All the world would witness that it was not a Tory paper.

All the world declined to do anything of the sort.

Harley, on the contrary, abruptly achieved a popularity as the result of an attack upon his life. A French émigré known as the Marquis de Guiscard, but who was, in fact, the Abbé de la Bourlie, had been in touch with Marlborough and Godolphin in connection with descents upon the French coast. Unsatisfied with his pay, however, he turned traitor for the second time, and offered his services to the French court. His letters were intercepted, he was arrested, and while undergoing an examination in Harley's presence, suddenly stabbed him with a penknife.

The wound was slight, and Harley treated the whole incident calmly. At attack of fever followed the shock, however, and he was confined to his room for some weeks. His wretched assailant died in Newgate a few days after the attack.

The affair was dramatic enough to excite the imagination of the dullest citizen. On the 13th both houses presented an address to the Queen expressing the belief that Harley's fidelity and zeal had drawn upon him "the hatred of all abetters of popery and faction". Anne obviously concurred, for on May 23rd she created him Earl of Oxford and Earl Mortimer, and in the same month appointed him Lord High Treasurer of England, upon which he surrendered the post of Chancellor of the Exchequer. Later still she made him a Knight of the Garter.

It was the zenith of his career.

On May 2nd the Queen agreed to Harley's scheme for funding the National Debt, the total of which at that time was less than the cost of a first-class battleship to-day. She also allowed the "proprietors" a yearly interest of six per cent, and granted them a charter of incorporation to trade in the South Seas under the title of the South Sea Company.

Of the débâcle of that unhappy concern; of the wholesale ruin, of the suicides, and of the wrecked homes and reputations which were the sequel to its crazy finance and the crazier prophecies of its promoters, there is no space to deal here, though there were individual repercussions which it will be necessary to record later.

De Foe laboured on. But he was, to use a cliché, not getting younger, and the remarkable resilience, physical and mental, which had carried him through so many battles was beginning at last to show symptoms of exhaustion. He needed, urgently, a rest, or, if not that, at least a complete change.

A period of quiet in the oasis at Newington might have been the solution. But at this period he seems to have acquired not only incessant restlessness but an active aversion from family life. He had always done what he conceived to be his duty by his children. Sophia, his youngest daughter, he loved greatly; perhaps she was the only thing in his life that he did so love. He is reported, on slender evidence, to have been on bad terms with one of his sons. Of his emotional relationship with Mary, his wife, we know nothing at all.

Harley and he worked effectively together. So, for that matter, did Harley and Swift. Between Harley's two paid protagonists there was never even a pretence of friendship. Their dislike—one might, indeed, call it hatred—seems to have been almost immediate, and mutual. Wrote Swift scornfully:

" One of these authors (the fellow was pilloried, I have forgot his name) is indeed so grave, sententious, dogmatical a rogue that there is no enduring him."

De Foe, his vanity properly stung, as Swift intended it should be, saw his enemy,

"Cynic in behaviour, fury in temper, impolite in conversation, abusive and scurrilous in language, and ungovernable in passion."

Two extremely angry men. But Swift's analysis was false, and inspired by his anger, whilst De Foe's, though inspired by anger, was completely accurate.

And their fortunes depended upon their serving the same master.

Had De Foe and Swift found it possible to work as a team, Harley would have found himself in possession of the most magnificently intellectual propaganda force that English people had ever known. The truth was, of course, not that Swift and De Foe differed in their views and in the best methods of emphasizing those views, but that they were fundamentally allergic. Swift's vitriol and De Foe's suave irony were not employed in attacking only their common enemy; they were employed in attacking De Foe and Swift.

The latter used a weapon at once snobbish and beyond effective parrying, a weapon so handy that others used it too. He attacked De Foe on his lack of education, an attack buttressed by his own qualifications, utterly beyond his enemy's achievement—a degree precariously achieved, but nevertheless granted, from Trinity College Dublin; a Doctorate of Divinity, the Deanery of St. Patrick's, to which must be added the early background of Moor Park and his relationship with Sir William Temple, its owner; the friendship, as an equal and not merely as a useful hireling, of Harley; and, above all, the unquestioned status of a gentleman that had always been De Foe's consuming ambition to attain—and retain.

The relationship between the two was further embittered and complicated by the fact that, while both of them were employed by Harley, Swift was running *The Examiner*, which supported "the utter exclusion of Whigs, as well as Dissenters, from office, the remodelling of the army, the imposition of the most rigid restraints on the heir to the Throne"; while De Foe was running *The Review*, the older-established Whig-Dissenter organ.

It is improbable that two such turbulent and opposing characters could have served any master less tolerant than Harley, himself a compendium of contradictions. Good-tempered, dilatory, always accessible in private life to his friends, of which he had many, including Gay and Pope; a book-collector with mild ambitions in the direction of poetry (Macaulay refers to his verses as being "more execrable than a bellman's"), in public life he was cautious and reticent, a systematic seeker of compromise whenever he found himself confronted with the necessity of choosing one of two divergent courses.

De Foe needed a holiday, but Harley needed De Foe.

There is in existence a letter written to his patron on August 12th, 1712, which exhibits De Foe either as a completely candid, deeply grateful man, or—a detestable alternative which I, for one, refuse to accept—as a consummate hypocrite even in his private dealings with the statesman who had, selfishly or unselfishly, stood by him steadfastly.

" God and your Lordship," wrote De Foe, " are witnesses for me against this generation in that your goodness to me was founded on no principles of bribery or corruption, but a generous compassion to a man oppressed by power without a crime, and abandoned even then by those he sacrificed to serve. The same witnesses are testimony for me that my services (however small) are founded rather, and indeed entirely, on a deep sense of duty and gratitude for that early goodness, than on any view that I can merit what may be to come. You have always acted with me on such foundations of mere abstracted bounty and goodness that it has not so much as suggested the least expectation on your part that I should act this way or that leaving me at full liberty to pursue my own reason and principles, and above all enabling me to declare my innocence in the black charge of bribery. . . .

"This, my Lord, gives me room to declare, as I do print every day that I am neither employed, dictated to or rewarded for, or in, what I write by any person under Heaven, and I make this acknowledgment with thankfulness to your Lordship, and as a testimony to your great goodness to me, that you never laid the least injunction on me of one kind or another, to write, or not to write this or that, in any case whatsoever."

CHAPTER V

NEWGATE AGAIN

D E FOE'S part in the floating of what later came to be known as the South Sea Bubble was not a small one. In a sense, he was the original begetter of the scheme, since he had actually suggested something of the sort to William as a convenient method of raising money to pay for the French war, to meet the expenses of which was Harley's aim, too. To its second incarnation De Foe contributed a pamphlet, *An Essay on the South Sea Trade*, published at the beginning of September 1711. By that time he was ready and anxious to set off on another visit to Scotland. Harley, however, checked him; it was part of His Lordship's technique never to allow his subordinates to know his plans too intimately. The preliminaries of the Treaty of Utrecht were in process of discussion, and De Foe, as the Government's handy man, had to remain handy. The Whigs would certainly attack some of its clauses; it was obviously advisable to have someone to attack the Whigs. The uphill job of explaining the political gains of the Treaty was left to Swift; to De Foe fell the task of convincing English merchants and traders of its business value.

De Foe's contribution was *Reasons why this Nation ought to put a Speedy End to this Expensive War*. The sequel was an action on his part which it is difficult not to label as double-crossing. Monsieur Mesnager, about whom he had a good deal more to say in later years,[1] belonged to a type which seems to appear in history towards the close of any war of any consequence—a nobody-in-particular given elastic powers precisely because he is a nobody. A French merchant, his business in England, where he had been sent by Louis, was not altogether dissimilar to De Foe's Anti-Jacobite excursions into Scotland on behalf of Harley. He was to find out the terms upon which the English ministers would be

[1] See page 228.

prepared to bring the war to an end. He found out, and communicated them to the French king. The much-condemned Peace of Utrecht was the sequel.

Mesnager read De Foe's pamphlet and admired it so much that he had it translated. He went further. With a general idea of securing the author's future services, he sent him a hundred pistoles. The gift was anonymous, but De Foe was given a pretty clear idea of its source. He pocketed the money, as a compliment to the book—and denounced the donor to the Queen.

The French ambassador might have taken some action, but judged it wiser not to, since Mesnager stood in no need of active diplomatic intervention. And nothing more was heard of the incident, at any rate for the time being.

Before the end of the year De Foe had launched a number of other pamphlets. But the steady drift of his master from tepid Whiggery to tepid Toryism, and thence to unqualified Toryism, was making things increasingly difficult for him. The climax was reached when the High-flyers brought in yet again the Bill for the Prevention of Occasional Conformity. The new House of Commons passed it; the House of Lords did the same, though only after a dozen new Tory peers were created to tilt the scales in the same direction.

And neither Harley nor the members of the Government offered more than nominal opposition.

De Foe did make one last effort, and to that extent is entitled to credit. On December 22nd he published *An Essay on the History of Parties*. In this he reminded the Queen that she still possessed the right to veto any Bill. The reminder was justified but futile. On the same day the measure received the Royal assent.

In February 1712 he again asked Harley for leave of absence. There was a further delay before it was granted, and De Foe continued to fill up his time writing. The year, journalistically speaking, included (as most years did) an extremely mixed bag, beginning with *The Present State of Parties in Great Britain* on January 30th, and ending with *Hannibal at the Gates, or the Progress of Jacobitism and the Danger of the Pretender* on December 30th. While it would be fairly safe to say that everything De Foe wrote was a challenge, two pamphlets were especially so: *The Highland Visions, or the New Scots Prophecy, declaring in Twelve Visions what Strange Things shall come to pass in the year* 1712, and *An Enquiry into the Real Interest of Princes in the Persons of their Ambassadors. . . . Impartially applied.* The ambassadors involved were the French plenipotentiaries at Utrecht and "impartially" was the last adverb one would have chosen.

Harley, at long last, gave him permission to spend a fortnight at Buxton, taking the waters there, as he had planned, and then to travel on, under his old alias of "Claude Guilot", to Edinburgh. His slogan—had he known the modern application of the word—was to be "Business first", varied by a few excursions.

He was back again in London at the beginning of the New Year (1713), and went almost immediately to Harley. Harley was unwell; De Foe and his report, together with a request from a company for permission to manufacture copper coins for the Government, would have to wait. Patience under rebuffs was not among De Foe's virtues; he retorted with a sarcastic note which might well have led to his dismissal.

"I had not given you the trouble of my calling last night, but by your command, and ask pardon for my mistake."

But Harley overlooked the insolence; he was prepared to overlook worse things from a man as useful as De Foe.

In the *Review*, which had completed its eighth volume in the previous July, De Foe continued to attack his enemies. His chief lamentation, stated a preface to the collected volumes, was that so many of his friends went over to the other political camp. He compared himself to Acteon,

"hunted full cry by, I won't call them hounds—in spite of protested innocence and want of evidence, against all fair arguing, against all modesty, and sense, condemned by common clamour. As writing for money . . . by great men's direction and the like, every tissue of which is abominably false."

It was, on the contrary, undeniably true.

He concluded with the statement that he had a large family (it was by this time at least an adolescent one),

"Who never want what they should enjoy, or spend what they ought to save. If any man ask how he has always been cheerful, easy and quiet, enjoying a perfect calm of mind, I answer him by serious application to the great, solemn and weighty works of Resignation to the Will of Heaven."

Perfect calm! Resignation!

Neither quality was conspicuous in the attacks he made in his papers—for *The Edinburgh Courant* was now his to wield as propaganda—on causes, on ministries, on individuals. Steele was one enemy; Ridpath of *The Flying Post* another, Swift, of course, another.

A Strict Enquiry into the circumstances of a late Duel [between Lord Mohun and General Hamilton] *with some account of the Persons on both Sides* is an interesting pamphlet of this year. So, too, is *The Secret History of One Year,* under which melodramatic title he masked yet another pious tribute to the evergreen memory of William.

De Foe's attitude at this time was that of self-conscious defiance, masking his knowledge of the fact that his position was precarious to the point of extreme danger. That it was also extremely complicated need not have worried him, for he had been creating and liquidating complications half his life. He might be compared to a juggler who is keeping half-a-dozen balls in the air, aware that at any moment Fate may add one or two others of her own.

He was ostensibly a Whig. But the majority of the Whigs in London—it might almost be said in England—believed him to be a traitor in the pay of another Whig, now turned Tory. And they had considerable grounds for their belief. His protests they regarded as a mixture of blasphemy and bluff.

The Tories, on the other hand, regarded him with the contempt due to a convert who dare not admit his conversion.

Harley, his friend, employer, and mainstay, even more politically suspect, was the last man on earth to provide him with anything in the way of support for his statements of innocence and honesty.

Finally there was the eternal puckishness (one hates the word, but it is the most appropriate) of De Foe's own character, a quality which can be fatal when exercised at the wrong time. And the year 1713 was to prove very much the wrong time.

The Queen's health, never good, was definitely failing.

All her life—she was still under fifty—she had been
dominated by circumstances and by individuals. An early
childhood in France had been followed by a return to
England when she was five. Her uncle, Charles II, had
insisted upon her being brought up as a strict Protestant,
and the support of the established Church of England had
been the one thing about which this generous, flabby,
obstinate, commonplace woman was definite and adaman-
tine. High-flyers and Nonconformists were equally anathema.

Her friendship with Sarah Jennings began long before
Anne was Queen. Sarah, Duchess of Marlborough, the
dynamic, domineering "Mrs. Freeman" to Anne's "Mrs.
Morley", was probably the most tremendous thing in her
life.

At eighteen Anne married Prince George, brother of the
reigning King of Denmark. He was an amiable, drunken
boor, with an accent that remained a permanent reminder
of his foreign origin. Nevertheless, the marriage, though
unpopular, proved a happy one.

She was twenty when her father became King. A year
before his abdication he did his best to settle the Crown upon
her on condition that she became a Catholic. Anne refused,
and the suggestion was dropped when James had a son,
subsequently the Old Pretender.

William, her brother-in-law, and Mary, her elder sister,
became King and Queen. Relations between the two women
varied from frigid to lukewarm; each bored the other. In the
words of contemporary doggerel:

> " King William thinks all;
> Queen Mary talks all;
> Prince George drinks all;
> And Princess Anne eats all."

Mary died of smallpox, and there were fresh quarrels with
William about money and about the Marlboroughs. Then in
1702 William died, and Anne began a twelve-year reign,
occupied with incessant political conflicts and intrigues
against a background of dazzling military exploits and
intellectual achievements.

Prince George died in October 1708, aged fifty-five.
"Mrs. Freeman's" domination, under the influence of a

new favourite and a totally unexpected exhibition of royal will-power, suddenly snapped; Anne was free. And with freedom went loneliness.

She had no living children; though there had been no fewer than fifteen occasions when the nation had hoped for an heir to the Throne, only one child had even survived babyhood. Throughout her reign she had served the State well according to her limited mentality. It *was* limited, even for her times: she took no interest whatever in literature, the drama, music or any of the arts. But she was kind, and she was considerate, and her court was an oasis of morality in the desert of eighteenth-century vice. Destiny should have given her friendly, humble surroundings; a small home to manage, small means, a family who loved her and laughed at her, and understood the narrow ruts in which her mind travelled. Instead it had placed her on the throne of England, where her obstinacy would be countered by clever scheming and her native generosity and her ignorance exploited by every type of adventurer. Only the Church remained; that stood firm. For its sake she swore to support the Hanoverian succession, and, though it meant the permanent elimination of her father and brother, that the Crown should pass at her death to George, Elector of Hanover and great-grandson of James I.

The deterioration in the Queen's health brought to the surface the unceasing underground warfare between the Jacobites and the Hanoverians. The Queen might nominate her successor, but that successor could occupy the Throne only with the assent and co-operation of those who survived her. The Stuarts were in exile on the Continent, but they were Royalty whom Englishmen knew: and their alternative was a German-bred princeling, also living on the Continent, whom the country at large did not know at all, and whose virtues and vices alike were a matter of sheer guesswork.

In the mounting restlessness and excitement De Foe was, of course, in his element. Equally of course, he was unreservedly anti-Jacobite. He exaggerated, he exhorted, and if he had mixed a little more discretion with the expression of his views, what he wrote might have resulted in nothing more than explosions of good-humoured laughter.

Unfortunately, laughter in De Foe's case involved a perception of irony. Carried away by his own exuberance,

ignoring the increasing danger of his position as one
suspected, and hated, by both parties, imagining himself
secure in his position under Harley, he grew more and more
reckless.

Between the last week in February and the last in April he
published anonymously three pamphlets in *The True-born
Englishman* tradition.

The first was *Reasons against the Succession of the House of
Hanover, with Enquiry how far the Abdication of King James,
supposing it to be legal, ought to affect the Person of the Pretender.*
In it he displayed a typical picture of a violently divided
England. He wrote:

" If you choose to listen to your cookmaids and footmen in
your kitchen, you shall hear them scolding and swearing and
fighting among themselves, and when you think the noise is
about the beef and the pudding, the dishwater or the kitchen
stuff, alas, you are mistaken; the feud is about who is for the
Protestant Succession and who for the Pretender."

Later in the same pamphlet there is an unfortunate
diatribe which was intended to convey to his readers the
fact that the author was ironically suggesting a drastic cure,
but the only one likely to be effective in England's underfed
and unhappy condition.

" If it be necessary to teach us the worth of things by the
want of them; and there is no other way to bring the Nation to
its senses; why, what then can be said against the Pretender?
Even let him come, that we may see what slavery means . . .
for no experience teaches us so well as that we buy dearest and
pay for with the most smart."

The second pamphlet was entitled *And what if the Pretender
should Come? Or Some Considerations of the Advantages and Real
Consequences of the Pretender's possessing the Crown of Great
Britain*, and the third, *An Answer to a Question that Nobody
thinks of, viz. What if the Queen should Die?*

According to De Foe, these tracts met with so much
approbation that half a dozen editions were printed: further,
if the Elector had given him a thousand pounds to make the
interests of the Pretender "odious and ridiculous" their
author could have produced nothing more effectual.

Perhaps. But his Whig enemies regarded them from a different, more sinister point of view. They saw in them, in short, the possibilities of his ruin.

Though De Foe was the ostensible object of their attack they had actually far bigger game in view—Harley, no less. If the journalist were in custody, it was reasonably certain that he would appeal to his employer for assistance. And if that happened, the whole story, the full connection of double-crossing employee and double-crossing statesman might be dragged to light.

Knowing their enemy, they planned the whole business with a careful eye to details. It was essential that De Foe should be arrested at his house in Stoke Newington. To achieve this, they bought from an old creditor—going as far afield as Yarmouth to find him—a bill of De Foe's. It was presented to him one evening as he was in the act of leaving home to visit Harley. As they calculated, he had not enough money in his possession to pay the amount there and then, and retreated into the house for sanctuary until he could raise the money, in the meantime sending one of his sons to Harley to ask for his overdue pension.

The leader of the attacking party was a man named Benson, already convicted of libel. He had previously gone to Janeway, De Foe's printer, obtained a personal interview, and then by threats induced him to part with the original manuscripts of the pamphlets. But at this point there had been a slight hitch. The pamphlets, as it happened, were in three different handwritings.

The reason for this was a trifle hard to discover, but it emerged when the printers were interrogated before Parker, the Lord Chief Justice. Janeway himself had edited the first, *Reasons Against the Succession of the House of Hanover*. Prior to its production De Foe had met him, mentioned the article, and its proposed title, and so excited Janeway that he had immediately commissioned De Foe to write it for a fee of four guineas and twenty-five free copies.

The other two had been printed by Baker, who had paid two guineas each for them. Both these had been written out partly by De Foe, and partly by his sons, Daniel and Benjamin; to the younger son had fallen the responsibility of verifying De Foe's quotations. The printer's employees, according to custom, had brought the proofs to his unofficial office which he then had in the Temple or to Stoke Newington. Also according to custom one of the boys had met the printer's man at the door, kept him waiting while he took the proofs to his father for correction or did the work himself, and handed them back.

The relentless Benson solved the problem of the handwriting by terrifying the printer into admitting that they were all De Foe's work, after which he went to the Lord Chief Justice and succeeded in obtaining warrants for the arrest of De Foe, Baker and Janeway.

The arrest of the chief defendant took place with every conceivable ostentation and publicity at eleven o'clock on a Saturday, the week-end being carefully chosen to minimize his chances of finding bail. Fortified, however, by assurances from Harley that he would receive the usual support, De Foe went quietly. Or, to be exact, was prepared to go quietly. But Ridpath, his old enemy, had issued warnings concerning a resistance, entirely fictitious, in which a barricaded house and mass assaults on its defences figured. And when De Foe emerged he found a crowd that arranged itself dramatically behind him. At this head of this preposterous procession he rode, ill and depressed, into the City.

On Monday, April 13th, he appeared before Parker. He offered bail to eight hundred pounds; two booksellers offered another four hundred pounds each. There were shouts from the enemy that this was not enough. Upon which William Borrett, De Foe's defender, coached by Harley, intervened to point out that it was all that could be legally demanded. Parker, uncertain whether the prosecution was a private one or whether the State itself was instituting proceedings, announced that he would enquire of Bolingbroke. De Foe overheard and informed Harley. Harley immediately contacted Bolingbroke to check any inconvenient facts concerning the relationship between himself and De Foe becoming public.

De Foe was temporarily released on the following day. But this time his return was far from being triumphal. The crowds were hostile; the hack writers, acting under Whig instructions, more hostile still.

" Judas discovered and caught at last," ran one pamphlet, " an animal that shifts its shape as often as Proteus, that goes backwards and forwards like a hunted Hare, a thorough-paced true-bred Hypocrite, a High Churchman one day and a rank Whig the next."

De Foe should by now have realized the extreme danger of his position. But on this occasion his common sense and prudence, both as politician and editor, seem for once to have deserted him completely. On April 16th and 18th he published in the *Review* unsigned articles, actually questioning the honesty of the judges concerned in his trial. When he appeared before them again to ask for an extension of his bail, it was inevitable that he should be asked if he had written these reckless effusions. (And even if he had not, the responsibility for their publication would have been his, as the *Review's* editor and proprietor.)

De Foe hesitated, then said "Yes".

Parker then said that he considered them insolent libels (which they indubitably were), but thereafter behaved with admirable and, in the circumstances, rather surprising fairness. He ordered the articles to be read aloud, but left any further action regarding them to his two colleagues. They heard them, and unhesitatingly declared that they were infamous insults, and that their author had shown the utmost contempt for the court and for the laws of the land.

De Foe was thenceforth sentenced to be imprisoned in the Queen's Bench. His protests that the three pamphlets which were the original cause of the trial were merely ironical was silenced by Sir Thomas Powis, the judge, who sternly reminded him that for such a crime he was liable to be hanged, drawn and quartered.

It was, of course, Harley, the Harley who, faithless though he might be to his principles, could on occasion be faithful to his friends, and especially to useful friends, who ultimately came to the rescue. He advised De Foe to make full apologies to the affronted court; he persuaded the judges to listen to the apologies. Under pressure—and one imagines that it required considerable pressure—they accepted it and a nominal fine of three-and-sixpence.

On May 2nd he once more found himself, not wholly free, but released on bail.

Released, but with his morale shattered. The bold and passionately independent spirit of twenty years earlier was at last broken. Sheer folly had brought him near to a horrible death; Harley, who had saved him, had probably warned him that the intervention was the last he might expect. His services were demanded as a *quid pro quo*, and it was no more than a fair price to pay. Bolingbroke was inaugurating a fresh political campaign; De Foe was to be the man at the head of it.

CHAPTER VI

DEATH OF ANNE; HARLEY IN ECLIPSE; MIST

HIS NEW and servile role was marked by the dexterous extinction of the *Review*, which for nearly nine years had been his clear-voiced megaphone and for the past twelve months had been growing feebler and feebler. Nevertheless there must have been a bitter, cynical smile on De Foe's lips when he had formally to announce that, owing to the recent appearance of a new journal, *Mercator*, subsidized by the Government and having sole access to all official statistics concerning trade, he had reluctantly been compelled to cease publication. His own future? Here the smile, we may imagine, became wholly cynical. He intended to retire into the country. There must have been many who pitied the exile of so brilliant a journalist, unaware that, so far from retiring, he had been appointed, if not Editor, at any rate one of the chief contributors to *Mercator* on extremely comfortable terms. According to Dottin he was editor. But this appears doubtful. It is in any case extremely difficult to be certain concerning his actual contributions. Whatever his precise role may have been, or whatever proportion of the five hundred pounds he received from the funds of the Government's Secret Service (the money being discreetly described as "bounty"), during the first seven months of 1714 was payment for such work, the periodical itself must have been one after De Foe's own heart.

Primarily it dealt with British trade,[1] "particularly as it respects Holland, Flanders and the Dutch Barrier, the Trade to and from France, the Trade to Portugal, Spain and the West Indies, and the Fisheries of Newfoundland and Nova Scotia." "Trading particularly" had always been one of De Foe's major hobbies. Each number consisted of only a

---

[1] " Mercator " means " trader ", and is so used in the celebrated map of the world, which, as " Mercator's projection ", is reproduced in present-day atlases.

single leaf, small folio size, and it was issued three times a week: on Tuesdays, Thursdays and Saturdays.

Yet *Mercator's* career, as it chanced, was to be far briefer than the *Review's*. But for that events completely beyond the control of the editor were responsible.

To return briefly to the offending pamphlets. Though nominally at liberty, it was not until October 9th that he was able to report to Harley that he had been advised by the Attorney General to petition for a general pardon. He did so, and on November 20th one arrived. It was signed by Bolingbroke on behalf of the Queen. She had been satisfied that, though his methods might have been wrong and his irony misplaced, he had no real intention of casting reflections on the Protestant Succession. The clouds lifted once more. If his new fetters were a trifle heavier, he had long ago grown used to fetters.

From the beginning of the year the uneasy Harley-Bolingbroke alliance had been in a state of steady disintegration. Bolingbroke, whole-heartedly Jacobite, found Harley's eternal shiftiness exasperating, while the Tory Government itself was becoming more and more unpopular. In March 1714 there was an open breach between Harley and Bolingbroke. The Queen's personal complaints about Harley's attitude towards her were, of course, utilized by Bolingbroke to the uttermost. He was fortified by the knowledge that Anne herself, whose general ill-health had by now become acute, had swung over towards the Jacobites and away from the Hanoverians.

Anne's resentment against Harley has an additional interest in showing how steadily, though insidiously, he had degenerated during the ten years he had been in power. She accused him of neglecting all business; of failing to keep appointments with her, and when he did keep them, arriving so intoxicated that he did not treat her with proper respect; she added that she frequently could not understand him, and when she did she could never believe him. . . . In brief, his heavy drinking had affected his manners, his morals and his intelligence.

Henry St. John Viscount Bolingbroke (1678–1751)—Tory politician, prolific author, and superb orator; friend of Pope, Swift, Voltaire, Walpole; part-negotiator of the Peace of Utrecht, ("an ignominious conclusion to a glorious war"), impetuous, brilliant and daring—bided his time. And before the final eclipse of the Queen's health he succeeded, in the course of a meeting that did not end until two o'clock on the morning of July 28th, 1714, in persuading her to dismiss Harley.

Bolingbroke, at only thirty-six, found himself chief minister. It was to be one of the briefest occupancies of power in English history. The Queen, her illness aggravated by the eternal dissensions, collapsed on the following Friday under an apoplectic stroke. Three days later she was dead. . . . The Tory regime, together with any real prospect of a Jacobite revolution, died with her. George, the gauche, unprepossessing Hanoverian princeling, was formally proclaimed King of England.

It marked the end of yet another chapter in De Foe's life. He had been William's man, utterly loyal; he had been Harley's man, not less loyal, perhaps, but with loyalty based on a different code, on lower principles. Until the arrival of George, the country was under the authority and guidance of a Council of Regents, and this automatically included Harley. To him De Foe wrote, with those assurances of support which must by now have become equally automatic.

Harley responded appropriately; the old De Foe was at his service again, with the old liabilities—a fact of which he was reminded when shortly afterwards his protégé became involved in trouble over a letter. This, printed in *The Post Boy*, violently insulted the High-Flyers, and Harley had to use his authority to stop a warrant that had been issued for De Foe's arrest.

Later still there were complications over another letter attacking the Earl of Anglesey, just back from a mission to Dublin. In this case the letter, one received from an outside correspondent, had been considerably, though insufficiently, watered down by De Foe. It stated that the object of the journey had been "to model the forces there, particularly to break no less than seventy of the honest officers of the army, and to fill up their places with the tools and creatures of Con. [Sir Constantine] Phipps".

The outraged Earl, who had returned to take his place as one of the Council of Regents, took prompt action. De Foe, as usual, along with the editor and printer, was arrested.

They were released on bail, but on August 28th, following the discovery of the original letter, De Foe was again arrested, and though given provisional liberty, was no longer a free agent.

Harley twice did his best to persuade Anglesey to drop the prosecution, the second time at the end of September. Both efforts were futile. When George, first King of the House of Hanover, arrived in London on September 20th and made his state entry, De Foe was not among those who rode in state in the official cavalcade.

On October 22nd, 1714, Samuel Tuffley, of Hackney, died. His will is uncompromisingly indicative of the attitude of the Tuffley family towards their distinguished, erratic and exciting in-law.

" To Daniel De Foe and his children, one guinea each. To my dear sister, Mary ",

went the bulk of his estates, lands, tenements and goods.

" For and to the only use of the said Mary De Foe, the wife of Daniel De Foe for and to her dispensing and appointment absolutely and independently of her husband, or any claim or demand which he or anyone claiming by for or under him by right of marriage or otherwise might have or made to the same . . ."

And so on, page after page, with elaborations guaranteed to make impossible the attempts of the most determined of De Foe's creditors to lay hands on the property.

The late Samuel Tuffley of Hackney was running no risks!

In October 1714 came the first part of *The Secret History of the White Staff*. The second part followed almost immediately, the third in the following January.

This is one of those books about which for ever circle the mists of doubt. The chief argument against De Foe being the author—to take the negative side first—seems to be his explicit statement in 1715 that he had written nothing since the Queen's death. Chalmers, on the strength of this statement, says that there was no doubt that De Foe was not the author. There is every doubt. The book—seventy pages—is a justification of Harley's policy; it insists that he was an upholder of the Protestant succession and upon his complete integrity. It indicates the possession by the author of a great deal of inside knowledge; it has all the stigmata of De Foe's style; it was from the first generally attributed to him. He admitted that he "revised" two sheets of the book while it was being printed. And finally, as Professor Sutherland points out, he refers to the Queen's death having prevented his completion of a piece he was writing to vindicate Harley's conduct.

Harley himself soon had need of every apologist and defender he could call upon, so dangerous had the position of him and Bolingbroke become. The danger intensified until in the spring of the following year Bolingbroke judged it wise to make his escape, disguised, to France; Harley, with more courage, remained to face the music. In July he and the absent minister were impeached on six counts. He was found guilty, and a little later committed to the Tower.

De Foe, a less magnificent but not less unpopular figure in the public eye, must have seen nothing ahead but extinction. A Whig, and a fanatical supporter of the Hanoverian regime was paying the price of loyalty to a man who had never been either, and finding himself execrated even more bitterly by the Whigs and Hanoverians in power than by the Tories and Jacobites who were out.

Whatever the precise effect of these political inversions upon De Foe's chameleon-like mentality, it is certain that his physical health suffered. On February 24th he published *An Appeal to Honour and Justice, tho' it be of his worst enemies, by De Foe. Being a true Account of his conduct in Public Affairs.* In this, he insisted that he had always been faithful to his first principles, a statement that many of his readers must have found difficult to credit. A publisher's note stated that the author had been unable to complete the narrative of his political career "owing to a violent fit of apoplexy".

"And continuing now, for above six weeks (resumes the note) in a weak and languishing condition, neither able to go on nor likely to recover (at least in any short time) . . . If he recovers, he may be able to finish what he began. If not, it is the opinion of most who know him that the treatment he here complains of has been the apparent cause of his disaster."

Thus De Foe, plaintively capitalizing his afflictions, though in point of fact the apoplectic stroke was a slight one, so slight that it had no obvious effect upon his customary cascade of literature. Only a month later he was issuing *The Family Instructor*, a three-part work running to between four and five hundred pages of dialogue, in which he gives highly moral and, as the sales proved, highly popular advice to the average citizen and the average citizen's wife and family. Within five years *The Family Instructor* reached its eighth edition.

The increasing tendency to moralize and instruct has led to inevitable comparisons between the characters of De Foe and Bunyan. It is obvious, on analysis, that a great gulf divides them. Bunyan's religious convictions were passionate, fundamental, primitive. De Foe, even when emphasizing his adherence to moral values and his belief in and practice of the major virtues, leaves one always with a feeling that he is so writing chiefly because it is politic, or because he is being swayed by a chance gust of conscience, or because he is anxious to put himself in the good graces of his readers. In short, that his piety is something of a veneer, and that in the long run he would rather rely on his own cleverness than put his whole faith in the eternal justice of the Deity. He prefers to tell the truth, the whole truth, and nothing but the truth, but is also prepared to tell only part of it, or dilute it with invention, or, if circumstances make the truth dangerous in any form, to lie. To take a single example, he specifically stated in defence of *The Secret History of the White Staff* that he had neither seen nor spoken to Harley since the King's landing, whereas there is actually in existence a letter written to the Lord Treasurer at the end of September. In short, at times he exhibited himself as an opportunist, a careerist, even a liar and a humbug. (But almost always with mitigating circumstances.)

Harley went to the Tower. His political finale had qualities oddly in keeping with his character, with all its insincerity, jealousy and general moral weakness, faults that combined to make his friendship insincere and his promises unreliable. Even during his imprisonment he was in correspondence with the Pretender, offering his service and advice.

In the summer of 1717 the impeachment was commenced. To the original sixteen articles another six had been added. But his luck held. Lords and Commons disagreed concerning procedure, and in the end he was acquitted because neither appeared to support the charges. Nevertheless, he was specifically excluded from the Act of Grace, which meant that he could never again appear in court, though he made various speeches in the House of Lords. He continued to keep in touch with the Jacobites, but declined, with obvious wisdom, to act as the Pretender's representative in England. He died at his Herefordshire home on May 21st, 1724, in his sixty-third year.

It is doubtful if De Foe greatly mourned his passing from their world of political scheming, plotting and subterfuge and double-crossing. He had served Harley because he needed the money that exigent taskmaster paid him, and the support that could be relied upon to save him from his own impetuosity and indiscretions. A new master would un-doubtedly be a new support. Though he was nominally free, the shadow of his libel against Lord Anglesey still lay across his path. To vary the metaphor, his enemies still had him on the legal leash.

He had always been terrified of losing his freedom; stone walls made a prison, and the poet's philosophy was never his. His health, until this seizure, had, with rare exceptions, been excellent; now visited with serious, possibly mortal illness, he was assailed with fears and compunctions. The latter, where his family was concerned, he could always counter with excuses. If he had seen little of his wife and children since the early Tilbury days of nearly thirty years ago, the political world in which he had become more and more deeply submerged, and necessarily so, made it impossible for him to live at home as much as other husbands and fathers did. Apart from which, there was the "ill-behaviour" shown towards him by various members of the family. They treated him, complained De Foe, with provoking language, and frequently put him into indecent passions and urged him into rash replies.

The occupations that compelled him to neglect his family might have met with more appreciation of his unceasing industry on their behalf, if his recklessness and impulsiveness had not cancelled out his more admirable qualities. The net result was demoralizing periods of wealth, alternating with periods of acute poverty which the knowledge of the breadwinner's real abilities made all the more exasperating and difficult to endure. He was, in short, one of those people upon whom money, or the mere prospect of money, acts as a stimulant rather than as a support. Henry Baker, husband of Sophia, once wrote of him:

"Your father loves to hide himself in mists. . . . Ruin and wild destruction sport around him, and exercise their fury on all he has to deal with."

But the heaviest trial to his dependants was not frustrated poverty. With a confused idea of punishing both those who provoked him, and himself for being provoked, De Foe decided suddenly to refuse to utter a word in the presence of his family. A psychoanalyst of to-day could doubtless have dealt effectively with the case, but unfortunately the only eighteenth-century equivalent to such treatment was the good bedside manner. And De Foe was not a bedside case. Mary did her feminine best to break down the barrier, failed, left him, and finally became mentally affected herself. His children, with the exception of Sophia, also left him. For years she endured the grotesquely pathetic situation of tending a man who remained determinedly dumb, though perfectly capable of speaking . . . until, at long, long last, illness and delirium brought back speech and he talked to Sophia and others again, though tersely and grudgingly even then.

But that strange and gloomy period still lay ahead. The dangers implicit in the immediate future pressed heavily upon him. As he surveyed the situation, his nimble and desperate mind must have realized that he was entangled, and indeed trapped, in the web of subterfuge he had himself for years been spinning. Inspiration came at last! God-sent, according to De Foe.

Instead of evading all future complications by a secret dash into exile on the Continent—his original intention—he listened, he says, to a spirit voice that repeated over and over again, "Write to the judge. . . . Write to the judge", the judge concerned being Sir Matthew Parker, the Lord Chief Justice, no less, before whom Lord Anglesey's case against De Foe had been heard in July. The supernaturally inspired letter he sent brought what the writer can only have regarded as a supernaturally inspired reply; all proceedings against him, he was informed, had been dropped.

The matter did not end there. Parker saw Lord Towns-hend, until December 1716 Secretary of State. The con-versation between the two men must have been worth hearing. (But when De Foe was the topic, almost any conversation must have been worth hearing.) Its upshot was that De Foe was re-enlisted in the Secret Service that he understood so well and had served so expertly. Towns-hend was a Whig; De Foe was a Whig. De Foe ventured on a suggestion a good deal more creditable to his brain than his sense of honour.

"In considering which way I might be rendered most useful to the Government, it was proposed by my Lord Townshend that I should still appear as if I were under the pleasure of the Government and separate from the Whigs; and that I might be more serviceable in a kind of disguise than if I appeared openly, and, upon this, a weekly paper, which I was at first directed to write in opposition to a scandalous paper called *The Shift Shifted* was laid aside, and the first thing I engaged in was a monthly book called *Mercurius Politicus* . . . In the interval of this Dyer, the *News Letter* writer having been dead, and Dormer, his successor, being unable to carry on that work, I had an offer for a share in the property as well as in the management of that work."

De Foe then went on to assure His Lordship that although the style would continue Tory, "the sting of that mis-chievous paper should be entirely taken out".

The "stingless" *News Letter* represented something unique in English journalism, something that only De Foe could have handled adequately and, moreover, have enjoyed handling. From being uncompromisingly Whig, he had created a secondary and unsavoury reputation as a Tory. Under Harley he had controlled, or at any rate kept a watching eye upon, the Whig press on behalf of a Whig-turned-Tory statesman; now he reversed the process, and controlled the Tory press on behalf of a Whig government. But this time more subtly. His attitude now was that of a complete con-vert to Toryism, who dared not go too far for fear of the disfavour of the Government. In such guise, he mixed with the Tories as one of them, he had access to Tory secrets and plans, he worked in the editorial departments of Tory periodicals as editor of foreign communications, and finally, stroke of near-genius, insinuated himself into the post of translator of foreign news, under Nathaniel Mist, director of a weekly paper with a strong Jacobite bias. It was, in fact, the Pretender's journalistic organ in England.

Mist himself deserves a good deal more than incidental reference. Beginning his career as a sailor, he became at some time prior to 1716 a printer in Great Carter Lane, and there started *The Weekly Journal or Saturday Post*, a newspaper of six folio pages. As editor of the organ of the Jacobites and the High-Flyers he was obviously suspect, and in April 1717 he was arrested for libelling the Government. He was released, arrested again in the following week, and again released. In August appeared an editorial manifesto disclaiming any disloyalty, and undertaking to supply early and direct news from abroad, "translated by the ablest hands"—a phrase of hidden but immense significance, since the "ablest hands" were those of De Foe, who had by then succeeded in his object of obtaining a post in the *Journal's* office.

From then onward the careers of the two men were almost inextricably tangled. De Foe's connection with the *Journal* soon became an open secret; by the end of the year, when an article on debtors appeared signed "D.D.F." it was no secret at all. Surviving letters from De Foe give an account of his work, nominally under Mist, on behalf of the Whigs. Edmund Curll, a publisher of pornographic literature, and a peculiarly repulsive character, makes a brief appearance as an enemy of both men; Ridpath, the publisher of the rival *Flying Post*, was also involved. De Foe steered with considerable success a complicated course; it stands to his credit that he did his best to save Mist from the consequences of the publisher's major follies, and of Mist's own tactlessness, impulsiveness and touchiness, while at the same time he kept himself sufficiently detached.

Mist, however, was incorrigible. After a succession of arrests, releases, escapes and fines, he retired to France, where for a time he was said to be driving a hackney-coach at Rouen.

The *Journal*, however, continued until September 1728.

De Foe, writing anonymously in *Applebee's Journal* at the end of 1724, makes an oblique reference to being abused and insulted by one whom he had fetched three times out of prison, that this person had at length drawn a sword upon him, but that, being disarmed, he had been forgiven, a kindness (adds De Foe) followed only by more ingratitude. And again in 1730, De Foe then being ill and in hiding at Greenwich, spoke of having received a blow "from a wicked, perjured and contemptible enemy, that has broken in upon my spirit".[1]

That enemy was certainly Mist. He died of asthma at Boulogne on September 20th, 1737.

The following is a list, derived from William Lee's *Life*, of the periodicals to which De Foe contributed.

Mercurius Politicus. An historical record, appearing monthly from 1716 onwards. 64pp. 8vo.

Mist's Journal, otherwise *The Weekly Journal or Saturday Post*. 6 pages, foolscap 8vo.

The Whitehall Evening Post. Established by De Foe in 1718. A single quarto sheet. (This was continued long after De Foe ceased to be a contributor).

The Daily Post. Also established by De Foe. A single folio Sheet, chiefly consisting of advertisements, and non-political.

Applebee's Journal—Applebee being the proprietor—otherwise *The Original Weekly Journal and Saturday's Post*. Only the first number was written by De Foe, but it was continued for some years by Henry Baker.

Fog's Journal—a clumsily punning continuation of Mist's. Only one contribution, non-political, is scheduled by Lee as De Foe's.

De Foe had no proprietorial interest in *Mist's Weekly Journal*, and consequently was unable to reject what he considered were "improper communications". But the very fact was an asset in allaying suspicion that he might be a secret agent of the Government.

He summarizes the position thus:

"By this management *The Weekly Journal*, and *Dormer's Letter*, also the *Mercurius Politicus* will always be kept (mistakes excepted) as Tory papers, and yet be disabled and enervated, so as to do no mischief to the Government."

In accepting this post, De Foe realized that from the first he was doomed to associate with "Papists, Jacobites and enraged High Tories" such as "my very soul abhors". He

[1] See pages 289–90.

not only heard traitorous expressions against the King, but was compelled to take scandalous and villainous papers, and keep them by him, as if he would gather materials from them to put into the news. What he actually did was to suppress them.

It was a fantastically dangerous rôle, almost certain to end in discovery, ignominy and, if his enemies came into power, the worst that political traitors could expect. And he knew it. But the risks were part of the job, and for the time being at any rate he had the right sort of Government behind him.

Every biographer has been intrigued over this phase in his career. Their views on the amount of odium that De Foe deserves vary considerably, but it may at least be said in his favour that what he did was no more culpable than the work of any spy on behalf of any cause, that he was faithful to those who employed him, and that he advocated what he had always advocated, a reasonable acceptance of facts and a general spirit of moderation and compromise.

On the other hand, the strict moralist with a tenderness for De Foe's reputation finds a good deal to censure. It is all very well to argue, as one biographer does, that "he had found a unique employment for his unique talents and experience". De Foe speaks with a kind of scornful unction of "bowing in the House of Rimmon", but he entered it of his own free will. In short, he became a spy because a spy's work involved the qualities that he possessed and practised, and were part of his complex make-up. One can only accept the fact with regret and resignation.

The year 1715 ended, and Harley was still in the Tower. The Jacobite upheaval, continuing in the north, as such upheavals did, ended, as they all did, in futility, and in the ruin of fiery, badly organized and incompetently led participators. Preston Pans saw the end of that particular Jacobite dream, and the death of the treasonable leaders. The Ministry was reconstituted in December with Lord Stanhope at its head, and the three years' life given to previous Parliaments wăs extended to seven. Abroad, the Whigs concentrated upon maintaining peace, the machinations of King Philip of Spain notwithstanding.

Harley still lived, an extinct political force, a man hardly worth either trial or release. But De Foe had not forgotten his old patron. Like the mouse in the fable who released the trapped lion, he began to busy himself, the mouse's teeth in this case being *The Journal*.

He appears to have begun his formal connection with it in August 1717, his salary being a pound a week. In the following March he was responsible for an innovation of first-class journalistic importance—an essay written in the form of a letter on some subject of popular interest, addressed to the editor and signed by any sort of pseudonym that occurred to the writer—an odd beginning to what has long since developed into the leading article. De Foe wrote a number of these.

He was, of course, still turning out pamphlets: *A Sharp Rebuke from one of the People called Quakers to Henry Sacheverall, the High Priest of Andrews, Holborn. . . . A Seasonable Expostulation and Friendly Reproof with James Butler, who by the Men of this World is styled the Duke of O . . . . d.; A History of the Wars of Charles XII; A Hymn to the Mob; A View of the Scots Rebellion; Some Account of Two Night's Court at Greenwich; Memoirs of the Church of Scotland; A life of Count Patkul, a Nobleman of Livonia who was broke Alive upon the Wheel, together with the Manner of his Execution. Written by the Luthurian Minister who assisted him in his last hours.* The list is a fascinating example of versatility and industry.

In June 1717 appeared *Minutes of the Negociations of Mons. Mesnager at the Court of London*, a book of three hundred pages. Its publication was quite incredibly opportune. Harley's petition for a trial, in an atmosphere now far calmer, and consequently one in which he stood a far better chance of getting something like a fair hearing, had at last been granted. And the book which, if trustworthy, would be of obviously vital importance in proving whether he had or had not been guilty of treasonable correspondence with the Pretender, antedated the day of the trial by precisely a week.

If it were trustworthy. But there were certain inconsistencies and inaccuracies in the text which made that more than doubtful. Abel Boyer, for one, had no hesitation whatever in denouncing the *Minutes* as forgeries and charging De Foe with being their author.

Boyer, a miscellaneous writer, educated in France, was himself the author of a number of pamphlets, histories, plays and poems of no particular literary value. His only real claim to fame was an Anglo-French Dictionary of some distinction. He had also compiled a monthly periodical, *The Political State of Great Britain*, and later edited *The Post Boy*, later still *The True Post Boy*. De Foe refused to admit the authorship; to that refusal he added completely irrelevant charges of criminality against Boyer.

The precise value of the *Minutes* to Harley's case remains unknown; possibly they had no value at all. He was acquitted, largely through the efforts of his friends in the House of Lords, on July 1st.

Harley, as already stated, lived for seven years after, years largely occupied in correspondence with his old friends and supporters—Swift, Pope and others. Their letters were found after his death. They included none from De Foe subsequent to 1715.

De Foe's relationship with Mist became more and more complicated with the passage of time. It is beyond belief that De Foe could have continued to exercise an anti-Jacobite influence, however Machiavellian, upon the chief pro-Jacobite paper in England without its editor realizing what was happening, especially as he must have been aware of his contributor's reputation. I have no doubt whatever that Mist *did* realize the true position of affairs. Going even further, it is quite possible that he decided that it might be safer—and, incidentally, more profitable—to indulge in a little double-crossing on his own account, and to accept money from both sides. A letter from De Foe to a friend concerning Mist does at any rate make it evident that the two men had come to a satisfactory working agreement concerning what would to-day be termed the political "slant" of the *Journal*. Mist "resolves his paper shall for the future amuse the Tories, but not affront the Government". De Foe, further, "has told him that this is the only way to preserve his paper, keep himself from jail, and to secure all the advantages which now arise to him from it."

But if Mist came to heel so conveniently and complacently, others outside the *Journal's* office were more sceptical. Three or four months after he had begun to contribute, De Foe was flatly accused in a rival paper, James Read's *The Weekly Journal or British Gazeteer*,[1] of being one of Mist's authors. In the autumn of the following year (1718) the attack was renewed with a vehemence that goaded Mist to a flat and

[1] Mist's paper was *The Weekly Journal or Saturday Post*.

lying denial. De Foe he stated, apart from formerly acting as an occasional translator, had no concern in the paper at all, or ever had had any. Mist wonders, in conclusion, how "men that pretend to other things can publish such audacious untruths."

From this point onward the relationship between De Foe and Mist and the proprietors of the other periodicals becomes so involved that it is hopeless to attempt to place events in proper perspective. The Government itself constituted an additional complication; De Foe and Mist between them were conducting their sham fight against it so vigorously that Stanhope, Secretary of State, was beginning to get uneasy. The climax came in October, when Mist published a letter signed "Sir Andrew Politick", sharply criticizing the state of affairs between England and Spain.

He was arrested. Questioned about the authorship of the letter, he said that De Foe wrote it. Asked how the letter came to be in his own handwriting, Mist said he had merely copied it out for the printer, because De Foe invariably insisted on having his original manuscript destroyed.

Then Warner, the publisher, was questioned. He also swore that the letter had been written by De Foe. His full statement is too long for reproduction, the essential fact being that it bore every evidence of being true. Granted that it becomes equally evident that yet again De Foe had allowed his recklessness to carry him beyond the bounds of prudence.

The affair blew over. Read's *Journal* summarized De Foe's career in scathing doggerel, which concluded:

> "This wretch if possible will cheat Old Nick
>   He's so inured to fraudulence and trick,
>   Great Bulzebube (sic) himself he does outvie
>   For malice, treachery and audacious lye!"

De Foe at this time began to contribute to a Whig paper, *The Whitehall Evening Post*. Almost simultaneously his contributions to Mist's *Journal* ceased. Then on the third day of the New Year the vigilant Read announced that "the famous Daniel was again to undertake the dirty work of writing for the *Journal*".

In 1720 Mist printed a paragraph so offensive that De Foe, foreseeing trouble, hastened to deny its authorship. Mist was put in the pillory and imprisoned. Months later there was another similar prosecution. De Foe came to his rescue by publishing a collection of miscellaneous letters selected from Mist's Journal. Meanwhile, he was continuing to write for half a dozen papers, including a twice-weekly periodical called *The Manufacturer*.

Volume Two of the *Family Instructor* also appeared in 1718.

PART FOUR

ROBINSON CRUSOE

CHAPTER I

PRELUDE

SEVENTEEN-NINETEEN came. De Foe, nearly sixty-one—and that in the eighteenth century implied old age, not to say senility—must have regarded his career as nearing its end and his reputation, such as it was, established. He had been tradesman, traveller, pamphleteer, and poet, with brief but not unspectacular incursions into landscape gardening, the army, and the Nonconformist Church. Collectively the occupations form an interesting example of versatility combined with an immense capacity for hard work. But hardly more than that.

Now, had he known it, he was about to enter the corridors of the Hall of the Immortals.

He reached it, as one would expect De Foe to reach any objective, by an oblique route.

His interest in the adventures of a morose and dissipated son of a poor Scotch shoemaker probably originated in the man's arrival in London in 1711, two years after his successful rescue from an uninhabited island off the coast of Chile.

The man called himself Alexander Selkirk, though his name was actually Selcraig. (He was buried under that name when, in his forty-fifth year, he died.)

It seems reasonably certain that De Foe met Selkirk in London while the aura of his adventures was still making him an object of excitement and public interest, in spite of his uncouthness and general lack of personal attraction. It is, furthermore, practically certain that they met again, according to tradition, at the house of Mrs. Damaris Daniel, in Bristol, whither Selkirk, "his head turned by public attention and then by public indifference", had retired. Sheer pressure of other work probably prevented De Foe from turning Selkirk's story to account at the time; alternatively, the brilliant essay which Steele wrote for *The Englishman* on the subject may have made De Foe think it better to wait awhile.

Selkirk was born in 1676, and seems to have been one of those boys destined by Providence to furnish a God-fearing family with a perennial succession of headaches.

As a youth, he wanted to go to sea, but paternal opposition kept him at home until 1695, when, according to the parish records, he was cited to appear before the local magistrates for scandalous conduct in church. He did not appear, however, having at last achieved his wish and gone to sea, probably with the connivance of a family hoping to see the last of a black sheep.

They had not, however, seen the last of him, for in 1701 he was back in Largo again. Here an ingrained quarrelsomeness led to scenes with his brothers, and ended in his being "rebuked in the face of the congregation".

He must have had a considerable amount of nautical training during his six years' absence, for when he left his home town for the second time in 1702, and sailed to England to join Captain Dampier's privateering expedition, he was immediately given the highly responsible position of sailing-master of the ship *Cinque Ports*.

The story of the expedition begins, properly speaking, several years earlier. It is linked with the career of Doctor Thomas Dover, whose powders and writings, but especially powders, were later to make his name familiar to every sufferer from fever. Trained in London under the famous Dr. Sydenham, and cured by him of smallpox, he became a permanent testimonial to one of the most extraordinary treatments ever used to combat that malady. "I had no fire in my room," Dover wrote, "though it was January, my windows were constantly open, and my bedclothes ordered to be laid no higher than my waist. He made me take twelve bottles of small beer, acidulated with spirits of vitriol, every twenty-four hours."

Astonishingly enough, it was the smallpox virus which died.

In Bristol Dr. Dover proved himself a humane and generous physician, giving free treatment to the destitute, and being notably successful in curing cases of fever among the poor

But his hobby, his burning passion, was the sea and the ships sailing thereon. And when a group of similarly adventurous spirits decided to collect enough money to set out on a filibustering expedition against French and Spanish ships returning from South America and the West Indies to Europe laden with incalculable treasures, the call proved too strong to be resisted. He became a partner in the enterprise, and not merely a sleeping partner. His financial help was made on the condition that he was allowed to sail as a member of the crew.

Two ships were eventually fitted out—the *Duke* and the *Duchess*. Dover was on the *Duke* with the curious double rank of "second captain" and Captain of the Marines, his superior being an officer named Woodes Rogers. The navigator of the expedition came from Somerset; his name was William Dampier, and he already had the unusual distinction of having twice sailed round the world.

Nothing momentous happened until, in the following February (1709), they approached Juan Fernandez and its satellite islands believed to be uninhabited. The belief was, however, demonstrably false, since from a distance they could see smoke arising. The crew's first and most natural assumption was that they had had the bad luck to blunder upon the French fleet at anchor.

After some hesitation it was decided to send the *Duke's* marines ashore ₊to reconnoitre, with Dover in command. The landing-party were staggered at being greeted by a solitary tanned and bearded figure dressed in skins, and talking, though with the jerky harshness of one long unaccustomed to human conversation, their own language.

The figure was Selkirk, and the story he told was complicated.

He had joined Dampier's expedition in 1703, his ship being the *Cinque Ports*, and its captain Charles Pickering. Pickering however, died, and Thomas Stradling succeeded him. A number of prizes were taken. At some point after that, for obscure but probably personal reasons—privateering and its illegitimate brother, piracy, tended to bring personalities violently to the surface—Stradling and Dampier decided to part company.

In the following September a long-smouldering quarrel between Stradling and Selkirk had come to a head—Selkirk seems to have been one of those people who contrive, sooner or later, to quarrel with every acquaintance—and when the *Cinque Ports* called at Juan Fernandez to collect two sailors who had been accidentally left behind there on a previous visit, he demanded to be set ashore. Probably no one was better pleased at the demand than the *Cinque Ports* captain. Selkirk and all his possessions were promptly dumped on the island. Then he suddenly changed his mind. Probably a vision of what his isolation would involve confronted him. He begged to be allowed to return to the ship. Stradling refused. The *Cinque Ports* sailed on her way, leaving her quarrelsome ex-mate to the society of seabirds, crabs, and wild cats and goats.

He had at first a distressing time. But he was young, active and intelligent, and, as a sailor, used to roughing it. In a few months he became reconciled to his exile. He built himself two huts; he hunted the goats, at first by shooting them, then, when his precious supplies of gunpowder began to run low, by chasing and capturing them alive. Some he kept for their milk, and as pets; from the skins of others he made clothes. He contrived knives from old barrel-hoops. He did all the things, in short, which marooned sailors have laboriously done in real life and small boys have always longed passionately for an opportunity to do.

Twice a ship made its appearance. The first ignored his signals; the second he identified as Spanish. Selkirk, deciding that he preferred a desert island to the risks of a Spanish prison, hid until the vessel sailed away after firing a few vindictive shots.

Such was Selkirk's story. He was identified by Dampier, who was in the boat with Dover, and Dampier immediately caused him to be appointed mate of the *Duchess*—a remarkable tribute to Selkirk's previous record as a seaman.

Selkirk soon had every inducement to forget the monotony of the years spent on the island. The ships attacked and captured a Spanish vessel bound for South America. Unfortunately all she had on board was an immense number of Papal bills, five hundred bales of them, intended for sale by the priests to their South American flocks, a cargo of problematical spiritual value, and from an honest privateersman's point of view of no value at all. So some were used to burn the pitch off the ship's bottom, and the rest thrown overboard. The prize itself was converted into a third privateer, and rechristened the *Marquis*.

Adventures continued. Four more Spanish galleons were attacked, and in April 1709 Guaquil was sacked (seven thousand pounds was obtained as the price of its subsequent ransom). At night the sailors stowed their booty in the church, intending to take it back to their ships on the following morning. They then prepared to sleep. But no sleep was possible; the stench of the place was too appalling. It arose—though they did not know it—from the bodies of victims of a recent invasion of bubonic plague. And two days after leaving Guaquil a hundred and eighty of the crew were down with the disease.

Dover, the indomitable doctor-cum-Captain of Marines, rose to the emergency. He ordered all the plague-smitten men to be bled, and then dosed them heavily with diluted sulphuric acid. The sequel was a miracle in which simple faith probably played a part. All but eight recovered. The expedition sailed for home.

The syndicate financing the expedition netted the stupendous sum of one hundred and seventy thousand pounds from the loot captured.

Selkirk, who in the meantime had been given command of the *Increase*, and in January 1710 had been made sailing-master of another Spanish capture, arrived eventually in England. His personal share of the booty amounted to eight hundred pounds.

The next chapter of his life-story begins with Captain Woodes Rogers's decision to publish a full account of the expedition, complete with useful nautical and other technical details. The book, entitled *A Cruising Voyage round the World*, and published in 1712, was dull and uninspired. But it did include the story of Selkirk. There had also appeared a catchpenny pamphlet—*Providence Displayed, or a Surprising Account of One Alexander Selkirk . . . written by his own hand*—a statement to be taken with a very large grain of salt. The interesting point is that the Woodes Rogers book was sent to Steele and reviewed in his journal *The Englishman*. With the instinct of a born journalist, Steele at once saw the real focus of interest in the story. He knew Woodes Rogers, and through him obtained an introduction to Selkirk. The sailor seems to have made a good impression. "A man of good sense," says Steele, "with a strong and serious but cheerful expression."

Steele devoted nearly all his review to Selkirk's adventures. In 1718 a second edition of Woodes Rogers's book was issued. Did that suggest Robinson Crusoe to De Foe? Or did he, prowling through old copies of Steele's magazine, rediscover the eight-year-old story of Selkirk and become inspired to make its "man of good sense" the model for a far more famous fictitious hero? There are stories that De Foe contacted Selkirk personally before *Robinson Crusoe* was published. But there are no direct proofs that he ever did so.

Selkirk himself came back to Largo early in 1712. His island experiences seem to have left something of a hangover, for we are told that "he there lived the life of a permanent recluse, making for the purpose of meditation a sort of cave in his father's garden". His meditations, however, came to an abrupt end when a girl named Sophia Bruce appeared on the scene. He persuaded her to elope with him to Bristol, and from there the couple went to London. Their relationship, however, does not seem to have involved matrimony, for in a will he made four years later he refers to her as "my loving friend, Sophia Bruce, of the Pall Mall, London, Spinster". He made her his sole executrix and heiress, leaving her a house he had inherited from his father. After that, Selkirk appears to have for ever parted from his Sophia—of whom we hear no more—and eventually gone back to his only true love, the sea. But before that he legally married a widow named Candid. In December 1720 he made another will, describing himself therein as a "mate of his Majesty's ship *Weymouth*." a vessel that he had joined two months previously, and leaving his wife everything. An entry in the ship's paybook furnishes the last word concerning his restless and violent career—"Dead, 12th Dec. 1721".

Captain William Dampier, who played a part in Selkirk's complicated career, also deserves a more than casual mention. The son of a West Country tenant farmer, in his sixty-three years of life he contrived to pack enough adventure to supply material for an entire library of juvenile thrillers.

He was born near Yeovil in 1652, and received a haphazard education, mainly at Weymouth Grammar School.

His father died when the boy was ten, his mother four years later, and after the second event he was packed off to sea. After a series of voyages, he joined the *Royal Prince*, flagship of Sir Henry Spragge, in 1673, as an able seaman, and was involved in two hard-fought battles. A spell in hospital followed, then a job as assistant manager of a Jamaican sugar plantation. This he threw up to join the crew of a coasting trader, and in 1675 left the Bay of Campeachy with a cargo of rum and sugar to exchange for logwood. It was a voyage planned by Providence to enchant and occupy a youth of Dampier's particular type. To a love for seafaring was allied a passionate interest in the twin sciences of pilotage and chart-making. And the ignorance, incapability and drunkenness of the master involved so many accidents on the way home that, as Dampier commented, with a genial irony that might have been De Foe's own, "we got as much experience as if we had been sent out on a design".

It took three months for the ketch to make that return journey. When the voyage ended, Dampier decided to rejoin the logwood cutters and spent the next two years in the society of a crowd of the toughest, wildest, most drunken blackguards in existence. But the pay was high.

In the autumn of 1678 he returned to England again, a budding capitalist of twenty-six, with the intention of investing his money in the logwood trade. He also married "a young woman out of the family of the Duchess of Grafton".

Six months later he sailed again for the West Indies. At Negril Bay he was tempted into joining a party referred to by him as "privateers", though the crews were, in fact, nothing more nor less than pirates. Crossing this isthmus, they sacked and burned their way as far south as Juan Fernandez. A defeat at Orica led to quarrels among themselves. Dampier and about fifty others went off to find their own adventures and eventually fell in with a French ship cruising "on the account"—a pleasant euphemism for "piratically"—and joined it.

The further record of Dampier's adventures is too complicated to be told in detail. In July 1684 the captain died A man named Davis succeeded him, and in company with several other "free cruisers," manned by a mixed crew of English and French ruffians, a cheerful twelve months was spent "scourging the South American coast". Under Davis were Captains Eaton and Swan, but when Davis decided in August 1685 to remain at Peru, Swan parted company with him with a view to extending scourging operations down the Mexican coast. Dampier joined Swan, "not from any dislike to my old captain, but to get some knowledge of the northern parts of this continent".

In the spring of 1686 the Dampier-Swan contingent sailed for the East Indies. By the time they reached Guam, there was only three days' provisions left, and the crew were cheerfully contemplating cannibalism. They reached the Phillipines safely, however, and passed six months in the wildest excesses. In January Dampier left Swan and thirty-six others and put to sea. Eighteen months cruising ended in a quarrel, following which he and three seamen and some native prisoners were dumped ashore on Nicobar Island.

From this they escaped in a canoe, and after further hair-raising adventures, including a terrific but highly edifying storm, in the course of which "I looked back with horror and detestation on actions which I had previously disliked but now trembled at the remembrance of", Dampier eventually reached his native land on January 2nd, 1691, bringing with him, as his only possession, a tattooed native prince whom he hoped to exhibit. The prince, however, failed him, dying of smallpox shortly after his arrival.

In 1697 Dampier published his voyages. The book achieved considerable popularity, as well as establishing his reputation as a hydrographer. He entered Government employment as captain of H.M.S. *Roebuck*, surveying vessel, but proved himself not merely unaccustomed to naval discipline but far too harsh and violent-tempered to be successful as a commander. His brutal treatment of an elderly lieutenant named Fisher led to his recall, a court-martial, and a decision that he was not a fit person for Government employment. Yet in less than a year we find him kissing the Queen's hand prior to his departure on another Government-sponsored voyage to the West Indies.

From this last combination of surveying and privateering he returned with nearly two hundred thousand pounds' worth of specie and merchandise.

Unfortunately the prize money due to him was not paid until 1719, four years after his death.

He showed himself, says one biographer, "an incompetent commander, whose highest idea of discipline was calling his insubordinate officers rogues, rascals or sons of bitches".

Perhaps. But they still occasionally use strong language in the Navy. And if ever there was a typical sea-dog, Dampier was he.

What of the lesser characters in the drama?

Dr. Dover left Bristol and migrated to London. But he could not settle there, and after a time he returned to his native Warwickshire, where he wrote the minor classic which has crystallized his reputation, *The Ancient Physician's Legacy to his Country. Being what he has collected in Forty-nine years Practice. Or an Account of the Several Diseases incident to Mankind, in so plain a Manner, that any Person may know the Nature of his own Distemper, and the several Remedies proper for it, where the Extraordinary Effects of Mercury are more particularly considered   Designed for the use of all Private Families.*

Mercury became Dover's obsession to such an extent that he was known as "the quicksilver doctor". His book was a best-seller both in England and in France. (Incidentally, however, there is no mercury in the powders which bear his name and which are used to this day. They contain opium and ipecacuanha.)

As a footnote to the story, it may be mentioned that John Rumsey, Town Clerk of Bristol and a shareholder in the privateers' venture, perpetuated the success of the voyages by presenting a noble pair of silver candlesticks to the Cathedral, where they may be seen to this day. Made by Gabriel Sleath, a master silversmith, each candlestick has three engraved shields on its base, one bearing the donor's arms, one the arms of the See of Bristol, and the third a representation of the ships—the *Duke* on one candlestick, the *Duchess* on the other.

CHAPTER II

THE BOOK

D E FOE acquired all this intriguing information in 1711. But, as stated, for various reasons he delayed presenting it to the public until eight years later. By then he had more leisure, while at the same time his financial position was rendering it urgently necessary to employ that leisure profitably. He could have had no conception of the place his first lengthy work of fiction-based-on-fact was ultimately to occupy in the world's literature. But that he wrote it with immense gusto and personal enjoyment, in the same spirit which irradiates *Treasure Island* and the best of Dickens, is obvious. The type of book was entirely new to him, although, upon analysis, it will be found to contain all the old ingredients, employed by him for so many years that he had become an expert who did not realize his dexterity in employing them.

The story is told, as all the finest adventure stories are, in the first person. It includes all the typical De Foe references to the eternal watchfulness of God in protecting the interests of the righteous and afflicted. Providence, one feels, was as permanent an inhabitant of the island as the goats. No book ever more diligently insisted on the rewards of Virtue. De Foe was even more anxious to point a moral than to adorn a tale.

In a brief preface, which he called the "Author's"—a word which he appears to regard as synonymous with "editor"—he says:

"If ever the story of any man's adventures in the world were worth making public, and were acceptable when Published, the Editor of this account thinks this will be so.

"The Wonders of this man's Life exceed all that (he thinks) is to be found extant; the Life of one Man being scarcely capable of a greater Variety.

"The Story is told with Modesty, with Seriousness and with religious Application of Events to the Uses to which wise Men always apply them (viz.) to the instruction of others by this

Example and to justify the Wisdom of Providence in all the Variety of our Circumstances, let these happen how they will.

"The Editor believes the Thing to be a just History of Fact; neither is there any Appearance of Fiction in it. . . ."

In the last sentence he is, of course, superbly, even insolently right—there *is* no appearance of fiction in it. The "Thing" rings true.

Is its simple, Biblically direct English the reason for this? The chief, perhaps. But not the sole reason. I suggest that De Foe's early commercial training, involving, as it necessarily did, the making out of exact and detailed lists of goods, plays no inconsiderable part in our belief in Robinson Crusoe's existence and adventures. He views his own little world with a gaze intensely selective, yet which misses nothing.

His hero's name, incidentally, was, as already mentioned, derived from Timothy Cruso, a schoolfellow of De Foe's:[1] "Robinson" was a common surname in the neighbourhood. The island itself he transferred to the coast of South America, near the mouth of the Orinoco. A lengthy correspondence in the pages of *John o' London's Weekly* in conjunction with the wireless talk referred to on page 247 appears to make Tobago the likeliest original. He chanced the presence of turtles and wild goats and cats there, and by a lucky chance was justified, but was less lucky in adding penguins and seals to the inhabitants. He supplied his island, as the inventor of every imaginary island has had to do, with the essentials of any castaway's existence—a stream of fresh water, a hill to serve as a look-out for passing ships, trees, a soil that could be excavated or tilled.

With what care he planned the details of the story may be deduced from the following notes in possession of the Guildhall Library and now published for the first time:

Goats: plenty
Fish: abundance, Split and Salt
Seals: Do
Sea Lions: Do. and Seals make Oil; the fat of Young Seals good as Olive Oil
Wood, Water: plenty
carry Plans and Coppers to make Salt and Oil

[1] Similarly "Fagin" was the name of the boy who worked next to Dickens in the Hungerford Bridge blacking factory, while Sherlock Holmes embodied the names of two of Doyle's favourite cricketers.

Par: 804 Young Seals, the Meat white as Lamb; best a little Salted

807 Salted Seals and Penguins: very good; keeps well a long time

808 Seals will keep in Salt very well, at least 4 months, if bleeded well & ca.

804 Seals 14 to 18 ft. long, as big as a But; very fat

808 Penguins, 8 *li*.

To distill fresh water at Sea

Note Every ton of Pro: (? provision) procured in the South Seas would Cost about £50 to carry from hence, besides the disappointment or loss thereof in so long a Voiage makes it much more Valuable.

[On inside of same sheet]

If intend a Trade to the South Sea by the Straits Magellan, Now Immediately send 2 small Vessels of 40 or 50 Tonns to discover R [io] d[e la] Plata.

Send to Lisbon and Spaine for the largest and best Drafts of The Coast of Brazil, R. d Plata, Coasts to Straits Magellan and all the South Sea Coasts from said Straits to Acapulco, All the Ports of Brazil, R. d Plata, Chili, Peru and Mexico at large.

The first part of *Robinson Crusoe* was published in 1719. But not by the first publisher to whom the story was suggested. The trade in general proved completely apathetic, until William Taylor, De Foe's editor, and a man with whom he had had other dealings, was shown the proposed title and grasped its possibilities. He advised an octavo volume of about three hundred and fifty pages. Actually De Foe's manuscript, when printed, extended to three hundred and sixty-four pages.

Its full title was impressive. It ran:

The Life and Strange Surprising Adventures of Robinson Crusoe, of York, Mariner; who lived Eight and Twenty Years, all alone in an Uninhabited Island on the Coast of America, near the Mouth of the Great River of Oroonoque. Having been cast on shore by Shipwreck, wherein all the Men perished but himself. With an account of how he was at last as strangely deliver'd by Pyrates. . . . *Written by himself,* concludes De Foe, lying in modest italics.

Such a long-winded and elaborate title-page was the rule rather than the exception two centuries ago; it combined, for the reader's enlightenment and explanation, introduction and justification. Writers in De Foe's day had a healthy contempt for the staccato and the snappy.[1]

Quotations are essential. But what can one select from a book of which at least half is clamorous with quotations?

"I was now safe on shore, and began to look up and thank God that my life was saved. . . . I walked about on the shore, my whole being wrapt up in the contemplation of my deliverance."

Followed a little later by a superb descent to the commonplace:

"As for them (the galleon's crew) I never saw them afterwards, nor any sign of them, except three of their hats, one cap, and two shoes that were not fellows."

Again:

"How mercifully can our Creator treat his creatures, even in those conditions in which they seem to be overwhelmed in destruction! How can He sweeten the bitterest providences, and give us cause to praise Him for dungeons and prisons."

And then, immediately afterwards:

"It would have made a Stoic smile to see me and my little Family sit down to Dinner; there was my Majesty, the Prince and Lord of the whole Island . . . attended by my servants: Poll, as if he had been my favourite, was the only person permitted to talk to me. My Dog, who now was grown very old and crazy, sat always on my right hand, and two Cats, one on one side of the table and one on the other, expecting now and then a bit from my hand, as a mark of special favour. (These were not the two Cats that I had brought on shore at first, for they were both of them dead.)"

He recorded, in parallel columns, the evils in which he found himself, and their compensations, for example:

[1] Mr. Walter de la Mare charmingly parodies the style in one of his most charming books, "*Desert Isands*: being the *Voyage of a Hulk*, called by Courtesy a *Lecture*, that was Launched . . . in 1920, was afterwards frequently in Dock again for Repair, and then refitted for *Farther Adventurings* and so at length became laden with an unconscionable cargo of Odds and Ends ", etc., for the best part of a page.

"*EVIL.* I have no clothes to cover me. | *GOOD.* But I am in a hot climate, where, if I had clothes, I could hardly wear them."

Either the climate or his views must have changed considerably later on, for we are given an elaborate account of the garments he constructed.

"A great, high, shapeless cap of goatskin, with a flap hanging down behind. A short jacket with the skirt coming down to about the middle of my thighs, and a pair of open-kneed breeches of the same. Stockings and shoes had I none, but had made me a pair of somethings, I scarce know what to call them, like buskins, to flap over my legs and lace on either side. I had on a broad belt of goatskin dried, which I drew together with two thongs of the same, instead of buckles, and in a kind of frog on either side of this hung a little saw and a hatchet. . . . At my back I carried a basket, on my shoulder my gun, and over my head a great clumsy, ugly goatskin umbrella."

And finally, prelude to the appearance of Friday.[1]

"It happened one day about noon, going towards my boat, I was exceedingly surprised with the print of a man's naked foot on the shore. I stood like one thunderstruck, or as if I had seen an apparition; I listened, looked round me, I could hear nothing, nor see anything. I went up to a rising ground; I went up the shore and down the shore, but it was all one. I went again, to observe if it might not be my fancy, but there was exactly the very print of a foot, toes, heel and every part. . . ."

He kept a diary from September 30th, 1659, with occasional gaps, until the following summer, and abandoned it only when his ink, which from time to time he diluted until it was almost too weak to make any mark on the paper, gave out completely.

That superb first part of *Robinson Crusoe* leaves one with a feeling that here is something in which no mental toil, no deliberate construction chapter by chapter, played any part; a masterpiece simply came into existence complete and unique.

Yet the driving force behind its creation was purely financial. De Foe wanted money badly, and for a specific

[1] A character whom De Foe is said to have borrowed from Captain Rogers's account of a " Moskito Indian " with the disappointingly prosaic name of William.

object, the object being, as it had been for so many years, the needs of his family. Only in this case it was for one particular member, the second of the lovely and accomplished Miss De Foes, Hannah. He wanted a dowry for her, and it is ironical to record that though he also wrote *Moll Flanders*, *Roxana* and *Captain Singleton* with the same object, she was destined to remain single until the end of her days.

To revert to *Robinson Crusoe*.

Where, precisely, and what was his island?

That Selkirk was marooned on Mas-a-Tierra, off Juan Fernandez (*not* Juan Fernandez itself), is certain. That Selkirk did not spend twenty-eight years there is equally certain. So is the fact that De Foe had never in his life visited the West Indies or the Pacific.

A few years ago Mr. C. E. R. Alford dealt with the Crusoe conception in a wireless talk in which he stated that he had arrived at two conclusions: firstly, that De Foe had amused himself, in the true De Foe tradition, by placing an island in a latitude and longitude where no island exists, and, secondly, that he had *described* an island which really did exist, and had indeed been very much in the public eye, owing to an ingenious, temporarily successful boom started in 1683 by one Captain John Poyntz, who had then offered plots of land on Tobago for sale to English settlers. And in 1689 Henry Pitman published his adventures. Pitman had been shipped to Barbados along with many others, for his participation in the Battle of Sedgmoor. He had escaped in a sailboat, but had the bad luck to be wrecked on Tortuga, a small uninhabited island off Tobago.

For Tobago, concerning whose topography the details described in *Robinson Crusoe* conveniently fit, Mr. Alford plumps. He was promptly challenged by another authority, Mr. R. L. Megroz, who insists that Mas-a-Tierra, Selkirk's island, would serve perfectly as the *basis* for Crusoe's. There, for the present, the matter must rest.

Wherever the Island, the success of the book was instantaneous and immense. William Taylor, who alone had been shrewd enough to realize its possibilities, and had taken the precaution of registering his right to the whole property, is said to have cleared a thousand pounds over his bargain. (What he paid De Foe is unknown.)

"In a short time," sneers Gildon, an envious contemporary, Crusoe was already famed from Tuttle Street to Limehouse Hole, "and there was not an old woman that could go the price of it but bought it and left it as a legacy, with *The Pilgrim's Progress, The Practice of Piety,* and *God's Revenge against Murther,* to her posterity."

There was, of course, the inevitable rush of unscrupulous publishers to take advantage of this popularity. One of these, Heathcote, made literary history. Beginning on October 7th, 1719, and running for sixty-five issues—Nos. 125 to 189—*Robinson Crusoe* appeared in *The Original London Post, or Heathcote's Intelligence,* the first story to be serialized in the English Press.

Apart from pirated editions and spurious abridgments, there were flagrant imitations. Two may be mentioned. The first, published eight years after De Foe's masterpiece, was entitled *The Hermit, or the Unparalleled Sufferings and Surprising Adventures of Mr. Philip Quarll, an Englishman who was lately discovered by Mr. Dorrington, a British merchant, upon an Uninhabited Island in the South Sea. . . . where* [inconspicuous contrast to Crusoe] *he still continued to reside, and will not come away.*

The second, published nearly twenty years after De Foe's death, was *The Life and Adventure of Peter Wilkins,* by Robert Paltock. The author evolved an uncomfortable blend of *Robinson Crusoe* and *Gulliver's Travels,* beginning with a desert island and passing on to a country inhabited by flying men and women. It had some popularity, but did not survive the century.

Into the almost limitless orbit of De Foe there swam at this turn one of those minor literary figures who, unfortunate, eccentric or dissipated, or all in conjunction, were so common in his century. He was the contemporary already quoted, Charles Gildon (1665–1724), who, by the time that he was twenty-three, had inherited a large estate, dissipated it, added a wife to the responsibilities he took so lightly, and come to London, there to settle down as what is described as "an unfortunate scribbler" in the pay of the Whigs. He scribbled much else, including five plays and a quantity of verse. He was ill-advised enough to attack Pope, who retaliated by including him in *The Dunciad.* Exasperated by the success of *Robinson Crusoe,* he published on September

28th a pamphlet in three parts under the title of *The Life and Strange Surprizing Adventures of Mr. Daniel De Foe. . . . of London, Hosier, Who Has liv'd above fifty Years by Himself in the Kingdoms of North and South Britain. The various Shapes he has appeared in, and the Discoveries he has made for the Benefit of his Country. In a Dialogue between them, Robinson Crusoe, and his Man Friday. With remarks serious and Comical upon the Life of Crusoe.*

He took the easiest line of attack—the blunders and inconsistencies in the narrative. How could Crusoe see the eyes of the dying goat in the cave if it was pitch dark? How could the Spaniards give Friday's father an agreement in writing when they had neither pen nor ink? What explained there being three *English* Bibles in a Portuguese ship? How came it that Crusoe had "no cloathes to cover him", seeing that he had already saved a large quantity of "Linnen and Woolen" from the wreck? And how could he fill his pockets with ship's "Bisket" after swimming out to the vessel naked?

These and others were legitimate criticisms, as De Foe partially conceded when in later editions he made the Bibles part of his own luggage, and swam out with breeches with pockets in them to hold the "biskets". ("And why he did do so," commented Gildon scathingly and ungrammatically, "I can see no reason, and tho' he did do so, I don't find how the pocket of a Seaman's breeches could receive any Biskets, that being generally no bigger than to contain a Tobacco Pouch or the like.")

But this pamphlet of Gildon's was dangerous from another standpoint. De Foe had emphatically asserted that Crusoe was a real person, and that his adventures had actually taken place. He now became acutely uneasy at the increasing probability of the book being exposed as nothing more than fiction on a shallow and shaky foundation of fact. Taylor was making persistent demands for a third part. He had good reason for optimism, since in spite of every form of literary sharp practice, four editions of the first part had been absorbed in three months.

On August 20th *The Further Adventures of Robinson Crusoe* appeared.

It suffered from two heavy handicaps. Firstly, Crusoe spends only twenty-five days on the Island; secondly, when he *is* there, he is accompanied by others: hence its essential charm as an uninhabited spot has evaporated. Nevertheless, De Foe made it a brisk and exciting story. And when finally he embarked upon a third part, it gave him an opportunity of making one of those sudden confessions which by their sheer naïveté inspire belief. He deliberately let the cat out of the bag with a flourish (except, of course, that there was no cat). The whole book was an allegory of his own life, honest-to-goodness Pilgrim's Progress. . . . His preface to the third part, explaining all this, was brilliant. Unluckily, it was the only portion of the book that was. The truth was that De Foe had grown as weary of his hero as ever Dr. Conan Doyle grew of his; moreover, Crusoe was now a man of seventy, and at that age one is ill-attuned to new and dashing adventures.

De Foe has been denounced as the only author who wrote a sequel that did its best to ruin the splendour of its predecessor. I think that statement is unjust, pathetically unjust, to De Foe, and that the same fate had overtaken his imaginative powers that had overtaken Crusoe's ink; however ingeniously diluted, it was bound to run short at last.

Taylor is said to have lost considerably over that unfortunate finale, which appeared in August 1720. He could, however, afford to lose. When he died soon afterwards he left—to quote Monsieur Dottin—"two very desirable properties". He also nominated two executors, Mr. Innys, a bookseller of St. Paul's Churchyard, and a Mr. Osborn, of Cornhill. Both were gentlemen of tact. Mr. Osborn acquired, for two thousand pounds, Taylor's business for the benefit of his prospective son-in-law, Thomas Longman, who subsequently became the founder of the well-known publishing firm of Longmans Green & Co. But Mr. Innys had other ambitions; he married Mr. Taylor's widow, a charming and amiable lady with a portion of thirty thousand pounds.

The history of De Foe's masterpiece—one excludes the réchauffé of odds and ends which makes up the third part—may fittingly end in a fanfare of praise. Scott knew no work more generally read or more universally admired; Dr. Johnson cried, "Was there ever anything else written by mere man that was wished longer by its readers except Don Quixote and Pilgrim's Progress!"; while Daudet considered that even Shakespeare did not give so perfect an idea of the English character.

That year, 1719, was one of stupendous industry, even for De Foe. Apart from *Robinson Crusoe*, and regular contributions to four periodicals, he also wrote the following:

The Anatomy of Exchange Alley, or a System of Stock Jobbing, proving that Scandalous Trade as it is now carried on to be Knavish in its Private Practice and Treason in its Publick. By a Jobber. Sixty-four pages. Price a shilling. Published on July 11th, 1719.

The Dual Philosopher, or Great Britain's Wonder, containing a Faithful and very Surprising Account how Dickery Cronks, a Turner's Son in the County of Cornwall, was born Dumb, and continued so for fifty-eight years: and how, some days before he Died, he came to his Speech. Also a sixty-four page pamphlet, published at a shilling.

This little book achieved a coincidental prominence from the fact that, appearing almost at the same time as the author's account of a man condemned to isolation on a desert island, it dealt with another man also cut off from human speech. Hence, its nickname of "The Little Robinson Crusoe". It is, one may add, fiction.

Charity still a Christian Virtue, or an Impartial Account of the Tryal and Conviction of the Reverend Mr. Hendley, for Preaching a charity sermon at Chisselhurst. And of Mr. Chapman and Mr. Harding, for collecting at the same time the Alms of the Congregation. Seventy-two pages, price one shilling. Published October 16th.

This last was a record of precisely the type of petty tyranny which could be guaranteed to move De Foe to fury. Mr. Hendley had taken the children of a London charity school to "Chisselhurst," otherwise "Chizelhurst," where on their behalf he had held a service and collected the alms of the congregation. The local justices proceeded against him and the collectors as "beggars and vagrants and rogues and vagabonds".

After being committed for trial the three men were tried at Rochester Assizes, and fined. Proceedings were later taken against the two justices, but the death of Hendley allowed them to escape punishment.

The King of the Pyrates, being an account of the famous enterprises of Captain Avery, the Mock King of Madagascar, with his Rambles and Pyracies. Wherein all the Sham Accounts formerly published of him are detected.

This was a bigger book, one of a hundred pages, and costing one shilling and sixpence.

It is interesting to note that these men, who introduced themselves as "good Christian pirates", as distinct from low-grade ruffians, visited Juan Fernandez and remained there for three weeks. There is no reference in the book, however, to either Selkirk or Crusoe.

Finally, written in 1719, though not actually published until the following January, is *The Chimiera, or the French Way of Paying National Debts laid Open. Being an Impartial Account of the Proceedings in France for Raising a Paper Credit, and Settling the Mississippi Stock.* Seventy-six pages, price a shilling.

This was the work of De Foe the economist. It dealt with the financial operations of that misguided and interesting financial genius, John Law, and prophesied the crash which, in point of fact, came six months later, ruining half France.

One detail should not be forgotten. All books in those days were written by hand and with a quill pen. Even if De Foe received some assistance in the actual preparation of the manuscript and revision of the proofs from his sons, as has been suggested, the amount of sheer physical as well as mental work involved is staggering.

PART FIVE

THEREAFTER

CHAPTER I

REPORTER AT LARGE

AFTER the climax the anti-climax; after a literary *chef d'oeuvre*, the waiting world is usually presented with something conspicuously second-rate, a tribute paid by technique and experience to an all-too-brief burst of inspiration.

It was so in De Foe's case.

His next work of fiction was derived from a deaf-and-dumb fortune-teller "living in Exeter Court, over against the Savoy, in the Strand". A book of over three hundred pages, embellished with four plates, it appeared on April 30th, 1720, *The History of the Life and Adventures of Mr. Duncan Campbell, a Gentleman who, tho' born Deaf and Dumb, writes down any Stranger's Name at first Sight; and their (sic) future Contingencies of Fortune.*

De Foe, with his usual flair for what would appeal to the public taste, had chosen a remarkable subject. The original Duncan Campbell, in spite of his double handicap, was a good deal more than a fortune-teller, being able to "play the violin with great exactness, and tune the instrument by putting it between his teeth". He was also an expert fencer. His fortune-telling brought him considerable wealth, which his extravagant habits rapidly dissipated.

The book was a success, running into a second edition before the end of the year, and encouraging De Foe to produce, on June 18th, *Mr. Campbell's Pacquet*, which "pacquet" comprised three parts, the first two being verses by what to-day would be termed "outside contributors", and the third an elaborate description of a series of encounters between a well-meaning minister named Ruddle, and the ghost of a lady named Dorothy Dingley who had been in her grave for eight years past. The story, like that of Mrs. Veal, was alleged to have been told De Foe by an informant he had no reason to mistrust.

Another story of the same type, called *The Friendly Daemon*, appeared in 1720. It was an account of a familiar spirit's visitation (in a white surplice, presumably to disarm suspicion) to "a famous deaf-and-dumb gentleman". But whether De Foe was responsible or not is uncertain.

De Foe was now fairly embarked upon what may be termed his historical novel period. In May he "edited" *Memoirs of a Cavalier, a Military Journal of the Wars in Germany and the Wars in England from the Year 1632 to the Year 1648. Written three score Years ago by an English Gentleman.*

Concerning this, modern critics have held sharply differing views. Dottin refers to the book as "a long-drawn-out succession of military manœuvres, described by a dull and lifeless individual". Wright says: "It has elicited admiration from critics of all opinions." Saintsbury says: "It is hardly surpassable. Many separate passages . . . have never been equalled except by Mr. Carlyle." While Lee terms it "one of the finest military memoirs extant in any language".

With regard to the proportion of fact to fiction, one can hardly do better than quote the preface to the second edition. Says the Leeds publisher:

" The republication of these Memoirs will renew the enquiry which has been oft made, ' Who wrote them? ' Some have imagined the whole to be a Romance; if it be, 'tis a Romance the likest the Truth I ever read."

It is certain that De Foe took even more trouble than usual to mislead his public into believing the narrative authentic, certain that he could not have written it at all without the backing of genuine historical documents, and certain that basically the whole thing was evolved from his own imagination.

He followed up this with *The Life, Adventures and Pyracies of the famous Captain Singleton*. It appeared on June 4th, and ran to three hundred and forty-four pages. It was reissued as a serial in *The Post Master, or Loyal Mercury* from November onwards. Possibly because here De Foe was deliberately cashing in on *Robinson Crusoe*, and his readers realized and subconsciously resented it, the book did not meet with conspicuous success, although it included a series of Peter Pan-ish adventures, with characters to match, including a Quaker named William who cheerfully became Singleton's second in command on the pirate ship, but eventually converted him.

" Now that you're rich," says William, " have you not had enough of this wicked life, which will certainly lead you to eternal damnation?"

Singleton, surprisingly, though sensibly, replied that he had, and demonstrated the fact by marrying the Quaker's sister.

In 1721 De Foe's fact-cum-fiction factory was comparatively idle, though he was still busy with his newspapers. But in 1722 he became really busy again. It was, indeed, a memorable year, for quality no less than quantity. On January 27th appeared a book of over four hundred pages with the truly horrific title of *The Fortunes and Misfortunes of the famous Moll Flanders etc. who was born in Newgate, and during a Life of continued Variety, for three score years beside her childhood, was Twelve Years a Whore, Five Times a Wife (whereof once to her own Brother), Twelve Years a Thief, Eight Years a Transported Felon in Virginia, at last grew Rich, lived Honest and died a Penitent.* Written from her own Memorandum.

It is hardly surprising that a second and third edition had to be printed during the same year.

It is redolent of De Foe, and his travels and experiences and philosophy. Bath, Bristol and Hammersmith form the background to a succession of landladies and friends to whom Moll tells the story of her life, to which story each adds a chapter in turn.

Moll's views, based on a certain amount of preliminary experience concerning the type of man she would accept and marry—or accept without marrying—are typical.

" I was not averse to a tradesman, but then I would have a tradesman forsooth who was something of a gentleman too; that when my husband had a mind to carry me to the court or

to the play, he might become a sword and look as like a gentleman as another man; and not be one that had the mark of his
apron-strings upon his coat or the mark of his hat upon his
periwig . . .

" Well, at last I found this amphibious creature, this land-
water thing called a gentleman-tradesman, and, as a just plague
upon my folly, I was catched in the very same snare, as I might
say I laid for myself."

"Gentleman-tradesman." There must have been the
deliberate touching of a raw nerve there.

There are, of course, the inevitable details. A thief, running from his pursuers, drops what he has stolen as he passes.

" I took my opportunity to take up what was behind me and
walk away.

" I got safe to my lodgings with this cargo, which was a piece
of black lutestring silk, and a piece of velvet, the latter was but
part of a piece of eleven yards; the former a whole piece of near
fifty yards; it was a mercer shop they had rifled."

And:

" Going by a house near Stepney, I saw on a window-board
two rings, one a small diamond ring, and the other a plain gold
one, to be sure laid there by some thoughtless lady, perhaps
only till she had washed her hands.

After considerable hesitation she rapped once or twice.

" But nobody came, then, seeing the coast clear, I thrust
hard against the glass, and broke it with little noise, and took
out the two rings, and walked away with them fairly safe."

One is tempted to quote almost indefinitely—extreme
quotability is always part of De Foe's charm.

A curious point in connection with the name of the heroine
may be mentioned.

Mr. Lee states that among books advertised for sale by a
Mr. John Darby in *The Post Bag* of January 22nd, 1722, is
The History of Flanders, with Moll's Map.

The coincidence is staggering—if it *was* a coincidence.

From *Moll Flanders* he turned to a work, or rather, two
linked works, of peculiar and permanent interest, inasmuch
as they raise the question as to how much personal recollec-
tion could have gone to their making.

FRONTISPIECE TO THE FIRST EDITION OF *The Life and
Strange Surprising Adventures of Robinson Crusoe of York, Mariner*

REPORTER AT LARGE 257

Both appeared in the same year. One was *Due Preparation for the Plague*, and is a book of nearly three hundred pages in which are described the vicissitudes of two families during the Great Plague. (It is upon this that Harrison Ainsworth's novel *Old St. Paul's* is based.)

Its far-better-known companion volume is *A Journal of the Plague Year*, also running to nearly three hundred pages, "Written by a Citizen who continued all the while in London".

That catastrophic period has already been dealt with in this book. At the actual time (1665) De Foe was only five years old. Five, nevertheless, is an age at which any normal mind—and De Foe's was far more than normal—is capable of permanently registering scenes and incidents; sounds and smells and sights are recorded with the fantastic selectiveness so common to the human memory.

To this must be added the fact that the Plague, with all its horrors and the multifarious sequels to those horrors, must have been a common topic for decades afterwards, and there were details that many people living in the 1720's could confirm or amplify from first-hand knowledge. Finally, there were contemporary official records available. To a journalist of De Foe's quality the whole business must have been childishly easy.

The late Walter Bell, to whose story of the Plague I have already acknowledged my indebtedness, gave it as his considered opinion that De Foe's account should be regarded only in the light of an historical novel, in other words, a fictitious excursion based, but merely based, on actual fact. It would have been an interesting experiment to see side by side the statements which he regards as due entirely to De Foe's ultra-prolific imagination, and what the actual records have to say about the same incidents. This paralleling process is, unfortunately, impracticable here. But I dare to suggest that the demonstrable inaccuracies and discrepancies are fewer and less important than Mr. Bell implies.

However much of the story belongs to genuine history, it is reasonably certain that his "citizen" did not. He was a saddler, living—the De Foe touch—"without Aldgate, midway between Aldgate Church and Whitechapel Bars, on the left or north side of the Street". The narrative begins with detached simplicity:

" It was about the beginning of 1664 that I, among the rest
of my neighbours, heard in ordinary discourse, that the Plague
was returned again in Holland."

But the absence of newspapers to spread the news, and
confidence that, in any case, the Government was capable of
tackling the Plague, even if it did become a serious menace,
helped people to forget the bad news until in the winter,
when "two men, said to be Frenchmen, died of the Plague
in Long Acre, or rather, at the upper end of Drury Lane ".

Follows, as the infection spreads, pages of weekly burials of
those certified as dying from the Plague. De Foe also includes
various advertisements for its certain cure, accounts of warning visions seen by certain semi-demented people, a list of
plague officials and what their individual duties were, and
"orders concerning loose persons and idle assemblies".

There are almost unbearably pathetic fragments such as:

" Passing thro' Token House Yard, of a sudden a casement
violently opened just over my Head, and a Woman gave three
frightful Screeches, and then cry'd ' Oh! *Death, Death, Death!'*
in a most inimitable tone, and which struck me with Horror,
and a Chillness in my very blood. There was no Body to be
seen in the whole Street, nor did any other Window Open, for
People had no Curiosity now in any case, nor could any Body
help one another."

And:

" Just in Bell Alley, on the right hand of the Passage, there
was a more terrible Cry than that . . . and I could hear Women
and children run screaming about the Rooms like distracted,
when a Garret Window opened, and somebody from a Window
on the other side of the Alley called ' What is the matter ?' Upon
which from the first Window it was answered, ' O Lord, my old
Master has hanged himself! ' The other asked again, ' is he
quite dead ?' The first answered ' Ay, ay, quite dead; quite
dead and cold!' This Person was a Merchant, and a Deputy
Alderman, and very rich. I care not to mention his name, but
that would be a Hardship to the Family, which is now flourishing
again."

The book concludes on a note of mingled gratitude and
lamentation:

" I should be counted censorious, and perhaps unjust if I
should enter upon the unpleasing work of reflecting . . . upon
the return of all manner of wickedness among us, which I was
so much an eye witness of myself. I shall conclude this account
of this calamitous year with a coarse but sincere stanza of my
own which I placed at the end of my ordinary memorandums
the same year they were written—

> A dreadful Plague in London was
> In the year sixty-five
> Which swept away an hundred thousand souls
> Away—yet I alive."

After which appalling doggerel the saddler living midway
between Aldgate Church and Whitechapel set his humble
initials "H. F.".

An interesting point arises. De Foe ignores the Great Fire,
though, as Pepys so superbly demonstrates, it possessed
equally dramatic possibilities. (Bell's edition of De Foe's
works includes an account of the Fire "by an anonymous
writer", who, the edition explains, was not De Foe, a super-
fluous statement to anyone familiar with that author's
style.)

The background of De Foe's next book was France. In
the "Foreign Affairs" column of his *Journal* he had already
had a good deal to say concerning a young criminal named
Cartouche, who, with his organized gangs of ruffians, had
been terrorizing the country, and had been finally captured
and executed. De Foe saw the possibilities of exploiting the
grisly excitement that the story aroused; there was obviously a
pamphlet in it, if not a book. The pamphlet, a thick one,
duly appeared on April 27th, almost six months to the day
after the villain's execution. *The Life and Actions of Lewis* (sic)
*Dominique Cartouche, who was Broke Alive on the Wheel at Paris. . . .
Relating at Large his Remarkable Adventures, desperate Enterprises, and various Escapes. With an Account of his Behaviour
under Sentence and upon the Scaffold, and the Manner of his Execution.*

Cartouche was dead, but—one is reminded irresistibly here
of Conan Doyle's Professor Moriarty—some of his lieutenants
remained still at liberty, and these continued the congenial
work of attacking, robbing and murdering travellers, their
chief victims being wealthy tourists and their servants. On

September 23rd, 1723, an Englishman returning home from Paris was murdered near Calais; a few minutes later three more Englishmen, together with their servants, were similarly attacked. One of the servants, Robert Spindelow, however, though desperately wounded, did survive to give evidence that eventually hanged two of the murderers. De Foe interviewed Spindelow, wrote his story in *Applebee's Journal*, and later, August 17th, 1724, produced another pamphlet on the crimes of the Cartoucheans. De Foe's statement that they were translated from the French means little more than that he obtained his facts from the News-Letters sent from France. His details concerning Cartouche's boyhood are almost certainly the fruits of his own imagination.

And after that?

Three days before Christmas the citizens of London were thrilled with *The History and Remarkable Life of the truly Honourable Colonel Jacque, vulgarly called Colonel Jack, who was born a gentleman, but Prentice to a Pickpocket; was six-and-twenty years a Thief, and then kidnapped to Virginia, came back a Merchant, was five Times married to four Whores, went into the Wars, behaved bravely, got Preferment, was made Colonel of a Regiment, came over and fled with the Chevalier, is still abroad completing a Life of Wonders, and resolves to die a General.*

No wonder a second edition was demanded a month later, and a third in 1724! No wonder, to quote a quaint phrase of Mons. Dottin's translator, the author's popularity "kept his nose to the grind".

The result of that grind was a double-barrelled book of over four hundred pages, published at five shillings: *An Impartial History of the Life and Actions of Peter Alexowitz, the Czar of Muscovy*, and *The Highland Rogue, or the Memorable Actions of the celebrated Robert Macgregor*—both in 1723.

And on March 14th, 1724, came *The Fortunate Mistress, or a History of the Life and Vast Variety of Fortunes of Mademoiselle de Belau, afterwards called the Countess of Wintselscheim in Germany. Being the Person known by the name of the Lady Roxana, in the Time of King Charles II.*

Again, into four hundred-odd pages, he packed a story of high and low life, but this time with a rather larger proportion of the high—"to describe Human Nature as it is for the Purpose of Contrasting it with what it should be", says the author smugly, although in point of fact the Gay Roxana—a full length portrait of whom, richly dressed and standing against an equally opulent interior, forms the frontispiece of the book—led a life of increasing worldliness and wealth until belatedly—very belatedly—she decided to abandon vice plus luxury for virtue plus luxury, this change of heart being hastened by the influence of a Quakeress with whom she lodged in the Minories. This Influence for Good (strictly in the De Foe tradition) is further supported by the arrival in England of the Dutch merchant whom she had met before in Paris. He had bought a foreign title of nobility, and, marrying her, made her the Countess of Wintselscheim.

One would like to add that a much-travelled, much-troubled and penitent Roxana lived happily ever after. But this time De Foe has no intention of protecting his heroine from Nemesis as he protected Moll. Perhaps he never really liked Roxana. Tormented by conscience, she is in contact again with the children she had borne and practically forgotten. The truth about her extremely lurid past becomes known to the Count, and they become alienated. Eventually Roxana is left a widow and, losing all her money in speculation, herself dies in prison.

"Roxana," says Mr. Saintsbury, "is on the whole the least good of De Foe's minor novels . . . and one of the most puzzling." (This second statement arises from the fact that the heroine is said to have been known as Roxana in the time of Charles II, whereas she was only ten years old when she came to England in 1683.) He adds that she is the most disagreeable of De Foe's heroines.

Professor Sutherland, on the other hand, makes the point that while one may not find her personally appealing, one can hardly help being attracted by her intelligence and astuteness, and her shrewd, common-sense attitude towards the life which she had made her own. And I am inclined to agree with him.

De Foe was ostensibly, one might say ostentatiously, a moralist; the mantle of the Nonconformist preacher might become considerably tattered and worn by friction, but he never entirely forgot it or cast it aside. He had also a passion for instructing, not because he was temperamentally a schoolmaster, but because he was temperamentally a journalist; an instinctive conveyor-belt of trivialities concerning humanity which, with limitless interest and delight, he was perpetually discovering. To study one's fellow-creatures and their reactions is a practical guarantee of intensified psychological insight, and in such small, unexpected revelations De Foe is at his best.

But with Roxana, the strange, belated flowering of De Foe's imagination into the region of fiction withered; and in *A New Voyage round the World*, published in the following spring, it may be said to have died. The *New Voyage*, an old one so far as De Foe was concerned, recounted the adventures of a London merchant travelling round the world *via* the Cape, and the Indian and Pacific Oceans, and returning by South America. It is referred to in detail on a subsequent page.

Before that, however, in fact within three weeks of *Roxana's* publication, he had reverted to his old style and his old grievance in *The Great Law of Subordination Considered, or the Insolence and Insufferable Behaviour of Servants in England duly enquired into. Illustrated by a great Variety of Examples, Historical Cases and Remarkable Stories of the Behaviour of some Particular Servants.* In Ten Familiar Letters. It ran to over three hundred pages, and was priced at two shillings "sticht" or three shillings bound. His chief argument was that, while servants were shockingly pampered, wives, owing to the prevalence of drunkenness among men, which made them "surly, cruel, tyrannical and outrageous", were shockingly ill-treated.

" To hear a woman cry murther now, scarce gives any alarm; the neighbours scarce stir at it, and if they come out in a fright and ask ' What's the matter? ' the common answer is ' 'Tis nothing, neighbour, but such a one beating his wife.' ' Oh, dear,' says the other, ' is that all? ' And in they go again, composed and easy."

In his next book De Foe suddenly assumed the role of courier. In three volumes published in May 1724, June 1725 and August 1726, respectively, he gave the world *A Tour through the Whole Island of Great Britain, divided into Circuits or Journies, Giving a Particular and Diverting Account of whatever is curious and worth Observation.*

The work was not, of course, the result of a single tour.

One commentator[1] goes so far as to state that De Foe obtained, and presumably recorded, his information during 1684–8, the five years preceding Monmouth's rebellion. If so, he kept his notes in cold storage for forty years—a long time, unless he was deliberately waiting until he could reinforce them with later material. In any case, those early travels, added to his subsequent tours, made an astonishing total— seventeen "large circuits ", i.e. (separate journeys in England), three general tours through the whole country, and further journeys over most of Scotland, the southern part of which he had, with the North of England, "viewed five several times over ". . . .

In these volumes De Foe, anonymous as "A Gentleman", is at his best. In the first volume he started from London and travelled through the eastern, southern and south-western counties. Included as an extra, so to speak, was a Diary of the Siege and Blockade of Colchester in the year 1648. The second volume contains a "Perspective Map" of England and Wales, and the third a similar map of Scotland, both the work of Mr. Hermann Moll, the Royal Geographer, whose *Flanders* has already been mentioned.

In the preface to the second volume he comments delightfully, though far from delightedly, upon the rapid changes taking place in or near the Metropolis.

" Since the finishing of the last volume," writes the sardonic De Foe, " the South Sea Company have been engaged in the Greenland Fishery and have fitted out a Fleet of twelve great Ships . . . and have made that great Wet Dock between Deptford and Redriff [Ratcliff], the Centre of all that Commerce, and the Building of the Works and the Management of all that they call their cookery, that is, the Boyling their Blubber into Oyl. 'Tis well if they do not make stink enough and gain too little."

In his preface to the third volume he reverts to the rapid expansion of London, to which was being added another little City of buildings, streets and squares at the west end of Hanover and Cavendish Squares. Later he refers to the turkeys and geese that travelled on foot in droves of three hundred to a thousand all the way from Norfolk to London market; to the swallows preparing in myriads for migration on the roof of Southwold Church; to the glories of Stourbridge

[1] Wright.

Fair—"not only the greatest in the whole nation, but in the world"; the delights and dangers of Tunbridge Wells, the charm of Ipswich as a residential centre; the high charge of the Harwich innkeepers; the animal market at Cambridge where "Woollens, Serges, Du Roys, Challoons, Cantaloons" are sold; and to Devonshire, "where Kersico is bought and sold ". And he tells how at Steyning Sir John Faggs received an offer of twenty-six pounds apiece for four bullocks by London dealers, but refused it because he wanted to take them up to Town himself. And at Amesbury the hay-crops were so rich that a single meadow was let at twelve pounds an acre for the grass alone. . . . So the happy traveller goes on his way, seeing, appraising, reporting.

He visited Norwich and Ely and Lichfield and Stratford-on-Avon, but neither cathedral cities nor poet's birthplace really interested our incorrigible middle-brow as much as horse-fairs and lace factories, and towns with legends. Burnham-on-Crouch particularly intrigued him, because he was told that owing to its marshy air the district had a peculiarly fatal effect on the female sex, with the result that numbers of the men living there had married anything from five to fifteen times. (One farmer had actually buried twenty-four wives and, moreover, found a young woman intrepid enough to become the twenty-fifth wife, with every probability of becoming the twenty-fifth victim.)

De Foe had always taken a special and personal interest in the world of social misfits. That interest continued throughout his own penurious and dangerous days—the days of Sedgemoor and Judge Jeffreys, of foreign travel with all its risks; of bankruptcy, the pillory and Newgate. Now, when he was famous, wealthy and solidly established as one of the gentry, the escapades of the outcasts of society still enthralled him, perhaps because their lives were crude and vivid and exciting and lent themselves so readily to dramatization.

In August 1724 he published his second pamphlet on the infamous Cartouche. In October of the same year he became more intimately involved with an English criminal of even greater distinction, this time no monster leading gangs of mass murderers, but a slim boy of twenty-two whose blackest offences had been thefts, and who to-day would have faced, at the worst, a few years of preventive detention.

His name was John Sheppard, and the story of his escape from Newgate still remains unique among real-life thrillers.

Born in 1702, he was the son of an honest carpenter who died early in 1703, leaving several children. One of them destroyed the family's record for respectability by being convicted of thieving, and was transported in 1704; Jack, however, was befriended by a woollen draper with the Dickensian name of Kneebone. The draper taught him to read and write, and eventually apprenticed him to Owen, a carpenter. At this point Jack seems to have taken a headlong plunge into the world of vice. As an expert thief, he associated with two female criminals known as "Edgeworth Bess" and "Poll Maggott" (Gay might have found immediate places for them in *The Beggars' Opera*) and a male villain, Joseph Blake, alias "Blueskin." Jack's subsequent career furnished plots for half a dozen stage dramas or at least one novel.[1]

De Foe took an intense, almost personal interest in the young criminal's exploits, a fact highly gratifying to Sheppard, who had all the vanity of his type. When first caught and imprisoned (through the machinations of Jonathan Wild, an infinitely viler specimen of London's scum), he was visited by Wagstaff, the "ordinary" or prison chaplain, as a matter of routine, and by a representative of *Applebee's*, otherwise De Foe, who had, of course, no official status, but who nevertheless did his best to second the efforts of the ordinary to impress the mind of the criminal with a proper sense of religion. Shortly afterwards Sheppard, with the help of Bess and Moll, succeeded in escaping, and five days after that wrote a letter to the hangman to which, as a postscript, he added, "Pray give my service to Mr. Ordinary and Mr. Applebee."

He was recaptured, tried unsuccessfully to free himself, was removed to safer quarters, and from those, on October 17th, made what was to prove his final and most spectacular escape. Two days later De Foe published *The History and Remarkable Life of John Sheppard*. Three editions were sold in as many weeks, but even more exciting to the author must have been a letter left at Mr. Applebee's Blackfriars residence by what was subsequently described as "a person like an ostler". The letter ran:

[1] Harrison Ainsworth's *Jack Sheppard*.

" Mr. Applebee—

" This with my kind love to you, and pray give my kind love to Mr. Wagstaff; hoping these lines will find you in good health, as I am at present; but I must own that you are the loser for want of my dying speech; but to make up your loss, if you think this sheet worth your while, pray make the best use of it.

" So no more from your humble servant,

" John Sheppard."

A postscript said, "I desire you to be postman to my last lodging," followed by a statement that the writer had fears of recapture, in which case he wished Mr. Applebee to write an account which should be published immediately after his death.

His fears soon materialized, entirely through his own folly. After a number of daring reappearances in the City he was discovered in a drunken stupor in a tavern near Clare Market and taken back to Newgate. This time the authorities were taking no risks. Guarded night and day, on November 16th, 1724, a few days before his twenty-second birthday, he was driven to execution at Tyburn. Efforts were made up to the last moment to obtain a reprieve on account of his youth, but the indictments were too heavy, his defiance of the law too barefaced.

De Foe was standing near the place of execution, one of a crowd of two hundred thousand spectators. Sheppard recognized him, beckoned him into the cart, and there handed him a full record of all his robberies and escapes.

There was rioting when they cut down the poor wretch's body; a regiment of foot was needed to restore order.

De Foe wasted no time over the sentimental side of the tragedy. Temperament and experience made him a realist and a philosopher; by training he was a hard-bitten journalist, with an eagle eye for front-page and exclusive news. And here was something magnificently exclusive. Only a day after the execution appeared *A Narrative of all the Robberies, Escapes etc. of John Sheppard. Giving an Exact Description of the Manner of his Wonderful Escape from the Castle in Newgate, . . . written by himself during his Confinement in the Middle Stone Room, after his being retaken in Drury Lane. To which is prefixed a true Representation of his Escape, from the Condemned Hold. . . . Curiously engraved on a Copper Plate. The whole Published at the particular Request of the Prisoner.* There were thirty-one octavo pages, plus the "curiously engraved plate", and the price was sixpence. The first edition was sold out on the day of publication; a second edition appeared on the following day, and other editions on November 19th, 20th, 21st and 28th, and on December 7th.

It was a curious reversion to the work of earlier years, a sound and indeed brilliant piece of reporting. But it lacked one thing—that inspired illumination of plain facts which constitutes De Foe's own unique magic. The truth was that with increasing age the arteries of his imagination were hardening. He could accumulate facts; he could deduce further facts from them; he could use those deductions as a basis for advice, censure, prophecy, and—though this occurred more rarely nowadays—praise. But no longer to delight, to charm.

His next book, previously mentioned, *A New Voyage round the World, by a Course never Sailed before,* emphasized this change. It appeared in May 1725, ran to over two hundred pages, and was illustrated with plates, "curious" and otherwise. Modern critics take widely differing views about it, although agreeing that it does exhibit the author's extraordinary range of geographical knowledge. Personally, I concur with Mr. Wright in considering the book a dull one by De Foe standards, containing too much geography and too little human nature.

He followed that up by a thirty-four page pamphlet called *Everybody's Business is Nobody's Business,* published in June 1725, in which he recurred to a grievance which seems to have become perennial—the pride, insolence and laziness and general unsatisfactoriness of domestic servants and others of their class. It was a popular outburst, for it had reached five editions before the end of July.

Contemporarily were two more thrillers: *The True Genuine and Perfect Account of the Life and Actions of Jonathan Wild,* and *An Account of the Conduct and Proceedings of the late John Gow, alias Smith, Captain of the late Pirates, executed for Murther and Piracy . . . with a relation of all the horrid Murthers they Committed in Cold Blood.* Both the above were published in June.

Wild was one of the most nauseating villains included in our criminal records. His trade was a simple one, with two separate branches. One was the training and organizing of bands of ruffians, each doing specialized work, to steal; the other, an equally organized system of returning the stolen property to its owners after a diplomatic interval and on payment of an adequate fee. Wild himself acted as the receiver and subsequently the recoverer of the goods. His methods, which included a ruthless system of blackmail and exposure if any of his employees showed signs of disloyalty, might have been the direct inspiration of the twentieth-century Chicago gangster.

Wild was eventually exposed, his specific offence being the acceptance of a reward for the return of some lace that one of his own band had stolen. After trying unsuccessfully to poison himself with laudanum, he was hanged at Tyburn on May 24th, 1725.

De Foe interviewed Wild—whose favourite slogan was Honesty is the best Policy—in prison, and doubtless by request published in two numbers of *Applebee's* lists of the criminals Wild had brought to justice. Neither the authorities nor the general public were impressed, however, and among the immense crowd that gathered at his execution "there was not," reported De Foe, "one pitying eye to be seen, not one compassionate word to be heard. . . . Nothing but halloing huzzas, as if it had been a triumph".

CHAPTER II

THE LOVELY SOPHIA

AT THIS point, on the publication of a work which on its own merits would have made the reputation of a lesser man, one may turn to the personal affairs of De Foe.

Though his mind had lost none of its activity, he was now sixty-four, and that agile body of his was becoming aware of the fact. There were spells of gout whose crippling reactions affected his never very patient temper; he was growing more quickly fatigued, and in consequence more difficult to live with.

Nevertheless, he had a good deal to be grateful for.

Within five years he had created a reputation, and with it a general popularity, totally detached from, and consequently unaffected by the political intrigues for which in the past he had sacrificed so much. He was a comparatively wealthy man. He had some years earlier acquired a square red-brick house in Church Street, Stoke Newington, then a village surrounded by open country, and to this added two flat-roofed wings which emphasized the barrack-like ugliness of the whole. It was, in the words of Henry Baker, later to become the owner's son-in-law, "a very handsome house"; the house-agent's favourite "commodious" would have been a fitter adjective. But there was plenty of room in it for De Foe's library, and deep window-seats, and many built-in cupboards, and massive doors.

There was also stabling for his horse and the "chariot", which was then, as Carlyle's gig was later, the hall-mark of a gentleman of means. Finally, and best of all, since the old man had developed rather unexpectedly into an enthusiastic gardener, there were grounds extending to four acres.

House and grounds have long vanished; only De Foe Road, now occupying the site, records their existence.

With increasing years, and fame, he became not only more remote from his very middle-class beginnings, but increasingly class-conscious. He had always been a dandy, with a hankering to consort with his social superiors; always, to speak plainly, something of a snob. If he had possessed a lighter, less ironic sense of humour, he might have laughed at his own foibles, but it was typical of his later touchiness that he became exasperated at the slightest failure of the lower orders to appreciate his position. A groom who turned a horse loose on De Foe's grounds moved him to such fury that eventually not only the groom but the horse's owner became involved, and the two men had to be dragged apart by friends. A group of rustics who disliked being cross-questioned by him led to another explosion; a third occurred when, entering a friend's house, he kissed by mistake a smartly dressed maid. Nobody would ever have echoed more heartily than he the Dickensian prayer, "God bless the Squire and his relations, and keep us in our proper stations"—after De Foe had successfully emerged from his own station.

Added to the insolence of social inferiors was the lack of respect shown by youth to its elders. "The general contempt put upon Old Age by others," he wrote bitterly, "is now such that it is hardly sufferable by Human Nature!"

So might an elderly and irascible cave-man have grumbled twenty thousand years earlier.

But there were pleasant sides to his nature. He could be, and was, charitable towards people less lucky than himself. "Mr. Deffoe hath acted a noble and generous part towards me and my poor children," testified Thomas Webb, a Quaker down on his luck. "Mr. Deffoe" is further recorded as having given ten pounds towards lightening the debt on the parish church.

Mary, his wife, a curiously shadowy figure in these later years, was still living. (She died in 1732, eighteen months after her husband.) His three unmarried daughters, Hannah, Henrietta and Sophia, were girls of whom any parent might be proud—as, indeed, he was proud—for their beauty, their education, their deportment. Maria, the fourth girl, had already married a "salter", or salt-maker, named Langley, and was no longer living at home. Of his sons, Daniel, the elder (or eldest), had married early, lost his wife after she had given birth to a son (christened Daniel, who also died), and made a second and wealthy match when he married his cousin, Mary, née Webb, in 1720. This Mary De Foe had, in turn, a boy, who was christened Daniel, and who, like his half-brother, died young. There were two other children, Tuffley and Samuel.[1] The latter lived until 1783. The precise status of the second son, Benjamin, presents the biographer with a first-class problem. On the one hand, we have the indisputable fact that there was a second son of that name, the fourth child born to Daniel De Foe and Mary his wife, and baptized at Norwich, a son to whom she left one pound in her will (Daniel, the elder son, received a similar legacy). On the other hand, there is a son, also named Benjamin, but with the additional name of Norton, stigmatized as the result of De Foe's brief intimacy with an oyster-woman. This Benjamin was known, at any rate for a time, as "Mr. Norton", and never disputed his illegitimacy. The originator of the oyster-woman story was Savage, who had a particular grudge against De Foe. Pope, who also hated him, though for other reasons, echoes the charge with his usual slick malevolence in *The Dunciad*.

"Norton, from Daniel and Ostrea[2] sprung,
Blest with his father's front and mother's tongue."

Biographical authorities have been dogmatic rather than enlightening on the matter. Dottin affirms the illegitimacy of Benjamin Norton; Wright scouts the whole thing as a ridiculous scandal; while Professor Sutherland, after considering the possibility of De Foe having a legitimate son named Benjamin as well as an illegitimate one by the oyster-woman, christened Benjamin Norton, ends by abandoning any attempt to decide one way or the other. But whether there were two Benjamins or not, it is certain that Benjamin Norton De Foe was no son to stir a father's pride. Wright, though protesting vehemently against the bend sinister, agrees with every other authority concerning his mental and moral qualities, and labels him as one who "inherited little of his father's genius, and all his father's faults". If the two Benjamins were indeed one and

---

[1] Wright is obviously in error in stating that the second Daniel, Mary's first child, died in 1724, and Tuffley and the second child in 1720.
[2] Latin form of "oyster".

indivisible, they were fused into a singularly unpleasant personality, with no Jekyll to mitigate the Hyde.

In the summer of 1721 Benjamin, who had become a hack journalist, wrote several "scandalous and seditious" articles for *The London Journal*, following which he was promptly arrested, together with Wilkins the printer and Peele the publisher. The two latter were released on bail, but Benjamin was committed to Newgate.

De Foe took action, but with no particular vehemence, in the form of a pseudonymous contribution to *Applebee's Journal*, in which he stressed the fact that authors who involved themselves in libels were usually more foolish than malicious (this from De Foe!). He added that the libel laws should be amended. "The indictment," he says, "is loaded with the usual adverbs—seditiously, maliciously, or traitorously and seditiously, and the like—when perhaps the unhappy scribbler has no sedition or treason or malice in his head."

Later on Benjamin was released on bail of two thousand pounds, an extraordinarily large amount in eighteenth-century terms of money. His father wrote in *Applebee's* on August 20th: "'Tis known that the young De Foe was but a stalking-horse or a tool, to bear the lash and the pillory in their (the printers' and publisher's) stead".

But in the end he bore neither; from the complete absence of any further records, it seems practically certain the whole thing was dropped.

To revert for a moment to Dottin's insistence upon there being two Benjamins, a legitimate and an illegitimate: he says that the legitimate Benjamin remained for a long time at Norwich and that he married in 1728 a girl named Hannah Carter; that he later emigrated to America, and that a direct descendant of his was recently heard of in Australia. Benjamin *Norton*, on the other hand, "continued his harrowing occupation of writing for wages"—a condition in which even the most distinguished journalist is liable to find himself —and lived in constant fear of prison. In 1739 he wrote a series of heartrending articles to the Duke of Newcastle, begging for help in bringing up his three remaining children, and adding the remarkable statement that he had "just come from burying his wife and his fourteen other children". If that were true, he could scarcely have been the same

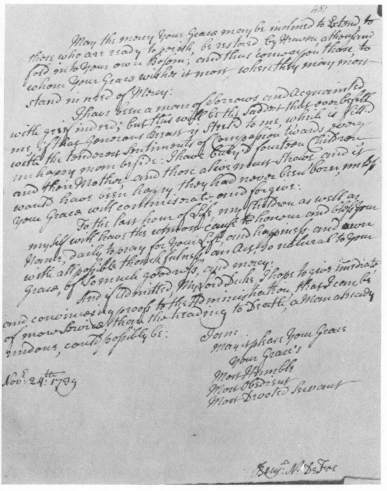

PART OF A LETTER DATED NOVEMBER 24TH, 1739 FROM
BENJAMIN NORTON DE FOE TO THE DUKE OF NEWCASTLE

Benjamin De Foe who was married in 1728. Of the remaining three children, one, Joseph, became a highwayman, and was executed at Tyburn in 1771.

At which unsatisfactory point one may, for the time being, leave the males of the De Foe family and revert to the three unmarried daughters.

They were all—to quote Henry Baker, concerning whom a good deal more will be said later—"admired for their beauty, their education and their prudent conduct". But Hannah, the eldest, was "getting on", and while beauty and education and deportment were useful assets, a girl in her thirties with no compensating dowry ran a very good chance of missing the matrimonial market altogether.

De Foe, from the publication of *Robinson Crusoe* onwards, should in his wife's opinion have been perfectly able to cope with the dowry problem. She insisted that his principle of reinvesting all the capital derived from his books and lesser interests was wrong and that it was his duty to do something about Hannah's future. And this eventually he did. He put eight hundred pounds into South Sea Stock for her, buying at a low price and banking on a rise. The stock duly rose, and Hannah netted a comfortable profit. Then he plunged into a far more complicated transaction. Employing an old friend, the Reverend William Smithies, Rector of St. Michael's, Mile End, as negotiator, he obtained a ninety-nine years' lease on Hannah's behalf of an estate owned by the Borough of Colchester within that city. It possessed the romantic name of "Severallo", was otherwise known as Kingswood Heath, and included two extensive farms, open heaths, woodland, and a fish-pond. The price of all this was one thousand pounds, payable in two equal instalments, the first on Michaelmas 1722, the second a year later.

The financial arrangement was, on the face of it, straightforward enough, especially as the sale of part of Hannah's South Sea Stock provided ample to cover the first five hundred pounds instalment. But when Michaelmas 1723 came De Foe found himself short of cash. The property had been leased to a Mary Newton, of Ipswich, at one hundred and twenty pounds a year—a twelve-per-cent investment for Hannah—and to Mary Newton "Severallo" was mortgaged for two hundred pounds, either by De Foe or Hannah.

At this point De Foe suddenly and inexplicably took a

further step. In spite of his prosperity, he remained at heart a restless, unsatisfied man. Perhaps his Nonconformist conscience was taking a belated revenge. Perhaps the sacrifice, by ever-speeding stages, of his personal integrity had left memories to which only further feverish activities could act as an anodyne. He had his library, his garden, his stables, but a vacuum remained.

His old friend John Ward, the hosier, was involved in his new schemes. To him, without consulting Hannah, De Foe granted a lease of a part of the property, and shortly after the lease was signed told him that there was extraordinarily good clay for making tiles there. De Foe further suggested, obviously as part of a preconceived plan, that a factory should be erected on the estate. Whether he had some idea of making a belated fortune as an offset to his early and unlucky experiences at Tilbury is unknown; but he did suggest that he and Ward should enter into partnership. According to a later statement made by Ward in the course of a legal action he brought, De Foe also asked him to keep the facts a secret from the rest of the De Foe family. Ward obligingly signed an agreement for exhibition to the family, and another—the vital and private one—which not only made them equal partners, but equal contributors of capital.

The factory was started. De Foe was left in charge; Ward, according to his own statement, paying out the whole of the wages involved. Eventually Ward became bankrupt, threw in his hand, and retired to Warwickshire. In the meantime, the family had discovered the truth. Hannah herself was prepared to continue the factory, but her mother flatly refused to consent, and De Foe finally dropped the whole business. In November 1727 he paid off the mortgage, and Hannah found herself freed from all complications and left to enjoy a comfortable income in what, to quote Mr. Wright, was "respectable gentility". She never married, but, dying in 1759, left the Colchester property to a nephew, son of Henrietta. (He subsequently married the daughter of John Boston of Much Hadham, in Hertfordshire, and died in 1760.)

Mrs. De Foe's firmness of will and common sense later went into action on her own account. Realizing the difficult position in which she would be left if her husband died suddenly and she were confronted with the problem of

extracting a regular income from his tangle of semi-secret
enterprises, she put pressure on him to create for her an
annuity derived from the value of the Stoke Newington
estate. To which was added in 1725 a legacy of over a
thousand pounds left her by her brother, Samuel Tuffley.
There remained the two younger girls. Particularly there
remained Sophia, the charming, the coolheaded, the darling
of her father's heart, and, occasionally, so startlingly like
him in character.

In 1724 she met Henry Baker, another among that band of
near-geniuses so numerous in De Foe's career that biographers tend to do them less than justice. Professor Sutherland introduces him, a trifle patronizingly, as "an intelligent
young bookseller". Baker was, in point of fact, a good deal
more.

A Londoner, like De Foe—he was born in 1698 in Chancery
Lane, and was the son of a Clerk in Chancery—he had been
apprenticed at fourteen to a bookseller named John Parker.
His description of his childhood is typical of the high-falutin
sentimentalism which was so curiously combined with the
logical and scientific qualities of his intellect. He describes
himself as "left at an early age by an unhappy father to a
relentless world"; he "knew not which way to turn for
bread", and was "destined to all the ills of poverty, to
pining, want and ill-endured contempt, to misery and ruin".
In spite of these handicaps, however, he contrived to
complete his seven years' apprenticeship, after which, in
April 1720, he left Mr. Parker's service and went to stay
with a relation, John Foster, "an eminent attorney", at
Enfield. Foster had a daughter, Jane, aged eight, who was
deaf and dumb. "Heaven," records Henry, "put into my
thoughts a method of teaching her to read, write, understand
and speak the English language."

He told the eminent attorney of this inspiration; the
attorney was only too anxious to take advantage of it, and
Henry, by a method which he kept rigidly secret to the end
of his life, did cure the girl. Two other deaf-and-dumb
children of Mr. Foster's, who seems to have been as unlucky
in his family's infirmities as he was lucky in getting them
removed, were similarly treated. News of the cures spread;
other afflicted children, many of the upper classes, became
Henry's patients. De Foe heard of him and invited him to

his house. There Henry met the three lovely Miss De Foes. There he fell immediately, passionately and permanently in love with the loveliest of the three, Sophia.

But before that happened he had begun to develop the other, the literary side, of his character. He was only twenty-five when he published a volume of original poems. Luckier than most poets, his first effort was popular enough to go into a second edition two years later. In 1727 he wrote *The Universe*, "a *Poem*," announces the second title modestly, "*intended to restrain the Pride of Man.*" That also was reprinted, though not until after the author's death. He followed it up with a two-volume selection from the Roman poets, with translations, and a translation of Molière's works.

For four patiently progressive years he was destined to prove his devotion to Sophia before he married her. We can follow its progress in detail, since the methodical wooer copied out, in later years, all the letters involved in his courtship, including those between him and his future father-in-law. They extend from that summer day when she accepted him, though only tentatively, to April 30th, 1729, when, all obstacles surmounted, they were married.

The proposal took place on August 17th, 1725, in the Stoke Newington garden, which was large enough and romantic enough for any love-affair. He besought her to tell him if her heart was engaged. Sophia, properly embarrassed—he had by now captured one of her hands, and was pressing it to his lips—answered: "Yes, to God and my Father." She then added, doubtless with an enchanting blush, "but to none beside".

After that, Henry interviewed her father to ask his assent to a formal engagement. (Her mother does not appear to have been consulted.) De Foe was not unwilling, for young Baker's reputation stood high, and gave every indication of standing higher, and he found him a conspicuous exception to the average young man, of whom, as an old one, he had an extremely low opinion. Nevertheless, he delayed his full consent, no doubt to discount any impression that he might be glad to get Sophia off his hands. He also took the opportunity to dramatize the situation. Henry was reminded that he was asking for the dearest jewel De Foe possessed, a best-loved child in whom his soul delighted. How, demanded the agitated parent, could he bear to part with her! Henry sensibly left this rhetorical question unanswered, and shortly afterwa ds received permission to continue his courtship. Sophia formally consented to marry him. From this point the real trouble began. Baker was desperately in love. In his letters he rhapsodizes, and indeed raves about Sophia's charms. "Your lovely image haunts me day and night, where'er I go, whatever I do," he cries. For half the week he is debarred from seeing her; and every moment of that time is filled with anxious hopes and desires. With an unfortunate lack of humour, he tells her that he spends his Sundays reading the Song of Solomon, and encloses her extracts. "It cost you little to borrow words," replies Sophia tartly, and very humanly. "Is the subject grown so dull that you are fain to be beholding to so antiquated a lover?" Poor Henry!

Nevertheless, he retained his practical outlook, even in the throes of a love-affair such as this. He had assumed, from fairly sound evidence, that De Foe was a rich man; rich men endowed their daughters, lovely or otherwise, with comfortable portions. Henry hinted as much. Unfortunately if there was one thing that De Foe disliked doing it was entering into money commitments in which he had no controlling part. He said that no formal marriage settlement was necessary; that when he died Sophia naturally would inherit her share of his property; that for the time being all his capital was tied up in other investments. Henry was shocked, dismayed, indignant. If he had not genuinely loved Sophia, there is little doubt he would have dropped the whole thing. But in spite of his protests De Foe remained obdurate.

Sophia, poor girl, was the most to be pitied. She was young and in love, and here were the two people she cared most about haggling over her price as though she were a horse or a plot of land. In a pathetic and bitter note she accuses Henry of writing her father a letter which "seems to have too much of the air of barter and sale". At the time she wrote it the two men had narrowed the difference between what her father would give and her lover accept to a mere five pounds a year.

Not that the two were haggling all the time. There was, for example, a truce when Baker, writing for some obscure reason under the pseudonym of "Henry Stonecastle", entered into partnership with De Foe in founding *The*

Universal Spectator and Weekly Journal. De Foe wrote the first number. It appeared in October 1728, when the bargaining had been going on for nearly four years. Three months later the climax came. Henry, though remaining adamant about the terms of the dowry, seems suddenly and illogically to have come to the conclusion that he could no longer live without his Sophia. On February 1st, 1729, he wrote a wild letter to her suggesting a suicide pact. The pair of them were to take poison, die in one another's arms, and leave the world, "telling with wonder our amazing story, pitying our youth and our too cruel fate".

Sophia threw cold water on this melodramatic proposition —and then collapsed under the prolonged and sordid strain of the negotiations. She became, in fact, so ill that the two negotiators abruptly agreed to compromise, and De Foe formally undertook to give Sophia a bond for five hundred pounds, payable at his death and secured on the Newington property. On April 30th Henry and Sophia were married. And though financial friction of one sort or another with the old man continued, the marriage was a complete and unqualified success.

The Bakers had two sons. The elder, David Erskine, who was born in January 1730 and had the Earl of Buchan for his godfather, showed early abilities as a mathematician. Moreover, at twelve years old he had translated the twenty-four books of Telemachus; at fifteen he had published a translation of physics from the Italian, and at seventeen a treatise on Newton's Metaphysics. "He is a pretty good master of Greek and Latin," wrote his proud father, "and I hope by the Grace of God will become a virtuous and useful man." Perhaps it was the inherited versatility of his grandfather that made him abandon these austere studies, and caused him, having first married a clergyman's daughter, to form a company of strolling actors, the sequel being in 1764 his *Companion to the Playhouse*, in two small volumes, which in 1782 were expanded under another editor to *Biographica Dramatica.* Later, he appears to have been adopted by an uncle who was a "silk throwster" in Spitalfields, succeeded him in the business, and "wanting the prudence and attention necessary to secure success in trade, soon failed". He died in obscurity, leaving no family, in Edinburgh. (The actual date seems uncertain, fluctuating between 1767 and 1780.)

The second son, William, became Rector of Lyndon and South Luffenham. His great-great-granddaughter is still living.

As for the original Henry Baker, he gave his adored Sophia every reason to be proud of him, as the *Dictionary of National Biography* amply testifies and the *History of the Royal Society of Arts* testifies more amply still. He was one of the eleven gentlemen who, under Lord Folkestone's chairmanship, formally founded the latter society at Rawthmell's Coffee-house, Henrietta Street, Covent Garden, on March 22nd, 1754. And although William Shipley was elected secretary, it was Baker who actually recorded the minutes. With Shipley, he was elected a "perpetual member" when the society was formerley constituted in the following February, and became Chairman of Accounts. He founded the Bakerian Lecture, and had the pride of seeing his elder son enrolled as a member.

He suggested a prize list of three premiums for sowing the greatest acres of land with acorns, four bushels to the acre, a minimum of five acres. He was on the committee of the first picture exhibition, and the awarding of gold, silver and copper medals instead of money prizes was first suggested by him, in a magnificently pompous introduction beginning, "Whoever would lead Mankind, even to their own Good, must take advantage of their Passions, among which the Desire of Gain and the Desire of Esteem are two of the most prevailing".

In January 1740 he was elected a Fellow of the Society of Antiquaries, and two months later a Fellow of the Royal Society. He plunged into microscopy, wrote a handbook on the microscope itself, received a medal for experiments on crystallization, and introduced the Alpine strawberry and the rhubarb plant into England. He died in his rooms in the Strand in November 1774, two years after the death of his beloved Sophia, leaving twenty thousand pounds to Henry, his surviving son, and an epitaph of his own composition:

> " Of all my cares and all my pains
> If aught commendable remains
> Be that my epitaph; if not,
> May I for ever be forgot."

The sale by auction of his library in the following March occupied nine days.

A fairly good record for an "intelligent young bookseller". Posterity bears him only one legitimate grievance. He took with him to the grave his secret method of teaching the deaf and dumb to speak.

CHAPTER III

WANDERER

IN THE autumn of 1725 De Foe set himself the task of writing what was in effect an encyclopaedia. Published on September 11th, *The Compleat English Tradesman, in Familiar Letters, Directing him in all the Several Parts and Progressions of Trade*, ran to over four hundred and fifty pages. A second edition, published a year later, contained a supplemental one hundred and forty-eight pages.

It is a work which, had the writer been anyone less eminent than the author of *Robinson Crusoe*, would probably have been recognized and established as a popular classic. As one critic[1] remarks: "Few persons, perhaps, would expect to meet with amusement upon so dull a subject as trade; yet inspired by the genius of De Foe, it has furnished material for one of the most entertaining works on the English language."

Beginning with "The Tradesman in his preparations while an Apprentice", the book, divided into sections, covers every conceivable aspect of commercial life. De Foe, as always, is severely factual; theories, however sound, are invariably driven home by example. In the section dealing with "The Ordinary Occasion of the Ruin of Tradesmen", we get:

"For a tradesman to open his shop in a place not resorted to, or in a place not agreeable, and where 'tis not expected, 'tis no wonder if he has no business. In most towns, but particularly in London, there are places appropriated to particular trades, and where the trades that are placed there would do very well, but would do very ill anywhere else, as the orange merchants and wet-salters about Billingsgate and in Thames Street; the Costermongers at The Three Cranes; the wholesale cheesemongers in Thames Street, the Mercers and Drapers in Cheapside, Ludgate Hill, Cornhill etc.

[1] Wilson.

" What would a bookseller make of his business at Billingsgate or a mercer in Tower Street or near the Custom House? Many traders have their peculiar streets and proper places for the sale of their goods . . . as the booksellers in St. Paul's Churchyard, about the Exchange, the Temple, and the Strand etc., the mercers on both sides Ludgate, in Gracechurch and Lombard Streets, the coachmakers in Long Acre, Queen Street and the like. When a shop is ill-chosen, the tradesman starves. What retail trade would a milliner have among the fishmongers' shops on Fish Street Hill, or a toyman about Queenhithe? Suppose a ship's chandler should set up in Holborn, or a block-maker in Whitecross Street or an anchor-smith at Moorgate or a coach-maker at Rotherhithe? "

But there are other reasons, risks of disasters. One he terms:

" . . . pleasures and diversions, especially such as they will have us call innocent diversion.

" When I see young shopkeepers keep horses, ride a-hunting, learn dog-language, and keep the sportsman brogue upon their tongues, I am always afraid for them. . . . For a tradesman to follow his pleasures, leaving his shop to servants and others, it is evident that his heart is not in his business. He will never thrive that cares not whether he thrive or no."

He passes to "Extravagant Expensive Living":

" There is now a weight of taxes upon almost all the necessities of life, bread and fish excepted, as coals, salt, malt, candles, soap, leather, hops, wine, fruit and all foreign consumption. . . . For the tradesman I speak of, if he will thrive, he must resolve to begin as he can go on; and if he does so, he must resolve to live more under restraint than ever tradesmen of his class used to do."

There is another section on the bad consequences of a tradesman marrying too soon. This includes the harrowing story of a young man with two thousand pounds capital who married his father's serving-maid; he "sank gradually, then broke, and died poor". And yet another—perhaps the most fascinating of all, "Of the Tradesman letting his wife be acquainted with his Business." De Foe was emphatically of the opinion that she should be so acquainted.

Chadwick, himself a tradesman, thought it De Foe's best book. Lamb—surely the antithesis of a shopkeeper—thought its bent too narrow and that it degraded the heart.

De Foe's next literary excursion took him in an entirely

different direction. It was *The Political History of the Devil* and the author combines originality with an unexpected burst of anti-feminism.

" How many hoop petticoats," he demands, " complete the entire mask that disguises the Devil in the shape of that thing called a woman?" And " Bad mother, bad child."

Furthermore, a female devil can kill at a distance; "the poison of her eyes is very strong". She may talk like an angel and sing like a syren, but every woman had within her a devil more or less malignant.

" *None rosa sine-spinis,*" quotes De Foe. " Not a beauty without a devil. Lord ha' mercy, and a + may be set on the man's door that goes a' courting."

One rather odd feature of this "History" is De Foe's attack on Milton.

" Though I admire Mr. Milton as a poet," he says, " yet he is greatly out in matters of history, and especially the history of the Devil."

One would like to know how De Foe knew.

Peter, the Wild Boy, a child of about twelve, discovered speechless, naked, and in a state of complete animalism in July 1724 in a field near Hamelin, in Hanover, brought him down (or up) to earth again.

The Wild Boy had been lured into the town of Hamelin and from thence taken to a hospital. His story reached England. Caroline, Princess of Wales, ordered him to be brought to London, where he was placed under the care of Dr. Arbuthnot. He remained, however, incapable of learning or uttering more than two or three words; it seems probable that he was, in fact, merely an example of arrested mental development. But De Foe saw him and the financial possibilities of a pamphlet supporting a more exciting theory, and after visiting the boy, produced *Mere Nature Delineated, or a Body without a Soul.*

Peter, unlike most abnormalities, survived to be over seventy. During his last years he lived on a farm near Northchurch, wearing a leather collar inscribed, "Peter the Wild Man from Hanover" and the offer of a reward to Peter's finder should the Wild Boy be lost.

And here, though he could not have realized it, ended a chapter in De Foe's career. Or perhaps one might better call it the point at which the top of a hill has been reached and beyond which the road slopes inexorably though slowly downwards.

He was sixty-six. For over forty years his pen had been busy, furiously driving over page after page, yet always under the clear and cool command of his intelligence. The mistakes he had made had never been stupid mistakes; they had resulted not from too little intelligence, but too much. He had hated many people, many things; had been hated with equal heartiness in return and accepted such hatred as something to be expected and despised. His limitations did not spring from the fact that he lacked emotion, but that such emotion was intellectual rather than something that surged, glowing and generous, from the heart. And when the tremendously active brain stiffened and moved creakingly, like an old man's limbs, there was no compensating generosity and tenderness towards those who knew less, or whose chief fault was that they were young; no kindliness to compensate for dwindling mental powers.

There was much he had still to write about. But henceforth he was under a double handicap—his attitude towards the world against which he had so many grievances, and his long and chequered past. On the one hand, he was becoming more and more didactic; on the other, the world he knew, and who knew him, contained many enemies, or, alternatively, acquaintances who did not trust him.

In November 1726 he published a pamphlet, *The Protestant Monastery, or a Complaint about the Brutality of the Present Age. Particularly the Pertness and insolence of youth to aged Persons.*

The last sentence is tragic in its implications. He was on bad terms with his elder son; while with his son-in-law Baker he had a succession of quarrels which might almost be called endemic. His private world was very much awry, and the wider world, the world of publishers and editors, no longer regarded him as interesting enough to be worth cultivating.

" Assure yourself, gentle reader," says De Foe bitterly, " I had not published my project in this pamphlet, could I have got it inserted in any of the journals without feeing the journalists or publishers. I cannot but have the vanity to think they might as well have inserted what I sent them gratis. But I have not only had the mortification to find what I sent rejected, but to lose my originals, not having taken copies of what I wrote."

In other words, he had been told plainly that if he wanted his contribution accepted he must be prepared to pay for it as an advertisement.

Was it because, as De Foe himself seems prepared to concede, he was losing his grip, and that, to use a cliché, his palmy days were over?

Or was it because his journalistic past, dangerously complicated, indefensibly double-faced, had become more or less public property, tainting with suspicion any subject he wrote about?

Or that his whole attitude to his readers fatally combined arrogance with a perpetual grievance?

Perhaps something of all three. He weighted the scales still further in his own disfavour with self-pity. He had, he says, but small health, and was almost worn out with age and sickness.

" The old man cannot trouble you long; take them, in good part, his best intentions, and impute his defects to age and weakness."

In 1726 he published also two books which are of pathetic psychological interest, insomuch as they indicate De Foe's anxiety, since journalism and its profitable excitements are receding, to impress the world with his scholarship. The first was *An Essay on Literature, or an Enquiry into the Antiquity and Original of Letters*. The second was *A General History of the Principal Discoveries and Improvements in the Useful Arts*.

Together they must have represented many hours of labour. Both have vanished into the oblivion reserved for pretentious failures.

But the old man had still much to say to an increasingly inattentive world—grievances to ventilate, advice to give. His popularity might have waned, but it had not entirely disappeared; his pen was still furiously active.

In December 1726[1] he published his second work on the supernatural. It had the intriguing title of *A System of Magick, or a History of The Black Art*.

[1] The book is actually dated the following year.

It ran to over four hundred pages, and was enlivened by a frontispiece showing a magician busily at work, watched from the doorway by a genial little devil. The book is made a convenient receptacle for a remarkably mixed collection of the author's prejudices, theories, and beliefs on "magick" in general, with satire as its prevailing note. Incidentally, Milton, Whiston, Pope and Steele are all attacked.

An Essay on the History and Reality of Apparitions—his third work dealing with supernatural matters—appeared in March 1727. And in the following June he wrote a full-length book with a title that in itself would have aroused disquiet among the Home Office authorities to-day. *Conjugal Lewdness*[1] was, in point of fact, an extraordinarily shrewd and almost incredibly modern approach to the problems arising from selfishness and incompatibility in the average marriage.

It is said that De Foe had begun the book—a long one— over thirty years earlier. He certainly dealt with his subject with masterly thoroughness. Dividing his book into six sections, beginning with "The Nature of Matrimony, its Sacred Original and the true Meaning of its Institution", including "Modesty in Discourse", "Modesty in Behaviour", and "Modesty in Regard to Sexes", and ending with "Many other Particulars of Family Concern", this eighteenth-century Malthusian backed his arguments with the anecdotes which are as recognizable a feature of De Foe's writings as the trees are in a Turner landscape. One of these concerns a friend, "Mr. M——", who habitually ridiculed his wife in public.

"She coloured at his words, which showed she resented them . . . but keeping back all resentment, she with an inexpressible goodness in her face and a smile, said to him ' My dear, you would like it in anybody but your wife' "—a gentle retort that one is glad to learn, cured " Mr. M——"

There is also a story "attested to me by a person of unquestioned veracity", about an elderly lady who, to make sure that her niece should not touch her fortune, married

[1] He amended this in a later issue to *A Treatise Concerning the Use and Abuse of the Marriage Bed.*

(with his father's consent) a little boy, she being sixty-five, he ten.

The lady proved

" A most excellent person of innimitable disposition, and preserved the youth of her temper and the strength of her understanding, memory, and eyesight to the last, and, which was particularly remarkable, she had a whole new set of teeth, as white as ivory and as even as a youth, after she was ninety years of age ".

And—crowning miracle—she lived to be a hundred and twenty-seven, her boy-husband being seventy-two when he buried her!

The same year also included *A New Family Instructor in Familiar Discourses between a Father and his Children*—one becomes aware of a certain monotony about De Foe's approaches—*as well as Parochial Tyranny, or the Housekeeper's* [i.e. Householder's] *Complaint against the Insupportable Exactions and partial* [biased] *Assessments of Select Vestries.*

In 1728 he began two tracts, *Of Royall Education*, which he left uncompleted, and *The Compleat English Gentleman*, which, published in parts by Baker, his son-in-law, failed to live up to its title by also remaining unfinished.

In March of the same year he brought out a pamphlet entitled *Augusta Triumphans, or the way to make London the most flourishing City in the Universe.* His suggestions included (1) the establishment of a University; (2) of a Foundling Hospital, and (3) of an Academy of Music; (4) the suppression of private madhouses and (5) of prostitution; and (6) the prevention of the "immoderate use of Geneva" (or gin).[1]

[1] The easygoing excesses so easily excusable in the merry days of the Merry Monarch became under the harsher reigns of his Protestant successors scandalous and shocking. Drinking was on the increase. The war with France had cut illegitimate trade connections, and they included wines and spirits. But the English distillers had risen to the occasion; they had even evolved a new, aromatic and desperately-potent drink, which made from the juniper plant, is called by an abbreviation of the Dutch form of that name " gin " (also " jin " by Swift.)

Writing in 1714, an author (Mandeville) refers to " The infamous liquor the name of which is derived from juniper-berries in Dutch by frequent use ", while another speaks of it as " A spirituous liquor, the exorbitant use of which has almost destroyed the lowest rank of the people until it was restrained by an Act of P. in 1736."

De Foe bracketed the new spirit with the Devil, the Pope and the Pretender.

Far-sighted Mr. De Foe! The first three have all come to pass; private madhouses as he knew them have long disappeared, and the "immoderate use of Geneva" is no longer general. Only the suppression of the oldest profession in the world survives to break the hearts of the moralists.

He wrote other books; like that eccentric genius of a later age whose brush distilled the sheerest magic, one might have said of him, "I have never known him idle". He had no obvious financial, political or personal troubles to harass and disturb his old age. Yet disaster can flow along many channels.

Part, perhaps most, of the fiasco of those last few years undoubtedly sprang from De Foe's own character. His restless brain was still immensely active; he could still express his thoughts with a cogency and clarity that by now had become as instinctive and effortless as breathing. But the magnificent machine was showing signs of wear, reflected in its owner's attitude to the outer world. He was ceasing to find that world an eternal fair-ground of diversions and delights. Concurrently, he was making heavier and yet heavier claims upon the patience and understanding of his friends. His later works reflect this combination of aggressiveness and general dissatisfaction—no phenomenon, unfortunately, in intellectual old age. The quality of friendly and good humoured intimacy that had nullified so much of his irony was evaporating.

These processes were, of course, gradual; his interest in living had not entirely dissipated itself. There were still great things to be done and fine things to be seen. And he had still some warnings to utter, some pearls to cast. Incidentally, he used a pseudonym during the last three or four years of his life, writing inder the name of "Andrew Moreton".

On September 10th, 1729, he sent a message to his publisher, saying that he had been ill. The illness was unspecified; the date of his recovery is unknown. Then in the course of the following summer he left the comfortable house at Newington, never—did he realize it?—to return.

His motive must have been as powerful as, to his family (and, until very recently, to the world at large), it was mysterious. What steps his wife and friends took to find and persuade him to return are still unknown. Had his flight

been due to a sudden revival of his passion for wandering, a
sudden uncontrollable revulsion against a settled, circum-
scribed life, the adventure might have ended as abruptly as
it began.

But a cryptic letter he wrote, obviously in reply to a
communication which must have reached him from Baker,
strikes a note of deeper tragedy.

It is dated August 12th, 1730. He says:[1]

" I was sorry you should say at the beginning of your letter
you were debarred seeing me. I am far from debarring you.
On the contrary. It would be a greater comfort to me than I
now enjoy that I could have your agreeable visits with safety,
and see both you and my dear Sophia, could it be without the
grief of seeing her father *in tenebris* and under the load of insupportable sorrow. . . . I must open my grief so far as to tell her,
that it is not the blow I received from a wicked, perjured and
contemptible enemy that has broke in upon my spirit, but the
injustice, unkindness and, I must say, inhuman dealing of my
own son which has both ruined my family, and broken my
heart . . . *Et tu, Brute.* I depended upon him, I trusted him,
I gave up my two dear unprovided children into his hands, but
he has no compassion, but suffers them and their poor dying
mother to beg their bread at his door and to crave what he is
bound under hand and seal to supply them with himself at the
same time living in a profusion of luxury . . . I only ask one
thing for them as a dying request—stand by them as a brother,
and if you have anything within you owing to my memory, let
them not be injured and trampled on by false pretences. I
hope they will want no help but that of comfort and counsel.
" It adds to my grief that it is so difficult to see you. I am at
a distance from London in Kent; nor have I a lodging in London,
nor have I been at that place in the Old Bailey since I wrote
you that I was removed from it. At present I am weak, having
had some fits of fever that have left me low.
" I have not seen son or daughter, wife or child many weeks,
and know not which way to see them. They dare not come by
water, and by land there is no coach. It is not possible for me
to come to Enfield, unless you could find a retired lodging for
me where I might not be known. I would gladly give the days
to solitude to have the comfort of half-an-hour now and then
with you both. But just to come and look at you, and retire
immediately, is a burden too heavy to be borne.

[1] For the convenience of the reader, I have slightly condensed the letter,
and modified the eighteenth-century spelling.

" It adds to my grief that I must never see the pledge of your mutual love, my little grandson . . . Kiss my dear Sophy once more for me, and if I must see her no more, tell her this is from a father that loved her above all his comforts to his last breath.

Yours unhappy

D. F.

" P.S. I wrote you a letter some months ago, in answer to one from you about selling the house; but you never signified to me whether you received it or not. I have not the policy of assurance; I suppose my wife or Hannah may have it."

It is a letter of quite extraordinary interest from half a dozen points of view, particularly the psychological. They may be dealt with separately. I agree with Professor Sutherland that it is "undeniably puzzling", but also I think the puzzle is capable of solution.

To begin with, the "wicked perjured and contemptible enemy" has in the past been identified as Nathaniel Mist, his old rival of the *Mist's Journal* days, the assumption being that Mist had gone on the warpath again and was doing his malignant best to publicize De Foe's political gyrations, and so to discredit him in the retirement of old age. De Foe explicitly states that this is *not* "the blow which has broken in upon my spirit", the "spirit which has carried me through greater disasters than these."

What had actually happened appears to have been a sort of hangover from his second bankruptcy, sixteen years earlier, a hangover which to-day, with an official receiver, to say nothing of the Statute of Limitations in existence, would have been impossible.

In De Foe's case his creditors had agreed to accept a composition of so much in the pound, and Stancliffe, one of the chief creditors,[1] agreed to take on the additional duty of distributing the proportions of the more than ample sum of money that De Foe handed over. One would have imagined that the necessary legal documents would have been drawn up, making the arrangement definite and watertight, but apparently they were not, for on Stancliffe's death the administrator of his estate, one Samuel Brooke, or Brook, came upon De Foe for the money still owing his dead client.

De Foe explained the position. Brooke accepted it and undertook to draw up a document freeing De Foe from any

[1] Referred to at length on pages 103-4.

further claims. Before that could happen *he* died. His widow, Mary Brooke,[1] not only refused to accept De Foe's statement and to give him his discharge but prepared to sue him for the money.

The challenge was one which in the past he would have had no hesitation whatever in accepting. It is certainly one in which he would have stood an excellent chance of emerging victor. But De Foe, once capable of bluffing his way through any entanglement, was now a tired, crotchety old gentleman, incapable of facing up to the legal machinery; terror-stricken at the mere prospect of the confiscation of his property, perhaps another bankruptcy, with all its furtiveness and shame, perhaps even Newgate. He had, of course, friends—Henry Baker was one—whom he could have trusted, and to whom he might safely have turned to take over this burden.

But he did not turn to his son-in-law, or to anyone else; a lifetime of suspecting had probably made him incapable of making a confidant of anybody. Instead he decided to begin by neutralizing in advance any chances of success that the gold-digging Mrs. Brooke might have; he made over his property to his son. And Daniel, from the parental point of view, let him down badly.

Precisely how badly it is impossible to say. For that lack of knowledge De Foe himself is responsible; firstly, because thereafter he completely lost his head, and, secondly, because, in losing it, he grossly over-dramatized the situation. That he may have believed the statements he made in his letter to Baker is not unlikely; one of the commonest hallucinations of old age is that of poverty and general ruin.

But the fact remains that neither his wife nor his children— these, incidentally, grown women, with the elder in possession of a comfortable and secure income from the Essex property—were begging their bread at Daniel's or anyone else's door. De Foe does in the same letter admit as much when he writes, "I hope they will want no help but that of comfort and counsel."

Nor was Mrs. De Foe dying; she survived her husband by

---

[1] There has been a general tendency on the part of biographers—Monsieur Dottin is an example—to believe that Mrs. Brooke was merely De Foe's landlady, to whom he owed rent which she afterwards recovered, either in money or goods, from the family.

nearly two years. Finally, De Foe's own death did not take place until the following April.

The probability is that he wrote that *cri de coeur* not from first-hand knowledge but after receiving complaints from his wife that Daniel was exercising his new rights too rigorously. To quote Dottin, he allowed his imagination to "build up a frightful picture". One is almost surprised to find no references to Lear.

One biographer[1] has evolved the theory that the letter, and particularly its so suddenly businesslike and matter-of-fact postscript, represents a Machiavellian attempt on De Foe's part to evade a direct answer to a previous enquiry by Baker concerning the securities which represented Sophia's dowry. In other words, the impassioned story of the younger Daniel's harsh treatment of his mother and sisters is mere camouflage.

But I do not share that view.

He appears to have gone from Newington to London and found lodgings somewhere in the crowded little streets about Newgate. In August, however, as he indicates in his letter to Baker, he had fled the City for other lodgings in the vicinity of Greenwich: his enemy (or enemies) had discovered his street hide-out, or, what was as bad, he was convinced that they had.

But early in the following year he had drifted back to London. This time his hide-out was near his birthplace, St. Giles-in-Cripplegate. The parish was a maze of little crooked streets in which even an old man might hope to scuttle successfully at the approach of his creditors; furthermore, near Ropemakers Alley, in which he found a lodging, was White Cross Alley, where he owned three houses which members of his family might be expected to visit in the course of rent-collecting and, so visiting, contact himself.

Did they contact him again? That, and a hundred other questions, remain unanswered.

At some time during 1731 he published an octavo pamphlet of seventy-two pages: *An Effectual Scheme for the Immediate Preventing of Street Robberies and suppressing other Disorders of the Night; with a brief History of the Night Houses, and an Appendix relating to those sons of Hell called Incendiaries.*

[1] Minto.

CHAPTER IV

CURTAIN

O N April 26th, 1731, he died.
"Of a Lethargy," says the Parish Register. Eighteenth-century diagnoses were crude and casual, and the exact significance of the word is left to the imagination. A surge of mental and physical weakness, of lassitude; a drifting into unconsciousness and from unconsciousness into death—that, perhaps, is as good a guess as any. "I am suffering from only one thing," said a philosophical nonogenarian recently, "the recession of youth." Might not De Foe's last illness be so summarized?

To the grave and beyond the grave the Fates mocked him. When they carried him to burial in Tindall's Burying-ground—it apparently occurred to none that he was worthy of Westminster Abbey—the fool who recorded the fact wrote: "1731, April 26, Mr. Dubow, Cripplegate," while the *Universal Spectator* of May 1st records the event in precisely sixteen words: "A few days ago died Daniel De Foe, senior, a person well known for his humerous writings."

His tombstone was a mean stone slab, which stated that he "died April 24th 1731 in his 70th year"—two inaccuracies in as many lines. And the following century even that poor memorial was broken and crumbling. It had been struck by lightning, an enquirer[1] was told.

Was it even subtler irony that in 1870 an appeal should be made through the columns of *The Christian World* to all the boys and girls of England for funds to erect a more appropriate memorial? Or that on the white marble "Cleopatric pillar"[2] that resulted from that appeal, to which over seventeen hundred people contributed, only one book is mentioned out of nearly four hundred that he wrote, including half a dozen unique classics? Or is it more fitting that only *Robinson Crusoe* be separately and signally remembered?

Even there the story of neglect did not end. The "Cleopatric pillar" was in turn allowed to fall into such a

---

[1] Chadwick.   [2] Unveiled on September 16th.

dangerous state that by 1949 it was obvious that steps would have to be taken promptly to preserve it. This time no public appeal proved necessary; an admirer of De Foe furnished the funds required, and the repairs were put in hand.

To-day De Foe's Memorial, lately reconditioned to a dazzling whiteness, rises above the crumbling grey stones that, with an oddly incongruous air, surround it. Its renewed lettering, unfortunately, repeats the old error concerning the date of De Foe's birth, while recording the generosity of the admirer who was responsible for the restoration.

Ropemaker's Alley once led from Ropemaker's Street, but Alley and Street have, with the exception of one or two shops at the corner, been annihilated.

Some distance away you may discover Bunhill Street, also shattered, but still retaining Artillery Row, a flat-faced, primly respectable terrace. And beyond that lies Bunhill Fields, bisected by a wide-paved path with high iron railings on either side to frustrate marauding boys, and at the far end, a small building, from which an obliging keeper will emerge to unlock the gates and show you the five tombs which bring so many visitors—Blake, and Bunyan, and the two Wesleys, and the relations of the great Cromwell, though not the man himself, and Daniel De Foe. The City, it is said, plans to make this a playing field.

It is a platitude to say that the works of a genius are his best memorial; that the life he lived is, all too frequently, a foolish and lamentable affair compared with them, a heart-aching disappointment for those who look to find the greatness which his art reflects.

De Foe was no exception to this rule. Over and over again his private life lapsed distressingly from the standards he preached. On the other hand, if he had never written *Robinson Crusoe* or *The Journal of the Plague Year*, or *Moll Flanders* or *The True-born Englishman*, we should still be left with a life-story of enormous interest and variety. "The middle-sized man of brown complexion with a hooked nose, sharp chin and grey eyes" would still have been our creditor.

And if one is left with a feeling that the brain dominated the heart, that, even when he is writing fervently as well as logically there was some inner glow, some finer, purer passion missing, there was never a moment when he was disloyal to England and to what he believed to be her destiny.

BIBLIOGRAPHY

De Foe. James Sutherland; Methuen, 1937.
Life of Daniel Defoe. Thos. Wright; Cassell & Co., 1894.
Daniel Defoe, his Life and Newly Discovered Writings. Wm. Lee; J. C. Hotten, 1869.
Daniel Defoe. Wilfred Whitten; Kegan Paul, 1900.
Life and Times of Daniel Defoe. Wm. Chadwick; Smith, 1859.
Life and Adventures of Daniel Defoe. P. Dottin, Tr. by Louise Ragan; Stanley Paul, 1928.
Works of Daniel Defoe. Ed. S. Keltie; Nimmo, 1871.
Moll Flanders. Introduction. Hamish Hamilton, 1948.
The Athenian Oracle. 1703.
Votive Tablets. Edmund Blunden; Cobden Sanderson, 1931.
English Journalism. C. L. Pebody.
Aubrey's Short Lives.
The Concise Cambridge History of English Literature. Geo. Sampson; Cam. Univ. Press, 1933.
A Short Biographical Dictionary of English Literature. Dent, 1938.
Curiosities of Literature. Isaac d'Israeli.
Strange Readings. Grant Uden; G. Newnes, Ltd.
The Human Approach to Literature. Ivor Nicholson & Watson, 1932.
The England of Charles II. Arthur Bryant; Longmans Green & Co., 1932.
King Charles II. Arthur Bryant.
Samuel Pepys. Arthur Bryant.
The Diary of Samuel Pepys. Ed. by Lord Braybrooke.
The Chronological Historian. Salmon, 1733.
A Short History of the English People. J. R. Green; Macmillan, 1882.
A History of the Worthies of England. Thos. Fuller, D.D.
England under Queen Anne. G. M. Trevelyan; Longmans Green & Co., 1946.
English Social History. G. M. Trevelyan; 1944.
Social England. H. D. Traill; Cassell & Co., 1895.
English Men and Manners in the 18th Century. A. S. Turberville; Clarendon Press, 1924.
The Great Plague of London 1665. W. G. Bell; John Lane, 1924.
London, a Comprehensive Survey. G. H. Cunningham; J. M. Dent & Son, 1927.

The Growth of Stuart London. N. G. Brett-James; G. Allen & Unwin, 1934.

London in 1731. Don Manuel Gonzales; Cassell, 1888.

History of the Port of London. Sir J. G. Brocklebank ; D. O'Connor, 1921.

London for Everyone. Wm. Kent; J. M. Dent & Son, 1931.

London Stories. More London Stories. W. Whitten; G. Newnes, Ltd.

London Revisited. E. V. Lucas; Methuen, 1916.

A Wanderer in London. E. V. Lucas; Methuen, 1916.

Five Centuries of London. Constable & Co.

History of the Monument. Chas. Welch, F.S.A.

Bunhill Memories. Ed. J. A. Jones, 1849.

South London. W. Besant. Chatto & Windus, 1912.

South London. Harry Williams; R. Hale, 1949.

Nonconformity, its Rise and Progress. W. B. Selbie; Williams & Norgate.

Water-Supply and Drainage. Engineering in Everyday Life; Pitman, 1945.

Desert Islands. Walter de la Mare; Faber & Faber Ltd., 1930.

The Murder of Sir Edmund Godfrey. John Dickson Carr; Hamish Hamilton, 1936.

A History of the Royal Society of Arts. Sir H. Trueman Wood, 1913.

INDEX